DIGITAL TRANSFORMATION

Digital Transformation

Understanding Business Goals, Risks, Processes, and Decisions

Mathias Cöster, Mats Danielson, Love Ekenberg, Cecilia Gullberg, Gard Titlestad, Alf Westelius, and Gunnar Wettergren

OpenBook Publishers

https://www.openbookpublishers.com

All external links were active at the time of publication unless otherwise stated and have been archived via the Internet Archive Wayback Machine at https://archive.org/web

Any digital material and resources associated with this volume will be available at https://doi.org/10.11647/OBP.0350#resources

ISBN Paperback: 978-1-80511-060-6
ISBN Hardback: 978-1-80511-061-3
ISBN Digital (PDF): 978-1-80511-062-0
ISBN Digital ebook (EPUB): 978-1-80511-063-7
ISBN XML: 978-1-80511-065-1
ISBN HTML: 978-1-80511-066-8
DOI: 10.11647/OBP.0350

Cover photo by Love Ekenberg
Cover design by Jeevanjot Kaur Nagpal

This book is dedicated to our dear friend, esteemed colleague, and co-author Professor Love Ekenberg, who passed away in September 2022 during the writing of this book. We mourn his untimely death, and that he is not here with us to see the end result.

Contents

Preface

The world is more unpredictable than ever. Digital transformation, which in principle affects everything that surrounds us, has during the last half-century strongly contributed to this unpredictability. It has enabled a global trade that incorporates more and more people, organisations and states. It has enabled a larger international labour market than anyone could foresee. It has made possible a tremendous rationalisation of social functions and tasks. It has enabled a huge flow of information in all sectors of society. And it has enabled some sort of organisation of all of the above. Numerous human beings, for better and for worse, have had to dramatically change their lives. The ongoing digital transformation has thus created a wave of both problems and opportunities. This development has fantastic advantages, but there is every reason to consider it with some scepticism. Nevertheless, this is where we are, so let us shape the future so that it suits us.

Digital transformation is ubiquitous. Everywhere we look these days, at least in cityscapes, we can see or otherwise sense signs of this ongoing societal transformation. Old ways of organising the transfer of goods or services from sellers to buyers constantly have to give way to new ones. There are even multiple waves of transformation. Consider, for example, the video and computer game industry, which used to sell products on DVDs (and earlier on other physical digital media). Those were predominantly sold in brick-and-mortar shops such as game stores, toy stores, and department stores. In the first wave of transformation, online sales of DVDs gradually but largely rendered game stores obsolete. In the next wave (still ongoing), the DVDs themselves are being replaced with digital downloads. The same can be said for the music industry, but with the addition of streaming services. For books (sic!), the future path is maybe a bit less clear. While online stores have taken a large market share, bookstores still prevail to some extent. And there are differing opinions on how large a portion of future book sales will be digital, particularly for different categories of books.

These transformations often depend on changing behavioural patterns. Sometimes these changes are driven by economic factors, at other times by availability, and quite often by both. But there can be other change agents as well, something that not least the recent Covid-19 pandemic has taught us. Most of the authors of this book work in the Swedish university system, which on 17 March 2020 was advised to cease all campus education and move online, preferably within twenty-four hours. Previous studies at some universities had stressed the need for years of preparation and extensive pedagogical research before certain subjects or departments could go fully or almost fully online, but the urgent need for change made the digital transformation happen overnight. As another case in point, however, many theatres did not convert any substantial part of their business offering to online platforms, in part because of the unique experience of live theatre, but also because of the potential risk of considerable numbers of audience members not returning post-pandemic if patterns changed from the enforced societal transformation of lockdown. Thus, there is a need for a good understanding of the different facets of digital transformation, which is this book's *raison d'être*.

However, to be able to shape some parts of society at all in the future, we need to know what we want. This applies to both individuals and organisations. First and foremost, it must be clear to us where we want to go, what we want to achieve (what our goals are), and how we will get there (which strategies we will choose and which decisions we will make). This may seem simple, but it is not. Building a vision and a goal in a complex environment and understanding how to realise them is difficult. Nevertheless, the need for clear preferences is often underestimated and clear preferences are rarely spelled out. At the same time, digitisation provides better conditions for success than ever—if we understand how to use it.

Amazingly, many still believe that introducing automation and information systems in various forms is enough to make their operations more efficient. The outcomes of such actions often become very costly.

One reason for this misconception is that technical design is a sidetrack in the context of an organisation. Instead, the real issue is understanding your goals and your organisation.

- You need to understand how people and parts of the organisation should interact to achieve clear and instrumental goals
- You need to understand the different processes in the organisation
- You must understand how to assess risks and opportunities
- You have to understand how to make decisions

If you take this as a point of departure, there are good opportunities to build an adequate IT business to support the organisation's processes and functions. This book, therefore, differs from a typical book on digital transformation and IT strategies. It is not about the details of implementing different types of information systems. Nor does it handle database design and data excerpts. You can easily find information on these elsewhere. Many of the technical details are also becoming increasingly obsolete as information system development becomes less and less computer-related and readily available modular products basically satisfy all our needs, as long as we know what we want.

In a meaningful book on digital transformation, whose underlying processes we will henceforth refer to as digitisation, strategies must therefore be about something completely different, something more fundamental. Thus, this book is about taking advantage of the opportunities that the now rather mature digitisation offers in a world of abundant data—and sometimes even a lack of relevant data. It is about understanding your goals and strategies and how business utility relates to your activities. It is about how to structure information and how to make decisions. It is about risk assessments and uncertainty. It is about project portfolios and project management. It is about organising resources and capacities. And it is about how to procure services and products, often from far afield in our increasingly connected world.

The book therefore considers digitisation based on what an organisation really is and what it needs. We describe how to understand an organisation's goals, develop its strategies, and shape its business models. The book is aimed at advanced-level university students and reflective practitioners looking for a deeper understanding of digital transformation. It is intended for an international audience and we therefore provide examples from organisations on different continents. However, since Scandinavia is among the forerunners in digital transformation, we have included numerous Scandinavian examples.

Theories are often good for understanding reality, but equally often it is difficult to understand how to actually use them in practical activities. Therefore, we also describe in detail how to achieve this by developing organisations, processes, decisions, configurations, and project implementations. We strive to address everyone who wants to understand how organisations should handle, and seriously take advantage of, the risky gold mining that digitisation actually is.

Happy reading!

The authors, January 2023

1. Introduction

The starting point for this book is that digitisation works as a catalyst for society and the organisations therein. A catalyst is something that increases the speed of a process without itself being consumed. It simply produces results faster. Digitisation, if used in the wrong way, can also make a bad situation worse. And it can make what functions well function even better. It is therefore absolutely crucial to start by making clear—or finding out—what one wishes to accomplish, and how well the way that the organisation is planned suits the realisation of that goal. Starting to run will not help an individual headed in the wrong direction. Quite the contrary. But as both the surroundings and the internal operations increasingly build on digitisation, it is important that those who work within an organisation can identify how digitisation affects its operations—and based on that, which technical solutions (IT) are needed to capture the possibilities offered by digitisation, and to avoid its pitfalls.

This book thus deals with value, organising, and digitisation—how to direct and organise one's business so as to take advantage of the possibilities that transformative use of IT, digital transformation, can offer, and not just temporarily and in the short run, but sustainably and in the long run (strategically). By digitisation, we mean the use of modern IT to create, deliver and use products (goods, services, and combinations of the two). When we speak of benefit and value, we do not simply mean asset growth for shareholders (shareholder value), but also value for other stakeholders—co-workers, customers, suppliers, and the organisational surrounding. Sometimes a venture can be positive to many, and sometimes interests clash. We strive to note discrepancies, but our main perspective is from within the organisation looking out; how can those in an organisation work to strategically further the business results? We focus on the organisation and the business it conducts; we

 https://doi.org/10.11647/OBP.0350.01

do not specifically look at individuals. We write about strategy and targeting goals, but this is not a book about the business leader or the brilliant technician as an omniscient hero. Nor are we primarily external observers, studying and assessing how the organisation affects others. But when adopting a perspective from within, we do so well aware that all organisations act in a context. Some parts of this context are in direct interaction with the organisation; others indirectly influence or are influenced by it. And yet others are so far from it that there is no discernible connection.

Given the focus on digitisation, our interest is directed at the digital and at digitisation as part of conducting business, not as technology in itself, or with a primarily technical focus. No doubt that machine, system, and information architectures all play a role in what can be accomplished, but we do not delve into the technical issues. And "IT" (denoting any technology for information transfer) has always been around in society: cuneiform writing, smoke signals, printing presses, abacuses, telegraphs, radio, computerised data handling, telecommunication, GPS, etc. Today, IT, or sometimes "modern IT", if one wishes to be more precise, is primarily used to signify that which is connected with computers: the hardware, but also the software and what the computers accomplish when the programs are run—computers as tools. Your smartphone and what it can assist you in doing is "modern IT". So, too, is much of the control of your modern cooker, and the card reader on the bus.

Our book is about navigating and handling a world with an abundance of data—and sometimes also a lack of relevant data. It is also about navigating a world where products increasingly build on digitisation. Music reaches us as files—resident or streamed—and digital music players (often as a part of a smartphone); the functions of a car are increasingly based on software and digital sensor data; money is increasingly digital, even in transactions between individuals; the airplane engine, with advanced software controls, is rented per flight hour (which are recorded by software); the forklift truck registers how it is driven, to provide a basis for upkeep, but also to identify needs for driver training; socialising and collaboration are increasingly digitised—via social network media, collaboration software, telephone, and video calls, and via the ability to digitally access the material we discuss.

Broadly speaking, digital transformation is the integration of digital technology into all areas of societal activities and processes. Digital transformation is about transforming organisational and societal structures by introducing digital information systems and flows as well as managing such structures and routines utilising these flows. Thus, digital transformations rest heavily on digital information systems, which have long been used to support various activities in organisations and have steadily reduced processing and communication times, but are now changing virtually all sectors of societal activities. Organisations can be geographically dispersed, and agents of various kinds can still communicate, collaborate, and coordinate their activities through standardised and automated dedicated digital platforms. Computation, storage, and transmission capacity are standardised services that can be bought from a host of global suppliers. The possibilities for collecting, analysing, and reporting data using a large set of tools and techniques have increased dramatically with the emergence of business intelligence tools, competitive intelligence, dashboards, data warehousing, data mining, and big data technologies, which have emerged and changed societal activities at large.

Digital transformation has changed product and service delivery in a fundamental way by changing the technological and cultural environment. It is, in principle, affecting everything since both the surroundings and the internal operations in many activities are increasingly built on digital solutions. As a consequence, digital transformations have fundamentally changed, and continue to change, our lives. Naturally, there are a lot of accompanying challenges on different levels. The surveillance capacities are increasing, privacy issues become alarming, social inequalities are emphasised, and although globalisation offers many opportunities, it also contains some severe issues for people that perceive that they are losing understanding, overview, and control. It is therefore crucial for decision-makers in societies and organisations as well as for citizens at large to regain control of the development and its substantial factors to avoid the otherwise inevitable alienation effects. It is therefore necessary to obtain the means to be able to identify how digital transformation affects societal operations in various contexts and to take command in a sustainable way of the challenges and possibilities it offers so as to navigate, control, and manage effectively in our world with its data abundance and control systems.

During this transformation, societies, organisations, and individuals would be wise to define their goals and in which manner digital solutions should be utilised to achieve them. Likewise, they should strive to find means to control their internal and external environments in increasingly complex contexts. Here, processes for adequate decision-making are of great importance. Otherwise, it will become costly in a variety of aspects: financial, integrity, efficiency, decision-making power, etc. Despite access to large amounts of information, we still have limited capacity to understand what we need and how to achieve our goals. Consequently, we need support for analysing our data and formulating our strategies in order to take control of the development. Nevertheless, the situation today is that most organisations do not have any structured procedures at all for handling decisions. Both methods and the knowledge by which to identify and analyse even fairly simple problems are lacking. Whatever people tend to believe, making adequate decisions is difficult but can be substantially facilitated by a methodical approach since human judgement, in many cases, is simply insufficient. Decision competence must be enhanced in several respects.

The possibilities for digital communication also decrease the need to build organisations according to geographical proximity; it is possible to communicate, direct, and monitor at a distance. In turn, this makes it possible for a particular organisation to be more geographically dispersed and facilitates collaboration between specialised organisations. Production, payroll, recruiting, product development, customer support and helpdesk, sales: all of these functions were previously natural parts of an organisation, and can now be specialties of focused organisations that, by buying and selling services, can collaborate as a coordinated unit, a virtual organisation delivering products to external customers.

What, then, is an organisation? A classical answer is that it is a cooperation to achieve a goal. People organise in order to achieve together what they cannot achieve on their own. One purpose can be simply socialising and human contact. But here, we concentrate on businesses that produce goods and services for customers, users, or members, who in turn can be individuals or organisations. In a juridical sense, an organisation can of course be owned and run by a single individual, a self-employed person. Most organisations conform to this type. But we direct our attention here to the larger ones, those composed of more than one person. Not all organisations are for-profit, and we will mix examples from for-profit enterprises with examples from the public and non-profit sectors. (We use the word 'organisation' in reference to all types of businesses. When we specifically mean for-profit businesses, we use the word 'company'.) When we talk of organising, we mean the creation, entertaining, and changing of organised ventures—which may be a part of an organisation, an entire organisation, or a collaboration between organisations. (Organising is the subject of Chapter 4.)

What is the digitisation intended to support? A strategic view of digitisation needs to start by addressing this issue.

1.1. Roles of Digitisation in Operations

Product development, production, project management and coordination, supplier communication, and customer communication: which functions in the business should really benefit from IT, and how? When digitisation more clearly became an important business issue, people started to think about which digitisation steps were important (and how), from capture to distribution of data, to the production-chain steps from orders and inbound logistics, to sales and outbound logistics. The point of departure is a physical production organisation. What can be digitised? That which is already clear data in paper (or similar) format does not require much imagination. In 1967, the Swedish public-sector telephone operator (Televerket) proudly announced to its customers that "computers will be introduced for handling telephone bills". But when many organisations have realised how to efficiently digitise the handling of such data, it will not provide any strategic benefits. However, it can be a disadvantage not to keep up with such development, if it provides clear benefits. Just imagine a bank not offering Internet banking to its customers.

The control of machines and of processes are obvious targets for digitisation, in turn providing possibilities for automation. Numerically controlled lathes, paper machines and increasing numbers of robots are now commonplace. Self-driving vehicles are increasingly being introduced into the consumer and professional markets and are expected to affect how we travel and ship goods.

After data and control, one next step was to think about what could be digitised in a good or a service. Watches, copying machines, and telephones are examples of physical goods that are now digitised. Analogue models have become curiosities. In services, delivery (of letters, music, games, and film) has undergone considerable change. Physical letters have been replaced by electronic messages. We want instantaneous, online access to newspapers, film, and music. Nowadays, we expect to be able to track the progress of a physical delivery or journey digitally. And in manufacturing, industry 4.0 is a concept for supply chains and production equipment that is connected and coordinated through standardised and automated digital communication. The transition from physical or analogue to digital can be expected to continue at the pace at which new possibilities for increased efficiency can be found—and sometimes at the pace at which new possibilities can be found, even if they do not lead to clearly increased efficiency; nowadays, there is a charm in digitisation. In some cases, this development leads to a change in what organisations produce, and how. ABB, Toyota, and Ericsson are increasingly becoming software companies, and their physical production is less and less manual. In other cases, the step from physical to digitised product and production logic is too large; those who were good at physical production, physical distribution, and physically performed services may find themselves being replaced by new organisations built on digitisation. The old postal services are not the leading actors in digital exchange. Camera and film companies, like Kodak, have been replaced by Samsung and Apple.

Digitisation presupposes choices of infrastructure. Half a century ago, it was important whether you chose IBM, Tandem, or Olivetti as your computer supplier because different suppliers' products were not compatible with each other; specific pieces of equipment would be suited—or less suited—for specific tasks, and the computer suppliers' future (and thus the future of the chosen infrastructure path) was uncertain. Today, the standardisation of hardware and networks has reached a level where such choices are no longer strategic to most organisations. Infrastructure is today normally a service rather than a good. Computation, storage, and transmission capacity are standardised services that can be bought from a host of global suppliers. The same goes for business applications: product databases, accounting, customer records, purchase history, webshops, etc., no longer need to be bought as software; they are available as services that many suppliers can offer of similar quality, capacity and, in mature markets, at similar prices. As technical choices become less important, the important decisions tend to revolve around cost efficiency, availability, and security—and the ability to move your data to another service supplier if the contract terms or the functionality should be significantly better there (see Chapter 4 on different ways of outsourcing IT, and benefits and drawbacks associated with these).

Technical standardisation, and the supply of computer resources and infrastructure as standardised, easy-to-access services at competitive prices, is a trend that started some years ago. It makes the technical choices less decisive for what types of applications and what types of data one will be able to handle—and to modify as new needs arise. It also increases the visibility of how business-relevant IT decisions concern important business issues—which information one wishes to derive from one's information systems to support which activities, in order to achieve which goals. IT use is not an end in itself; at its core, it concerns which results or goals one wants to reach, and thus in which manner IT will be needed to achieve them. In the changeable world of today and tomorrow, we can rest assured that our needs, and perhaps even our goals, will change rapidly. These changes will partly stem from opportunities created by the technical development, but socially, economically, politically, ethically, and materially driven changes will also affect both business and goals. It will then be important to be prepared in such a way that the IT support needed continues to work and can be obtained in a manner that meets new or changing needs. Such preparedness will need to build on technical insights and skills, but above all, it will need to build on insights in, and monitoring of, the other sources of change.

The development towards standardised architectures and services also means that it becomes increasingly important to truly understand the business that is to be supported, even more so than to profoundly understand the technology delivering the support. We are not claiming that any insight into technological issues is now superfluous—it is difficult to choose wisely if the functions under consideration are completely black-boxed. But deep insight becomes less important in step with the increase in the number of suppliers who can deliver equivalent services. And business insight has always been important, but the more the business builds on IT solutions and is intertwined with them (is digitised), the more important it becomes that the procurement of IT services builds on a solid understanding of the business needs, functioning, and resilience to disturbances.

The strategic IT issues used to be more of a computer-science nature. It was important to have methods for designing information systems, for maintaining them, and for further refining and developing them. Today, it is increasingly rather about developing the general strategic capability and decision-making in the organisation in order to achieve the organisational goals. IT becomes one of many support functions for achieving the goals, and IT-related decisions are being taken in more and more places in the organisation. Today, meaningful and valuable digitisation is everybody's responsibility.

1.2. IT's Informing Function

As noted above, IT can have different roles in an organisation. One aspect is how it contributes to realising the value proposition of the organisation, for example in relation to customers or suppliers, or as support for the co-workers' competence development. (This will be discussed further in Chapter 3.) Another aspect is how important IT is to the business: how mission-critical is it, and how much emphasis is there on being at the forefront of the use of IT? A coarse yet fundamental division of the roles of IT is into *rationalising* and *informing*.

IT's rationalising role—partly or entirely replacing manual labour in certain areas and thereby saving both time and money—has long been acknowledged. IT's role in generating, storing, and supplying information is also not new, as digital information systems have long been used to support the financial and operative reporting in organisations. But the last decades have brought a marked increase in the possibilities for data collection, analysis, and reporting, as well as a large set of tools and techniques, such as business intelligence, competitive intelligence, dashboards, data warehousing, data mining, and big data. This is a good reason for taking a closer look at how IT can contribute to informing. We will not place much emphasis on labels—they are broad, and there is rarely consensus on their exact meaning.

For example, business intelligence will be used to describe just about any kind of support for control and follow-up, with widely differing demands for functionality and much else that lies outside the transaction systems used at a given organisation. We are therefore going to concentrate on frequently occurring properties and functions of these types of systems, regardless of what the systems are called. What they have in common is that they provide data that should be possible to interpret into information about the business and its environment, so that co-workers at different levels can get a picture of how the business is working—and how it could work—and based on that make sound decisions and act in order to move the business in a desirable direction. To understand what is desirable, goals, standards, and other points of reference are needed. These can be both internal and external, historic and forward-looking, quantitative and qualitative. From this information perspective, some characteristics are particularly salient:

- Speed
- Integration
- Detail
- Orientation
- Accessibility

Speed. That information is provided reasonably quickly by means of IT could seem self-evident, but for a long time, there was a widespread view that information on managing organisations was not accessible sufficiently quickly. IT has certainly helped bring processing and communication times down. From the earlier process of monthly reporting being prepared manually by accountants, today, many people click themselves through to the latest figures on revenues and costs fairly soon after the events have taken place in the business. With the types of tools mentioned above, speed is even more pronounced: in many cases, there is even talk of real-time information provision. Production standstills and customers becoming dissatisfied are examples of events that it can be important to be informed of quickly. Automatic warnings can be sent to those responsible if a machine starts to malfunction or an important customer chooses to cancel a contract. This can enable responsive actions that might make a considerable difference. But speed in information transfers also increases transparency. I can no longer handle my tasks or area of responsibility and choose what becomes visible to others. Many others within (and sometimes also outside) the business can also have become aware of the disruptions at the same time as me—perhaps even before.

What is considered as rapid depends on the type of information, who should receive it, and on the strategy and business models of the organisation. The production line that has come to a standstill or the scandal that has erupted can be important to know at once—minutes can count. To the stock trader, fractions of seconds can be important, since the transactions are carried out at the speed of lightning and business opportunities come and go at that pace. But for someone negotiating a large bridge construction contract, "quickly" probably equates to days.

Integration. If the information provided via IT was previously dispersed over several systems—for example, one for financial information, one for customer and market information, one for personnel records, etc.—we today find an increasing emphasis on the unified image that IT can help provide. This is not just about the practicalities of having access via an integrated system, rather than having to look up different pieces of information in different systems. More importantly, systems integration can help provide an image of connections between different parts of the business.

Financial results are practically always focussed, regardless of whether there is an ambition to maximise profits or if it suffices that revenues simply cover costs (see Chapter 3 on how the different parts of the business model can be related). But financial results can contain many different business events, and therefore do not provide complete signals regarding the health of the business. For this reason, it is increasingly common that results are measured in multiple ways within an organisation. Measurements and indicators along multiple dimensions can indicate connections between the different parts, and thereby teach the co-workers what drives, for example, profitability at different stages. Is there a clear connection between short processing times of cases and customer satisfaction, or between the number of sales meetings and the level of revenue? Is the combination of certain people on a project profitable? How does the distribution of staff across different roles match the needs that the commitments of the coming months will pose? Information that is integrated from different parts of the business can also indicate clashes between different dimensions of the business. The successful decrease of lead times in production coincides with a dramatic increase in costs for certain purchased services. The emphasis on a new customer segment has given rise to helpdesk overload. The increased delivery precision does not at all show up in the customer satisfaction indicators. Such signals can also be important and provide bases for discussions about priorities.

Detail. For many purposes, financial information—such as balance sheets, income statements, and cash flow analyses—is too aggregated and abstract to provide sufficient insight regarding the business. Integrating it with other types of data can then be a way of providing a more concrete and nuanced picture. Also, the possibility to "drill down" (to look at constituent parts, possibly all the way down to individual transactions) that digitised data provide can help inform the user. Financial (and non-financial) data can often provide insights, but interpreting them is also likely to raise questions that require further investigation or at least an increased level of detail, for example regarding a particular employee, rather than an entire department; a well-defined customer group, rather than all customers; a particular day, rather than the entire month. It could be, starting from a cost item in the income statement, to click your way right down to the individual invoice that caused the variance. It could be to use more sophisticated cost allocation to generate insights regarding the profitability of different customer groups (perhaps one ought to direct more attention to some groups than to others?). Or it could be to visualise the customer-service call load hour-by-hour over the month so as to better plan the manning of the helpdesk.

Orientation. Data processing can also provide indications of what could happen, rather than just telling us what has already happened. A classic example of this is making suggestions to customers regarding other items they may want to buy, in addition to what they have already placed in their digital shopping cart. Another example is banks' efforts to warn customers of possible frauds or to forecast which customers will probably not repay their loans (and through this forecasting, the ability to standardise the lending process more thoroughly). Retail chains can use weather forecasts to predict demand patterns for umbrellas, drinks, etc. Municipalities study migration and birth statistics to better forecast the required dimensioning of day-care and schools. Other areas, too, have been impacted by forward-looking IT applications. The police in several countries use forecasting to determine whether criminal events are related and could have been committed by one and the same offender, and if—and when—new crimes may be expected. In healthcare, digitised models are used to predict the survival rates for different types of cancer.

Accessibility. If many are to be able to use "informing" IT tools as a normal part of their work, rather than these being confined to specialists, then intuitive presentation of information, requiring less user experience, is needed. It can also be important to present data in a visually appealing manner, for example using colours effectively to enhance the clarity of presentation. This may sound obvious, but at least previous generations of informing IT tools were often deficient in these respects. The development of fast storage and computation capacity now allows for both fast analyses of large amounts of data and the possibility to instantaneously click on to further analyses of what a figure builds on (as described in the "Detail" section above). Also, comparison presentations are becoming more common, and show relevant standards and historical values, thereby indicating variances and needs for action more clearly. What can be regarded as diverging and what action will be required to address the deviation, is of course not universally given, but will rather build on what has been agreed on in the organisation, and on subjective assessment. But standards can be built into systems and help generate automated suggestions for actions in specified situations.

The information characteristics presented above overlap to some extent. For example, integrated information can also lead to faster access and provide a more detailed picture. Depending on the extent to which the characteristics are emphasised, the informing role of IT can include anything from a clearer visualisation of existing data—for example a financial monthly report with coloured graphs—to forecasts of customer preferences, detection of competitor product launches, or support of decision processes. The affordances are not limited to structured data; unstructured data, such as free text and images, can also be included. Examples include searches in patent databases, product launches, etc., to become informed about what competitors are doing, to find potential partners, or to identify talents to recruit. Another possibility is automated scanning of social media in order to assess how the organisation, or specific goods or services, are mentioned and discussed. This can lead to dialogues with customers and opinion leaders, to adjustments of the marketing, product design, complementing services, etc.

1.3. Information and Value

We want to emphasise that supplying information with the aid of modern IT does not automatically generate value. There are limitations in the systems and how they match the organisation. No tool solves all challenges and problems; flexible tools, too, have their areas of application, and their limitations. When investing in a system of this type, it is first crucial to determine the needs for structuration in the different decision situations in the organisation to ensure that adequate structure and correct bases are available to enable efficient and effective decision-making considering operational and business risks. Posing clear requirements on the decision processes and the bases for decisions enables the appropriate design of systems support for different types of decisions. Of course, however, it is difficult to determine exactly what information will be needed in the future.

We illustrate this with a case description of work to improve the accounting information setting at a construction company.

Construction Firm had a somewhat outdated accounting information setting, including a plethora of information systems that were deemed user-unfriendly. Accounting information here refers to a variety of financial and non-financial numbers that are compiled in an organisation to provide, for example, managers at different levels with an insight into how the business is progressing and bases for their decisions. It can encompass anything from the profitability of different products; staff cost in relation to total cost; the level of CO_2 emissions; the number of workplace accidents; and customer-satisfaction scores, to how many projects are finished on time—anything that people in an organisation choose to record to provide an image of the business. The same data existed in several places, and the choice of which system to rely on depended on the habits in a given department, business area or geographical region. Sometimes, there was a need to access data from several systems in order to compose a more complete picture, for example in preparation for the yearly discussion of how to act on the market during the coming year. Which customers and products have the greatest potential and should be given the most attention? Financially: which profitability patterns can be discerned in different customer and product groups? Strategically: is there a reason to start constructing a number of environmentally certified houses to signal (or meet) environmental consciousness? Which events can be perceived on the horizon, for example, is any potential customer planning a large construction, and should we then submit a tender for it? What is the distribution of professions/positions? Are too many foremen approaching retirement, causing a risk of a lack of qualified personnel when large projects start in the coming years?

Since the data to explore such issues resided in different systems, it was manually extracted and compiled in Excel sheets. Even the quarterly reviews of the business demanded a great deal of manual work in order to achieve a clear view of economic status, customer relations, procurement, safety, etc.

The head office called for a "more professional information use". Their ambition was, through new information systems, to both make the handling of management control information more efficient and create more relevant grounds for decisions. The latter would be accomplished by tailoring the information supply to managers based on level and department. Those managing production at a site probably need different information from those managing a district with hundreds of construction projects. By creating easily accessible accounting information views tailored to the specific management role, those at headquarters hoped that the managers would make better-informed decisions.

The head office initiators were keen to involve the members of the organisation in the work, so they performed solid investigations; surveys, interviews and workshops were used to capture how the managers experienced the accounting information setting and what their wishes for it were. Most of the views received concerned the need to simplify and make the information setting more efficient; accounting information handling should be fast so time can be spent on other tasks. Views and search paths were felt to be complicated; sometimes time-consuming, non-intuitive search commands for reaching relevant data led to compact tables in black, grey and white. The managers expressed that they would rather have integrated systems, so that manual transfers of data would not be required. They also wanted to be able to quickly report using smartphones and hand terminals regardless of their location and to have appealing and logical user interfaces with, for example, illustrative warning flags.

Thus, there was no lack of opinions about the processing and presentation of data, but relatively few suggested types of information that they thought were missing. Some wanted a better overview of prices of purchased goods and services in order to compare districts, or more feedback regarding previous projects in order to create more realistic budgets for future projects, but many found it difficult to think afresh. To instead ask managers to describe specific decision instances in their work, and what information they felt they needed there, did not help; the majority still found it difficult to identify something that they lacked and that could help make them better informed. In addition, many line managers held the opinion that more information and analysis was not necessarily beneficial. Being a line manager largely means handling customer contacts, keeping a time-pressed production on track, and being present in operations, or handling unforeseen events. To sit in the office and ponder information competes with other tasks. It can even lead in the wrong direction. One type of project can be successful in one instance, and in the next work badly, depending on who from the construction company is involved, who the customer is, and which suppliers are contracted. To believe that a certain type of project is always profitable or that a supplier works well, just because some numbers from a previous project say so, was considered naïve.

As a first step in improving the accounting information setting, a Business Intelligence solution was introduced to collect and visualise financial and HR data. The tools did not provide much new data; largely, existing data were provided. But they were presented in an appealing manner. For example, the financial results were presented in colourful graphs, while the HR tools collected dispersed information without missing any details. Even reminders of employees' birthdays were included. The BI tools were gradually rolled out and were appreciated. There was even talk of them in districts where access had not yet been provided, and even really sceptical managers had turned enthusiastic.

This case illustrates a number of necessary considerations in just about any organisation aiming to advance their use of the informing function of IT.

- It is typically easier to see the potential for a rationalising, rather than truly informing, use of IT. For example, making existing data and information timelier and more clearly visualised is more likely to come up as an improvement request than requests for retrieving entirely new types of data and information. The latter requires co-workers to think more outside the box.
- We humans cannot cope with unlimited amounts of information. There is a reason why we often term accounting information 'Key Performance Indicators'; the information should stress what is most important—key—in the business, not everything that is going on.
- Data and information are not sufficient *per se*. Rules, standards, and other means for sorting and evaluating data and information are also needed. For example, some tools can process data and summarise them in key indicators, but it is we who choose the indicators, and these choices matter; are we actually highlighting what is really key? Other tools sift through available data, summarising and selecting that which, according to set rules, is deemed worthy of attention and closer scrutiny. This could be sifting through a news flow to identify articles that deal with our organisation or with our competitors. It could be to find deviations from forecasts in structured data. The automated sifting decreases the need for

> human toil and attention, but we still need to assess that which is being presented and act on it. What are the consequences for us of the expected product launch of a competitor in a year? Should we do something to benefit more greatly from the current praise of our sustainability drive? Is our employee turnover at an appropriate level? Is our profitability sufficient? Is it a problem that the number of customers in a specific segment is low?

In every organisation (and in its sub-operations and departments) there is a need to establish norms and to set standards for what is to be viewed as desirable and worth striving for, or undesirable, and what requires action, and what does not. A part of establishing norms and standards is to formulate strategies and/or business models (see Chapters 2 and 3). Thereby, one defines what is important to do and to achieve, and what is less so. It is thus not sufficient to compile information from different parts of the organisation and its environment; that information needs to be related to something. A systematic way of supporting the use of available information is through the design of structured decision processes. In Chapter 5, we will therefore take a closer look at how an integrated decision process can be structured to use all of the information and synthesise it in a systematic decision process. Finally, it is also important to consider what is important in the available information. How quickly should it be available? How detailed should it be? Who requires what? The needs differ between organisations, between roles, and between individuals, as demonstrated above.

1.4. Type of Business Determines IT Needs

All organisations are unique, to some extent. But there are of course also similarities and common denominators. All enterprises need some type of accounting. Everyone who has co-workers needs to keep track of who they are, just as all those who have recurring contacts with customers need to keep track of who these customers are. Those who have active contracts with customers or suppliers need to keep track of what these contracts contain. Just about every organisation needs ways of paying out and receiving money. And so on. When any such generic need becomes extensive, IT solutions can likely be useful.

But what hides behind these generic needs? In what ways do enterprises differ in manners that matter to the choice of IT support? Look at the following list of enterprise types. Does it seem likely that they require similar IT support?

- Service company, mass service (hotel, taxi, home care)
- Mass-production (assembly line, process industry, prefabricated housing)
- Customised (unique) production (design your own shoe at Nike, Sculpture, 3D printing of unique items, unique buildings [advanced bridge, palace, ...])
- Trading platforms (generic/special goods and services)
    - Generic goods and services, like Amazon, Alibaba; hotels.com, ticketing.com, Uber, Lyft
    - Special goods and services, like via eBay, AirBnB
- Payment solutions (Amazon Pay, PayPal, Standard Bank, Société Générale, Visa, MasterCard, Bitcoin)
- News agencies, media companies

Of course they require different kinds of support. The challenges for the hotel differ from those of a dairy plant, a marketplace for transportation or a news agency. For that reason, the strategic decisions concerning IT support made by each kind of business will also differ. And two similar enterprises may even face similar IT-support issues, but still ultimately make different decisions.

Another dimension is how much of the enterprise the IT-related decision should affect. Is it intended to support a specific department, a collaboration between departments, a rethinking of how to conduct the business (provided suitable IT support)? Or is it about transcending the own organisation's boundaries and supporting the interaction with customers and suppliers, or increasing the level of ambition even more, changing the roles of the collaborating partners? The unit that is facing automation of certain tasks; the product development group that is seeking better contact with and feedback from customers; the record company that moves from selling records to selling music files, or even to streaming the music via a subscription-based intermediary;

the consumer-goods company that starts to use crowdsourcing as a part of product development; the camera manufacturer that moves into organising and making the customers' pictures accessible: all these changes have, or can have, extensive IT elements that require strategic positioning. The considerations leading up to such decisions can be more of a technical nature, like scalability, operational reliability, and data security, or novel versus well-tried solutions. But to a large extent, they could be expected to be operations- and business-related, such as appropriate degree of automation; possible customer reactions and the own ability to process and deal with feedback from customers; the impact of alternative sales channels and price models on the profitability of the business; the build-up of competence to be able to attract and keep a community of constructively imaginative individuals; the ability to develop, launch and monetise appreciated picture-management services. This does not mean that the considerations are operations- and business-related *instead of* being IT-related; it is a matter of IT-related operations and business issues.

1.5. Digital Transformation and Fundamental Rethinking

Many high-profile, much talked about and highly-valued ventures that build on extensive use of IT have emerged since the turn of the millennium. Amazon, Alibaba, Spotify, Uber, and Lyft have reshaped business networks by acting as new middlemen—electronic platforms that enable those who want to offer products to reach potential customers and to do business with them. *Huffington Post*, Kickstarter, and Airbnb crowdsource from individuals to individuals to offer services that compete with established actors such as the BBC and *The Times*, BNP and Standard Bank, Hilton and Accor. All of these companies appear innovative and require both advanced IT solutions and positioning regarding business focus and competitive opportunities. It is no coincidence that the new business models are not presented by the existing large actors in these markets. They already have functioning, often profitable and large businesses that are worth maintaining, rather than radically changing. Rapid IT development can influence the organisational climate in IT-intense operations. But that does not mean that all IT-related change is rapid. There can, as just noted, be commercial reasons for not rapidly and radically changing functioning operations and business models. Also, people are not machines, and it is the rule rather than the exception that compared with the rate of technical development, the rate of change involving a change of mindset and human behaviour is slow. Even if it is possible to build a new organisation with a business logic that diverges from that of existing competitors, it can still be highly challenging to convince intended customers and suppliers to accept the new approach as trustworthy, functional, and valuable.

When new models are launched and become successful, they are adapted by other actors who want to start similar ventures. Amazon's web bookshop soon elicited followers like the Swedish Bokus. Spotify inspired Apple to start Apple Music and the discount broker Charles Schwab showed the way for similar actors such as Avanza. For these followers/challengers, the strategic decisions to be made can differ somewhat from the challenges facing the innovators. Both the technical solutions and the business models already exist. The question is whether they can be improved and made more efficient, or if it is even possible for clones to enter the market and acquire customers without competing with the innovators. Sometimes, the IT solutions themselves can differentiate an actor, and be the reason why a customer (or a supplier) chooses one over another. Differentiation might lie in user friendliness or functionality. If so, then IT design is central. Alternatively, the IT solution may remain in the background, with the differentiation lying in the price model or range of the offer. In such cases, the IT design will only become relevant to competitiveness if it fails in some respect, for example if there are long or frequent service interruptions, incompatibility with new user devices, or insufficient security leading to the theft of user data.

IT is always used in a particular context. A department forms one part of an organisation, and has parallels in other enterprises. The organisation, in turn, is both a part of networks of customers, suppliers, and other stakeholders, and a part of a category of similar organisations—with or without competitive relations to each other. From a still larger perspective, we can see the organisation as a part of an ecology of enterprises, actors, institutions, and ideas which interact in ways that change over time. Today, there are not many ventures where smartphones do not form a part of everyday life, and of the organisation's active or passive infrastructure. Crowdsourcing and servitisation are ideas that have arisen in different places and have come to spread increasingly in the business ecology (the wide and far-reaching business surrounding), not just close to where the ideas originated. Strategic decisions tend to be presented as unique, but normally, they are rather a case of being able to recognise a good idea and realise how it can be made to fit the circumstances in which one is operating.

1.6. Significance of Systematic Decision-making

In a complex environment, it is crucial to be able to make reasonable decisions in an organisation. Having larger or smaller sets of data will not suffice as bases for decisions, and will not help if systematic decision processes are lacking. This is true not least when it comes to formulating a strategy for reaching a set goal. The ability to make conscious decisions is thus absolutely vital. The central decisions that are made are often important for the business and associated with varying degrees of risk. It is also easy to give competitive advantages to other businesses that have a better overview of their decision-making processes. Decision situations are generally characterised by unique assumptions, poor structure, and high complexity. Despite this, rather few reflect on why they act in a certain manner. Instead, one guesses and seldom understands one's own motives. Nevertheless, one must make the decision to survive. So, what should the organisational decision process look like? When people in an organisation formulate a decision, they face numerous questions:

- What are the relevant alternatives? And how do we know that all important alternatives are included?
- What are the relevant consequences?
- Which views and people are important to pay heed to? How important are these people and their opinions? Which perspectives are important to consider?
- Which values are important in the decision setting? How can these values be assessed?
- How can we correctly estimate the probabilities?

- Do we need additional knowledge to make the necessary decisions?
- How do we know that a decision is well-founded and correct?

Based on such questions, we will keep returning to theories and practices about decisions and decision-making processes throughout this book. The reason for having a decision-making process is to achieve a better quality of decision. This is, however, not easy to assess, but a reasonable quality requirement is that the decision-making process provides more effective methods for collecting and analysing knowledge communicated to employees and other stakeholders and that it does not become too costly in relation to its value. You then must ask yourself how to judge whether the basis for a decision is solid enough, and how to estimate the value of additional information to supplement the basis. Regardless of whether the decision concerns a problem or an opportunity, it is important to know what you want to achieve. If the decision is well-founded and you follow up on its consequences, it will generate knowledge about the business and its environment that may be applied in future decision-making processes.

1.7. A Global Perspective

Digital transformation is an opportunity and enabler for companies, organisations, sectors, and institutions worldwide, not least in the developing world. It is not something you enter, implement, and conclude. It is not a destination; it is a permanent state of evolution that one enters and re-enters to achieve one's goals. From promising but expensive IT activities to be used for different purposes, understandings of the digital and its enabling components have matured together with several powerful technologies, where artificial intelligence (AI) is one component. Fuelled by fundamental needs in the developing world, digital transformation (and AI) has moved to the top of the agenda of key international organisations such as the United Nations, UNESCO, the European and the African Union.

Both the upside and the downside of digital transformation were forcefully demonstrated during the Covid-19 pandemic. For example, in higher education, digitisation has become a challenge, opportunity, and threat to which universities around the world must respond. In value chains and value networks, digital transformation had allowed the development of logical coordination of geographically distant units spanning the globe, which proved vulnerable to physical and political disruptions during the pandemic and to political reactions to armed conflict and conflicting political ambitions. Thus, attempts at digital transformation should not be blind to physical and political aspects potentially affecting the transformation.

1.8. The Structure of the Book

We have noted that people in organisations act based on different time perspectives, both short-term and long-term. Acting for the long term is often viewed as acting strategically. The idea is that strategies should act as guidelines for the organisation in its short-term, daily operation. Digital transformation has potentially given us access to more information than ever to support the work, it enables automation of tasks, and can give rise to entirely new products, forms of enterprise, and ways of conducting business.

In the process of formulating and applying strategies, those responsible within the organisation need to include and reflect on how digitisation can contribute value to its long-term aims.

But what characterises organisational goals and strategy processes? And how are they affected by digitisation? We delve into these issues in Chapter 2. Then, in Chapter 3, we go on to illustrate how the concept of business models can contribute to the strategic discussion. Business modelling is about identifying activities that contribute to the realisation of strategies. We focus on how benefits can be achieved via digitisation, or even how digitisation can form the very foundation of a business model.

So far, the focus has been on strategies and business models, on goals and opportunities creation. In Chapter 4, we focus on how we can act to realise such opportunities. The basis is organising, how organisations can divide and coordinate tasks and decision-making for digitisation—within an organisation or between separate organisations. This involves roles to capture and realise the potential of digitisation, which role holders provide input and make decisions, competencies that are important for understanding the role of digitisation in the business and how people's experience and competencies can be united in a fruitful, rather than conflict-laden, way in the digitisation effort. Next, in Chapters 5, 6, and 7, we return to the issue brought up above in Subchapter 1.6: how to achieve a better structure of grounds for decisions and of decisions themselves, how this can be applied in the important area of procurement, and how uncertainty and risk, which always accompany decision settings and planned activities, can be managed through probability and risk analyses.

Digitisation and strategy work often bring change to the organisation, and such change can be handled via projects. Therefore, the book deals with two aspects of projects. At a strategic level, managing the entire set of projects is important. Which projects should we run, which should we discontinue, and how does the portfolio of projects contribute to realising the organisation's strategy? Thus, the first project-related aspect is project portfolios from both practical and theoretical viewpoints (Chapter 8). Having provided this context, we then move on to the second aspect, the projects themselves: how projects can be conducted, what must be considered in the organisation regarding running projects, and methods and tools available for project managers (Chapter 9).

Chapter 10 focuses on the issue of globally sustainable digital transformation, specifically looking at universities. Universities face a major challenge if they are to contribute to the United Nations' Sustainable Development Goal 4, "to ensure inclusive and equitable quality education and promote lifelong learning opportunities for all." In the eleventh and final chapter, we summarise the messages of the book. We start by exploring the business ecology perspective on digitisation that we have pointed to in previous chapters. Then, we relate what we have focused on in the book to an overarching model of organisational focus. From this wider scope, we return to our messages about strategies, goals and business models, decision-making and risks, and projects and project portfolios. To conclude, we remind readers of the catalyst metaphor with which we opened the book. Digitisation works as a catalyst—that which is good can become better, but that which is not functioning well and carefully designed can also effectively get worse. This is why it is so important to try to understand what the attempted digitisation should lead to, and how to work to keep guiding the process in the desired direction.

2. Organisational Goals, Strategies, and Digitisation

Many organisations rely on the assumption that they exist because they want to achieve something. Linked to this vision, there are (more or less) stated goals. Before we study how the digitisation of organisations can contribute to the fulfilment of goals, or the other way around, we first have to discuss and understand what organisational goals might be, and what it means to work strategically to achieve them. At the beginning of this chapter, we therefore give examples of different types of organisational goals. The strategy concepts are then presented, together with some challenges that may arise when organisations formulate and implement strategies. Throughout the chapter, we emphasise the role that digitisation may have in goal fulfilment as well as strategy realisation, and how digitisation may enable new strategies and goals. The chapter builds partly on strategy literature and partly on interviews with managers within organisations who work directly or indirectly with strategic business projects where IT plays a central, and in some cases crucial, role.

2.1. Organisational Goals

If the employees in an organisation are asked to identify the goals of their organisation, their answers will probably differ. There may be several reasons for these differences, but primarily it is a matter of different perspectives. What is the purpose of the organisation? Who should it benefit? How does it contribute to the development of its employees? If you are the CEO, the answer to the first two questions may be "the shareholders and other important stakeholders". The answer to the last question may be "through stimulating tasks". If you are a seller,

 https://doi.org/10.11647/OBP.0350.02

your answers may be "customers" and "opportunities for achieving sales bonus". This illustrates that there are many types of goals within organisations, some of which are written down and determined by the board and management, while others are more personal. From the perspective that IT should be contributing to organisational goal fulfilment, it is necessary to sort and prioritise the various goals.

2.1.1. Goals, Time Perspectives, and Goal Conflicts: Some Examples

There are some basic issues that can be considered starting points in a discussion about the goals of organisations. One is the need to factor in a time perspective. An organisation must be able to achieve some goals in a relatively short time, for example within a year. Others are more long-term and extend five, ten, or fifteen years into the future. The long term is especially important when organisations are identifying how digitisation affects them, and prioritising which IT systems to invest in. Are they investing to maintain the competitiveness of the current business model? Will the technology ensure that new products and value propositions can be developed in the long term? (We return to how digitisation can affect business models in the next chapter.) Within banks, for example, (but also in other industries) it is common for people to be organised into different business divisions or groups. These divisions have plans for IT investments that may extend over periods of three to five years. Such plans indicate how the business will allocate its resources, i.e., what they will invest in. In addition, there are elements within the overall organisation that take care of overarching infrastructure, such as databases. An IT manager for a business area in a large bank described challenges in prioritising IT investments:

> Of the resources spent on IT projects, about 19% goes to compulsory projects, 19% to maintenance projects, 30% to strategic investments and 32% to business ventures. What you first have to cut down on is the business part. Everything that is compulsory is prioritised as this is based on legislation. In second place comes maintenance projects, the do-or-die projects. The next step [the third] is strategic development. We have a really huge system park, so we need to plan for five to fifteen years ahead when it comes to strategic development. Such projects are like big dragons that cost a lot, but it can be hard to capitalise on the benefits

> they generate at once. It would be great if we could do that and also distribute it over a long period of time, but it is difficult to measure such immediate benefits. Then [in fourth place] comes the business ventures, if there is anything left. My main responsibility lies at this level. I have a project portfolio with different bricks, but no mortar. But it's even worse for those that are responsible for the big giants [steps 1-3 above], these are projects where you cannot stop individual projects without affecting the others.

Some frustration can be sensed in this quotation. An organisation carries a digital backpack in its everyday life that may weigh them down, as it contains, among other things, life support functions. It is therefore not always possible to simply open the backpack and fill it with new digital solutions to whatever extent an organisation desires. An important reason for this is that organisations are complex phenomena. A drawing of the organisation may show it as pretty well sorted, with straightforward linear operations, when it in fact is relatively multi-layered and multidimensional. This means that there is often consensus regarding the organisation's overall goals, but when moving down into the different layers, you soon find that there is a variety of goals in the organisation. These goals are given different priorities depending on where someone is active in the organisation.

The quotation is also an example of how time affects the nature of goals and priorities. Short-term goals, such as units produced per month, customer satisfaction per quarter, or sales per half-year, can often be quite easily measured and followed up. The longer the time horizon, the greater the likelihood that the goals of organisations are non-quantifiable (we return to the long-term goals connected to the dragons in the example above in Chapter 8, when we discuss project portfolios). These goals are an expression of the long-term endeavour and alignment of the organisation's operations, rather than anything concrete and verifiable. Here, the difference between what can be perceived as vision and goals also becomes somewhat unclear. These goals and visions also often change over time.

In relation to the time perspective, it is also necessary to take into account the fact that many organisations have multiple hierarchical levels. In larger companies and public organisations, these levels are often referred to as strategic, tactical, and operational levels. At the strategic level, we find the top management of the organisation, for example a CEO, with function managers such as the Financial Manager (CFO), IT Manager (CIO), Human Resources Manager (HR Manager), and so on. These are the people who are primarily expected to formulate the long-term overall goals, and are responsible for continuously monitoring how well they are fulfilled in the various functions of the organisation. At the tactical level (as in the bank example) the overall goals should then be transformed into unit-specific goals that are more measurable and can be implemented at the operational level, where the everyday production of goods and services takes place.

This ideal image rarely reflects real happenings in organisations, however. Working with different goals tends to be simultaneous with and parallel to various parts of the organisation. The everyday lives of business executives are often packed with operational issues, and an individual seller at the operational level may occasionally manage to derive strategically important contracts. Seen from a digitisation strategy perspective, there are many examples of individual initiatives at an operational level having led to changes in goals as well as strategies. Establishing email, using smartphones, and more, have come to affect working methods and business models without having been introduced or guided by business objectives. The digitisation of mass media in the form of digital cameras and photo editing has snuck through many small decisions, but has had great implications regarding, for example, staffing and news design.

In other words, effective IT utilisation has rarely been initiated by the top management or driven by organisational goals. It has often instead been the result of initiatives from individual employees or groups who have struggled to convince others in the organisation that digital initiatives can be of strategic importance.

For example, the newly appointed HR manager of a large global company group (operating in over 100 markets; an organisation with almost 5,000 employees, and 35 local sales organisations) found that the HR function was neglected. He found that information was unclear regarding, for example, competence among employees. There was thus a need to catalogue, categorise and structure master data (central data) and to automate the most common HR transactions, such as salary, leave, and vacation. The perceived deficiencies in the organisation's HR function involved, among other things, their origin in different views of its role. To communicate the need for a digital renewal of the HR function, the HR manager established a clear goal for the HR function:

> My predecessor believed that HR is a function that should wait for the business to express their need for HR support. I believe that we are a profession. The business does not always know what they want or what they need. We should therefore be able to look around the corner and foresee the needs that may arise.

The quotation is an example of the fact that the establishment of goals in organisations depends, among other things, on where in the organisation they are formulated. The HR manager further noted:

> The company's opinion was that HR was very slim, they believed that it was almost anorexic. The first thing I did was a current situation analysis, where I excavated all costs and what people did. I found that, for example, they did not report within the HR function. People who worked in HR reported instead to a country manager somewhere, or to someone who recruited them locally. I came to the conclusion that we had an overall HR cost of almost ten million euros. The management group had not previously understood, they had never seen it that way. Then I said that this is the cost basis on which we are to transform our HR function. My goal was to get down to a cost of seven million euros for HR, although we at the same time would invest in new digital technology. We could see that in comparison with other organisations, we were under-invested in terms of technology. So I gave it a number, we were going to reach seven million euros.

A quantitative goal, reducing costs for the HR department by three million euros, became the starting point for the HR manager and how he communicated with others in the management group. As a first step, it was determined that better IT support was needed, as the existing system was somewhat inefficient. They chose SuccessFactors, a cloud-based system for managing an organisation's human capital through payroll management, recruitment, personnel, and so on. The system is a standalone application that downloads data from the rest of the organisation. The system was introduced almost entirely through the HR manager's initiative:

> To accomplish this, I took chances as they appeared. When we had problems with incentive programs, I used them to initiate a new system. Then I got to implement the first module in this program [SuccessFactors].

> After that, I got no as an answer every time I argued for a new module. Each time! Everyone thinks it's fantastic, but the CEO is doubtful. So when we argue for it in the management team, they reply "No, we're waiting. It looks expensive." So I've had to prove it made a difference and so I finally got to implement it module by module. So instead of taking a year, I'm now in the third year of implementation.

Despite the fact that the HR manager felt that he had communicated a clear goal (to reduce costs by three million euros), his enthusiasm was not shared fully by the other members of the management group. Among other things, he noted that:

> The goals of the project were not formulated by the CEO. There is a difference in the view of whether we are a strategic department or just some kind of support. I believe we have strategic value. My boss only cares whether we are cost-effective. If he was interested, then maybe he would see the value creation that this could enable. He is beginning to realise it now, but that is because we now have managed to push forward the HR positions.

The introduction of the actual system is a project that involved different phases:

> First, we threw out the system we had used for measuring goals because it was far too arbitrary. It was a direct cost saving to implement a modern system instead of the homemade one we had used, because we got rid of a lot of maintenance costs. Then I managed to buy a module that you can use to identify development opportunities and performance and to build the basis for relevant benchmark figures. Now we are looking at connecting it to the payroll systems that the company group uses around the world.

As the new HR system came into place, it became obvious that it was not only the system that the organisation needed to update. The following illustrates that strategic work on digitising information flows is not obvious in an organisation if IT only is considered a support function:

> What we have done here is something the whole organisation needs to do, within each department and division. Today we have about forty different systems within the organisation, through untamed growth over time. Because some of these systems have reached their technological limit, this was also partly a forced IT change. Many departments work in too many systems, making it complicated to obtain data. Now, all the other departments talk about how well the HR department is doing—and

> that they have to do the same. This project has become a catalyst for the rest of the organisation.

The goals set by the HR manager have been important in gaining acceptance for the system and therefore pushing it forward:

> My boss is used to people selling things that never happen. So I just sold this digital project based on cost savings. I started with value but noticed that it was an argument that received no response. At the same time, I have been able to show results. No one else in the management group has saved 30% and is about to halve their staff—and in fact has almost done it. Nobody has dared to stick their neck out by proposing such a clear goal as I have.

2.1.2. Organisational versus Personal Goals

Another important aspect when considering organisations and their goals is that organisations, as we discovered in Chapter 1, are a collection of individuals. If, for example, we receive a salary from an organisation, we probably have the same interest as the rest of the organisation when it comes to making long-term positive financial results, because there is a clear connection between the cessation of the organisation and the absence of our salary. In the long term, however, payment is rarely, or perhaps never, the main reason why an individual works in an organisation day after day. There are additional values, such as being part of a social community and self-realisation, or even a desire to contribute to a better world. The individuals in an organisation have (more or less) explicit personal goals, that is to say, things they hope to achieve through all the time they spend working.

If an individual's personal goals deviate too far from the organisation's goals, there is a clear risk of conflict. In turn, this can affect the individual's will to make sensible efforts at work. If this is true for several key persons, then it may have consequences for an organisation's overall goal fulfilment. This can be the case particularly in organisations where the business model is based on a digital product (we will offer examples of such business models in the next chapter). In these organisations, the staff is generally made up of a few key individuals, such as designers, programmers, and project managers, even though the turnover is usually in the hundreds of millions. Such organisations can be particularly vulnerable to conflicting goals at the individual level.

It is therefore important to ask oneself: how can I understand and interpret organisational goals? A common way to do this is to make a rough and simplified division of the goals, categorised as either financial or non-financial. We start with a review of financial targets.

2.1.3. Financial Goals

It is often assumed that the overall goal of owners of a company, such as the shareholders of a limited company, is to maximise their return on investment (ROI = value of profits in the financial statement in relation to the value of the assets in the balance sheet). Of course, there may also be many other reasons why someone owns a share of a company, such as tradition, technological development, self-determination, good citizenship, and power. There are, in other words, many possible drivers. But financial goals, whether in terms of profit maximisation or just long-term survival, are important. Today, for example, the vast majority of citizens in Sweden are shareholders in, and thus owners of, various companies via the government-run pension system, although they are rarely aware of which companies. The ROI target is a priority for these pension schemes. Financial goals are also fundamental for a business, as they enable it not only to initiate new investments and survive in the long term but also to continue to provide financial returns to its owners.

The profit maximisation perspective assumes that a company's actions are basically rational. This means that all of the activities that take place at the company must aim to contribute to its financial goals. Activities that do not do this should be stopped. This type of rational argument for goal fulfilment is one reason why many companies continuously strive to streamline their operations. For example, the automation of certain functions in an organisation can reduce costs. The development of products via digitisation can contribute to increased competitiveness and revenues. Increased competitiveness is necessary for organisations that are active in a competitive market if they wish to survive in the long term.

It is not just in private companies with financial goals that striving for efficiency is central. Public organisations must ensure that tax revenues cover the costs of providing services to the citizens of, for example, a municipality. Income from members and donors has to cover the costs for non-profit organisations. Profit maximisation is probably not the overall goal for either public or non-profit organisations, though.

Instead, it may be providing the best possible healthcare, giving help to the vulnerable, or contributing to a safer upbringing for children. As financial goals are still central to such organisations, however, target conflicts can easily arise. A medical doctor will be frustrated when a county council budget does not allow the treatment of patients by use of a certain sort of medicine, or the manager of an orphanage may be frustrated when the organisation lacks the financial resources to accept more children.

Studies of digitally driven process transformation in various industries such as publishing and printing, grocery retailing, and healthcare show, as expected, that some succeed better than others, and some fail completely. It is common to these industries, however, that IT increases productivity. Of course, it can contribute to significantly more than that. Digitisation in these industries also leads to improved quality regarding goods and services or to new goods and services. We will return to this in the next chapter.

2.1.4. Non-financial Goals

Although profit maximisation and rational efficiency efforts increase an organisation's ability to become more competitive, they may also have negative consequences if they are an organisation's sole focus. In the short term, a company can become very profitable by being cost-effective, but if this is achieved at the expense of necessary investments and stressed staff, then the profitability may quickly subside. Companies are not fully rational, but rather are characterised by limited rationality. Decision-makers in a company do not have access to all conceivable information when making a decision, and can only process limited amounts of data (more on that in Chapters 5–7), and therefore, they are satisfied if the company achieves or surpasses a defined minimum goal. This is a common approach in many small businesses with one or a few owners, and no or very few employees. The reason for starting a company may be that the alternative is unemployment or, for example, that someone's greatest interest in life is to cook, which ultimately makes them dream of running a small restaurant of their own. Whatever the reason, the financial goal over time for many small businesses is to make enough profit for continued survival rather than profit maximisation, growth, and expansion.

Different types of focus on profit to a large extent represent an internal perspective regarding an organisation's goals. But an organisation is not solitary: it exists alongside other actors, with whom it has relationships, similar to those of the individuals working in it. These relationships are based on the fact that the actors have some form of interest in the organisation's activities, something that is displayed in the "stakeholder model". The starting point of this model is that organisations strive for a stable relationship with their environment. This is achieved when there is a balance between the contributions that stakeholders make to the organisation and the values the organisation offers to stakeholders. Of course, the owners represent an important stakeholder as they contribute capital and are rewarded with a return on that capital. The difference is that in the stakeholder model, the organisation cannot solely address its owners; attention must be paid to all stakeholders. The organisation therefore needs to establish both financial and non-financial goals. Employees contribute with work efforts and the rewards they receive from the organisation are salary, social community, and in some cases, opportunities for self-realisation (although far from all organisations offer that!). Customers contribute with payments and are rewarded with goods and services. The state and municipality contribute with infrastructure, education, and services, and are rewarded with taxes, fees, and jobs. The environment and future generations may also be seen as stakeholders if they are affected by the organisation's actions, or if they take advantage of its efforts to run a sustainable business. Thus, such parties should also be considered, regardless of whether they are represented by a strong voice or not.

Digitisation plays an important role in maintaining and developing stakeholder interests and engagement, but the most fundamental aspect of digitisation in this context is that it allows for more comprehensive communication and richer exchanges of information, which are crucial in all sound relationships, whether organisational or personal.

2.1.5. To Balance Different Goals

Finally, it is also important to highlight that there should not be too many goals, and at the same time, they should complement each other. Thanks to digital information systems, organisations have greater opportunities than ever to measure and follow up on their activities, for example, compiling financial information to measure against financial goals, or following up on time, material, customer satisfaction, and so on, to measure against non-financial goals. Information systems thus enable an organisation to set many goals, financial and non-financial, which reflect how well it is performing. Far too many goals can, however, obscure what an organisation is striving for and what it is actually managing to achieve. The goals should also be balanced against one another, because what good is it in the long term to have, for example, very satisfied employees if customer satisfaction is low? Balanced scorecards (BSC) is an example of a governance model for organisations that try to manage different types of goals and how they relate to the organisation's strategies. The fundamental idea of the BSC concept is that from a few key perspectives, all of which affect each other (in the original model, there are four: financial, customer, internal processes, and research and development), the organisation sets goals and indicators that provide information about how well it is performing in each. The BSC should also provide information about how well the organisation's strategies are working.

The scorecard is today often based on computerised information systems. If they are well-designed, they also reflect the effects of digitisation: the development perspective should capture the value of new products and practices that are partly or entirely based on digitisation; the process perspective should capture the efficiency and efficiency improvements (or deteriorations) brought about by digitisation; and the customer perspective should grasp how customers perceive contact, delivery, and service via digital channels and how customer loyalty and branding is enhanced (or adversely affected) by digitisation. Even the financial perspective may reflect the monetary effects of digitisation. For some investments, this correlation may be possible to identify, but often the connection between digital efforts and the monetary results of the business is too long-term and too difficult to isolate, making it difficult to pinpoint how digitisation affects a company's monetary performance.

Goals themselves have little or no value to an organisation if they do not lead to action. Follow-up is therefore necessary but applying goal stages and measurement is not just a numbers exercise. How the organisation achieves its goals, and how it can act strategically, are therefore also of great importance.

2.2. Organisational Strategies

If an organisation's goals, financial or non-financial, tell it what to achieve, then its strategies tell it *how* to achieve those goals. The purpose of a strategy will differ depending on the organisation. For a company, the purpose may be developing competitiveness. For a hospital, the purpose is probably to provide the best possible care with available resources and to get patients to choose (or not choose) their hospital (that is, to develop competitiveness and attract the "right" users).

It is often emphasised that strategies are about achieving long-term goals, and therefore guide the organisations' long-term commitments, regardless of the particular type of strategy. This means that the level of detail in strategy is limited, which often makes it necessary to break it down into different activities. In the next chapter, we will return to this idea through the business model concept. Here, however, we will describe some challenges in strategy work and then examine what strategies can be and how they can be evaluated.

2.2.1. Challenges in Strategy Work

An important starting point when discussing strategy is the assumption that people are always rational when deciding which strategy is the most appropriate. However, there are several challenges regarding rationality in strategy work. The biggest concerns are how to deal with uncertainty about the future and what we really want to achieve. We must understand in part how to take uncertainty into account, as well as precisely what we ultimately want to achieve, based on the goals we have set.

We have access to large amounts of information, but limited capacity to deal with them and understand exactly what we need. We easily miss relevant factors in the background information and even very complex decisions are often reduced to comparisons between simple numerical values. An additional worry is that when we think we understand our data, it is often missing important information on the projected effects of different strategies and how the future will unfold. At best, we have an idea about the future, but it is often quite unclear. Finally, it can be incredibly difficult to prioritise our stated goals and identify which of them are the most important. The goal for some organisations may be to maximise profits and from that point of view, this process could seem relatively simple. It can be very difficult to know the actual value of what is being accomplished. We simply do not have the exact data required. Nor is it obvious how much risk should be accepted to try to maximise profit, and the values of others also have to be considered.

To consider it metaphorically, we may imagine that we are on a ship in a port. The goal of our trip is to reach another port far across the sea within a certain timeframe. The sea is full of visible islands and hidden underwater reefs. We must first therefore develop a plan, a strategy, for how to travel across the sea. We then map how to reach the other port on a chart, i.e., we concretise our strategy. We then identify the data available on the chart. We note islands, calculate winds and water currents, plan for water and food on-board as well as fuel for the vessel, however, some data may be missing—for example, are we sure that all underwater reefs are included? Once we slip our moorings and head off on our journey, we must therefore be prepared to revise parts of our chart as we gain access to new data. Our original strategy must also be very well thought-out and robust so that our corrections do not disrupt it. Otherwise, there is a great risk that we will end up stranded on one of the islands, or even worse, that a reef will tear holes in the hull and sink the whole ship. Even if we do succeed in navigating between islands and reefs, there is still the risk of unforeseen storms.

For organisations, global financial crises, pandemics, and armed conflicts are examples of storms of hurricane strength and have proven themselves to be very difficult to foresee throughout history. In such drastic changes, it is important that an organisation's strategies are well thought-out and that they contribute to its stability. When sailing on calm seas, the challenge is to arrive before one's competitors, i.e. to ensure that strategy contributes to developing competitiveness. So how can this be achieved? Let us look at a company group within the telecom industry.

2.2.2. An example of strategy formulation

Despite, or perhaps because of, the challenges of formulating strategy decisions suggested by the above metaphor, many organisations expend many resources in doing so. The following example is a global company group within the telecom industry that offers IT-based products to a global market. They themselves estimate that about 40% of the world's mobile traffic travels via their networks. The annual report describes their overall strategy:

> Our vision is a connected society, where everything that benefits from being connected becomes connected. The conversion to the connected society brings about a clear customer segmentation, when different operators take on different roles in the changing ICT market, and we adapt our operations accordingly.

Here, the telecom company identifies the world they are to navigate: the connected society in which the company is a strategically important actor.

> Our ambition is to lead the market transformation to ensure that we continue to be relevant to both existing and new customers as the new ICT market grows. Our basic strategy is unchanged: we will achieve success in our existing core business and become a leader in selected growth areas, while we maintain industry-leading operating margins and strong cash flow.

The company emphasises that they have a basic strategy. A basic strategy should remain unchanged and representative of the company for a long period of time. The company has a core business, which should have a better operating margin (gross profit divided by turnover) than comparable margins in the industry. A strong cash flow means that payments into the company over time will be significantly greater than outgoings. To achieve this goal, the strategy is based on assumptions that the company will become a leader in selected areas and also expand its business to new areas.

> We have two core businesses: Radio, Core Networks and Transmission, and Telecom Services. Radio, Core Networks and Transmission is aimed at the network equipment market and includes a broad portfolio of offers that build on industry standards ... we generate our telecom services sales through a professional service that is focused on the operating costs of the operators. Some revenue is also generated through network installation services aimed at the operators' CAPEX (capital expenditure, investments, as distinct from operating expenses, OPEX).

In the quotation, the company's market is identified as network equipment, and their offer to this market should be broad and based on industry standards. Sales should be accomplished through the sale not only of gadgets but also of services (including the operation of entire telecom networks) that can help to develop customers' financial results.

> Become a leader in selected areas. We strive to meet demand and needs in the changing ICT market through mobility. Our leadership in technology and services in the core business, the company's global economies of scale, and competence, is a platform from which the company can develop and expand its operations to selected areas, so as to seize growth opportunities.

Here, the strategy formulation indicates that there are areas where there is not yet a market, or where the market is relatively small. The wording also suggests that a substantial part of the company's research and development is focused on defining these areas. Also, rather than focusing on current profitability, the focus is on growth, probably to provide a basis for future profitability.

IT plays a crucial role in realising the strategy. One reason for this is that the company's products are digital. The core business is physical products, such as switches and masts, but it is software that determines the products' capacity. Similarly, telecom services are based on a largely digital platform. But it is not just the products that are digital. Access to functional and powerful IT in, for example, research and development work, is crucial for the development of new products in new areas.

The company is thus also an example of an organisation whose strategy process cannot treat IT and digitisation as standalone functions, as is still common in many organisations. Technology is often a prerequisite; without it, it would not be possible to conduct a business at all. It is therefore necessary, when formulating strategies for different goals, to consider how IT contributes to their fulfilment. We will discuss how this can be done in the next chapter. First, in order to further illustrate what strategies can or cannot be, we shall describe different approaches to strategy.

2.2.3. Strategy Approaches

The term "strategy" is used in many contexts, sometimes without any relation to the term's actual meaning. To have a strategy regarding payments for a common fruit basket at work is hardly what the strategy literature addresses as strategy...

In companies, the term "strategy" is often synonymous with business strategy, i.e., a plan for how to go about developing competitiveness. There are no standard templates for what constitutes a strategy; the design depends, among other things, on the type of strategy and what aspect of a business it addresses. Nilsson, Olve, and Parment (2010) present a basic compilation of different strategy approaches, based on Mintzberg et al. (2009). These can be divided into two main types: those focused on design and those emphasising organic development. The design approach is characterised by a focus on planning and positioning. In this approach, the organisation assesses its environment and builds operations based on what it believes will create the greatest competitiveness. If we return to our seafaring metaphor above, this approach corresponds to establishing a plan and drawing it on the map. Critics of this approach point out that it does not matter how much one plans, and the ability to formulate and implement strategies depends primarily on the resources that an organisation possesses; that is, what kind of ship it has, the crew, their competencies, and the availability of, for example, fuel.

Critics of positioning also do not see strategies as static, and note that as an organisation's resources change, their strategy will also change. Organisations must be able to adapt during the course of the journey, in order to achieve their goals. In this context, adaptability can be regarded as a strategy in itself—i.e., having an idea of where one wants to go, but above all being able to quickly perceive when circumstances are changing and therefore that working methods, skills, alliances, and more must also change, and improvising to take advantage of such changes. Of course, this adaptability is more easily achieved in a smaller and newer organisation than in a larger and older one. The ability to achieve goals also increases when more and more of the necessary resources can be purchased as standardised services via digital interfaces.

In practice, there are few (perhaps no) organisations that consciously function according to only one of the strategic approaches outlined above, as each has its own merits. Strategy work is often characterised by a combination of both approaches. We assume, for example, in this book, that the benefits of digitisation are crucial to realising an organisation's goals. In this way, we can say that we agree with the design approach. We design digitisation based on what we want to achieve and what we perceive our competitors are achieving. At the same time, there are always existing IT-related resources in an organisation that must be taken into account when formulating strategies. Our employees have certain skills, we have certain systems, knowledge, and contacts for a certain type of system acquisition and development, and our suppliers and customers have certain equipment and preferences. As a result, strategy development does not necessarily mean new IT investments, and it could sometimes instead involve simply using existing resources in a better way. In that scenario, resources should affect the content of the particular strategy. From this perspective, we can agree that strategies primarily depend on the resources of the particular organisation.

2.2.4. Coordinating Strategies at Different Organisational Levels

Strategies and goals are found at different levels within organisations. Three categories that are commonly used, especially in larger organisations, are group strategy, business strategy and functional strategy. A group is where a parent company organises several subsidiaries. A group strategy may therefore include, for example, how coordination between subsidiaries produces synergies that strengthen competitiveness. The telecom example above is an example of a group strategy. A business strategy shows how individual units within a group or stand-alone business units should compete. In many groups, there are differences between business units, and therefore business strategies may also differ in character. The different business areas in the telecom company are networks, digital services, managed services, and technologies and new businesses, and these emphasise different parts of the group strategy in their business strategies.

Functional strategies are the strategies belonging to different departments in a business unit, such as purchasing, production, and marketing strategies. In other words, there are a great variety of functional strategies within any one organisation. Some of them are formalised and written down, and others are less clearly recorded but present nonetheless. There are those who say that it is important that these different kinds of organisational strategies can be disentangled from one another, and that they should not be extensively governed by official organisational guidelines, which is known as "de-coupling". In this book, we connect research that claims that the different strategies in an organisation need to be congruent or coordinated with strategy. This means that an organisation's different corporate, business, and functional strategies rely on compatible common logics and consistent critical success factors. When formulating a strategy that includes how digitisation contributes to goal fulfilment (either explicitly or implicitly), it is necessary to consider this perspective. IT is utilised, and designed, in all functions and all business units. Its importance may vary. In some cases, there is reason to coordinate across devices or functionality, while in others this is unnecessary or even unproductive. Business needs and goals should direct IT usage and there may be reason to check that different parts of the business do not unintentionally and unnecessarily counteract or conflict with each other. Commercially available services and compatibility between IT systems across different organisations are becoming increasingly important. The strategic digitisation choices of organisation therefore increasingly depend on what is happening in the outside world.

The IT manager for a business group at a bank, who we met previously in this chapter's earlier section on goals, also described some challenges in coordinating and implementing digitisation strategies:

> My office's role is to take the business plans and try to transform them into an IT plan that also extends over three years. It is up to us how to allocate resources, which blocks or areas that we will invest more in. Lo and behold, the wishes are usually 400% more than we will get from the finance side of the company. But also in relation to what IT is capable of delivering. This means we have to trade off. Financially, what can we spend on IT development? Then you have to also assess the extent to which we need to increase staff or if we need to move staff from one area to another. The crux of our bank is that both of these processes [the business group and the IT office meta-plan] are running simultaneously. Most of all, we would like the business plan to be completed and then IT can add its own plan, but the year is a little too short to work that way.

This indicates the challenge in moving from a strategic group plan to coordinating strategies from different departments, which in the quotation above, includes the business plan and the IT plan. It also illustrates that in organisations it is constantly necessary to prioritise, as resources are never endless. There are also practical circumstances that make it difficult to achieve ideal coordination of different strategies. But strategies should give guidance regarding priorities in order to achieve the organisation's goals. The IT manager talks about the challenge of prioritising IT projects:

> You have to keep many projects in the air simultaneously, in my case about 70. We therefore have continuous planning about which projects can be started. I can decide on these projects up to a certain level, but if we get over that level, they have to be decided on the next one, there is a hierarchy in it. Then, before any new projects are started, one must review the ongoing ones.
>
> In addition, all projects can be changed several times: when we have made wrong estimations, when we need more money for development that we could not foresee, when we have to extend project time because of events which we didn't include in the feasibility study. In other words: more money, changed time or changed focus. To manage it, we have monthly meetings and sometimes also weekly meetings to decide how to adjust and handle the portfolio. Then we need to assess and compare projects.

Here we also see how the plan and strategy meet a problematic and partly unpredictable reality, where it is necessary to adapt and re-prioritise. In Chapters 8 and 9 we will discuss priorities in projects and project portfolios. It is also important to notice here that the bank uses projects as a way of deciding which IT investments to prioritise. The IT manager further emphasises the need for, and the challenge of, directing digital investments in the organisation:

> In my business group, we own the channel infrastructure, that is, the office network, the internet bank and the mobile bank, all the channels that meet the customer directly or indirectly. We also own the next layer, service functions, such as keeping track of customers, CRM features, sending out reports, campaign management and segmentation of customers.
>
> Beneath this, there are all the product systems, but we do not own these. Instead, the product units [in the bank] own the product systems regardless of which customer category a system serves. They have their own budget and their own IT resources. In case of cross-directional interdependences, I have to negotiate with the product units. I also have to take into account the bank's Business intelligence unit, which handles all database infrastructure.
>
> So not only do I have to synchronise my business group's IT requirements, I'll also match with the other parties – the product and

> database units – and their IT providers. This is a puzzle that is not easy to solve. Here, it is very important how the organisation is controlled and directed, who decides what makes the most business sense.

This shows that not everything can be solved with plans and guidelines, and that there is no clear hierarchy for digitisation issues. A large part of strategic work involves negotiations and discussions between different managers. The banking example shows that in this context, a well-functioning management that clarifies goals and strategies is necessary. In Chapter 4 we will further examine some aspects of management control.

2.2.5. Strategic Dialogues

Strategic dialogues are another important aspect of strategy work. An organisation, as we noted in the first chapter, consists of individuals. In order for them to understand and perhaps share their opinions about organisation strategies, they need to discuss them. It is through conversation that strategies are brought to life and become comprehensible. Without discussion, the strategic plan and work are at risk of becoming only a hypothetical scenario in a document. There are challenges, however, to achieving a well-functioning strategic dialogue. For instance, it is complex to run such a dialogue on multiple levels and via multiple functions in an organisation. An organisation is a chain of interconnected relationships. A major challenge in strategic discussion is therefore to identify existing chains and to determine which ones should exist and if there are any links missing in order to get the strategy to develop from words and dialogue into action.

An abstract idea about the future of an organisation can be concretised in a strategy. This is especially true for strategic discussions about digitisation and how it affects an organisation. Digitisation is in itself an abstract concept. On the one hand, it relates to digital information flows, a fact which probably seems obvious to most people, but on the other hand, it relates to building and maintaining organisational structures and routines that gainfully utilise these flows: for example, what are the effects, and what role does IT play? The mere introduction of technology rarely leads to the organisation's goals being fully achieved. There are many concepts and tools that can contribute to the strategic dialogue.

One such concept, the business model, will be further discussed in the next chapter.

2.3. Chapter Summary

In this chapter, we have discussed the importance of goals and strategies for organisations. It should be the very starting point when an organisation wants to decide how to work strategically with digitisation. IT has no intrinsic value; it only becomes valuable when it contributes to valuable digitisation and enables goal fulfilment. We have illustrated certain challenges when it comes to developing an organisation's goals. It is important to be aware of different time perspectives and target conflicts that may arise, as well as the fact that the smallest participants in organisations, e.g. employees, have their own personal goals involving both work and life. A plan or strategy document is therefore not adequate for coordination of organisational goals. Discussion, reconciliation, and negotiation are equally important. We have also explained that organisations often formulate financial and non-financial goals. Depending on the stakeholder, different goals have different levels of importance, which in turn places demands on an organisation in terms of the steps it takes to successfully balance its goal fulfilment.

The way to succeed in this balancing act is to develop and formulate strategies. Working strategically therefore means having a long-term plan for the realisation of organisational goals, although there are also several challenges in strategy work. We have highlighted that the organisation rarely (and perhaps never) has full access to useful and high-quality data. Conversely, access to data may be so extensive that it becomes hard to sort it sensibly! We will consider how best to address that challenge in Chapter 4. We have also illustrated that strategy views are important, as is the coordination of strategies at different levels within an organisation. We emphasised the importance of digitisation being a part of strategy (at different levels within the organisation) and not merely a task for a specialist department. Conducting strategic dialogue therefore becomes important in order to move from words to action. Describing the resources and activities within an organisation that will help it to reach its goals is another important step on the road from strategy to action. It has become common to try to describe these functions in the form of a business model. This is why our next chapter is devoted to business models.

2.4. Reading Tips

The Canadian Henry Mintzberg is a commonly cited strategy researcher. His numerous publications include many thoughts about what strategy can be, and what it is not. Some of these are collected in this book:

- Mintzberg, Henry; Ahlstrand, Bruce and Lampel, Joseph (2009). *Strategy Safari: Your Complete Guide through the Wilds of Strategic Management* (2nd edn). Harlow: Prentice Hall/ Financial Times.

Another strategy researcher who has made a big impression is Michael Porter, whose basic textbook from 1980 is still relevant. Porter was also relatively early to identify the strategic importance of IT:

- Porter, Michael E. (1980). *Competitive Strategy: Techniques for Analyzing Industries and Competitors*. New York: Free Press.
- Porter, Michael E. and Millar, Victor E. (1986). How information gives you competitive advantage. *Harvard Business Review* 63 (4), pp. 149–160, https://doi.org/10.1016/b978-0-7506-7084-5.50007-5.

The approach to strategy that Porter advocates has come to be called "the positioning school". Critics point out, among other things, that it is an organisation's resources that are crucial to its strategic choices. Criticism along these lines can be found in the below articles:

- Prahalad, Coimbatore Krishnarao and Hamel, Gary (1990). The core competence of the organization. *Harvard Business Review* 68 (3), pp. 79–91, https://doi.org/10.1016/b978-0-7506-7088-3.50006-1.
- Prahalad, Coimbatore Krishnarao (1993). The role of core competencies in the organization. *Research Technology Management* 36 (6), pp. 40–47, https://doi.org/10.1080/08956308.1993.11670940.

Attention is paid to the relationship between organisations' governance and strategy development in the field of strategic financial management. The control is considered here as a support when formulating and implementing strategies; it will also be adapted to the specific strategies. The importance of dialogue is also emphasised as an anchor for strategies, as described in the following books:

- Nilsson, Fredrik; Olve, Nils-Göran and Parment, Anders (2011). *Controlling for Competitiveness – Strategy Formulation and Implementation through Management Control.* Stockholm: Liber, Copenhagen: Copenhagen Business School Press.
- Nilsson, Fredrik; Petri, Carl-Johan and Westelius, Alf (eds) (2020). *Strategic Management Control – Successful Strategies Based on Dialogue and Collaboration.* Cham: Springer, https://doi.org/10.1007/978-3-030-38640-5.

3. Business Models and Digitisation

In this chapter, we will give examples of how business models can support a strategic dialogue, by identifying activities that contribute to the realisation of strategy. We focus on how IT can contribute to value creation through the digitisation of activities, or how digitisation can constitute the very starting point of a business model. The chapter concludes with a consideration of how a business model analysis provides knowledge about how digitisation contributes to the development and implementation of strategies, goals, and goal fulfilment.

3.1 The Relationship between Strategy and Business Model Concepts

When we discussed the concept of strategy in the previous chapter, we emphasised that an organisation has different strategies at different levels, but that their overarching purpose is the same: they should indicate a direction, a long-term path for the organisation's goals. However a strategy is not in itself an action plan. It is therefore necessary to identify how to work according to the strategy. In response to this question, the business model concept has gradually received more attention in recent years. Some of the definitions of a business model resemble those for strategy, and the difference may be seen as hierarchical. In Figure 3.1, strategy is depicted as the pathway from current position to desired goal. Strategies emphasise an overall perspective and can therefore accommodate one or several business models. They in turn act as a conceptual layer between strategy and the processes included in an organisation's activities (that is, what an organisation does in practice). The business model concept can thus be useful when organisations

 https://doi.org/10.11647/OBP.0350.03

must decisively identify factors in order to develop their processes and implement strategies.

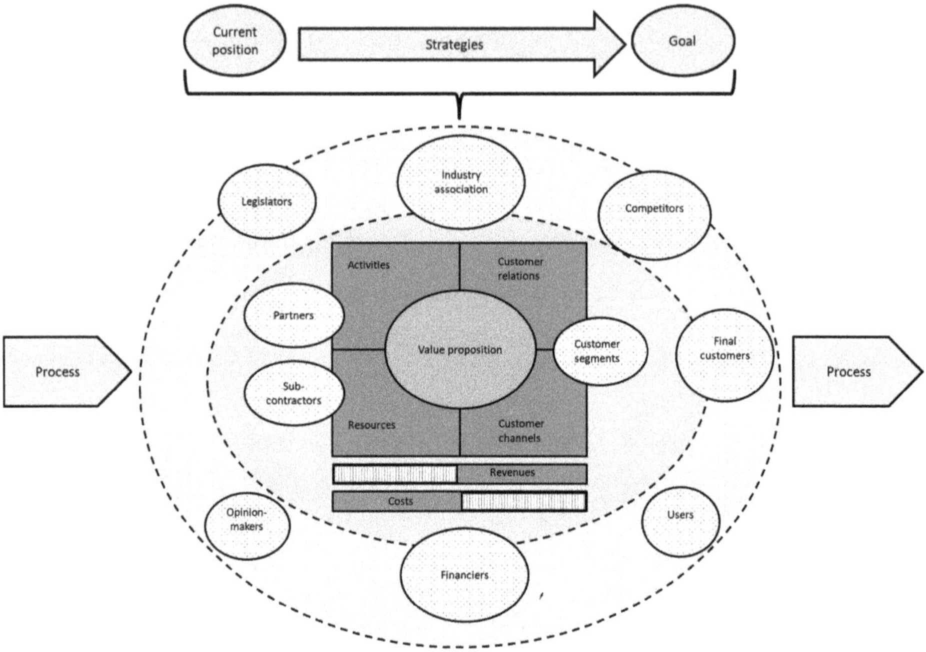

Figure 3.1. The relationship between goals, strategies, and business models.

From this perspective (which is the perspective we choose to assume in this book), a business model can be seen as a simplified and clear representation of an organisation's critical activities. By analysing its business model, an organisation can assess which activities are critical for creating and capturing value, and can thus also maintain competitive advantages. Put more simply, the organisation imagines the extent to which a certain business will be financially successful and thus viable. The business model describes those parts of the organisation that are necessary to generate products and identifies important supplier, customer, and market conditions. It is also important to remember that business models are dynamic, as relevant events within and outside the organisation constantly need to be evaluated and reflected.

3.2. The Different Parts of a Business Model

What are the different parts of a business model? Since there is no uniform definition of the business model concept, descriptions of its components will also vary. Figure 3.2 shows those components that are most often included in descriptions of business models.

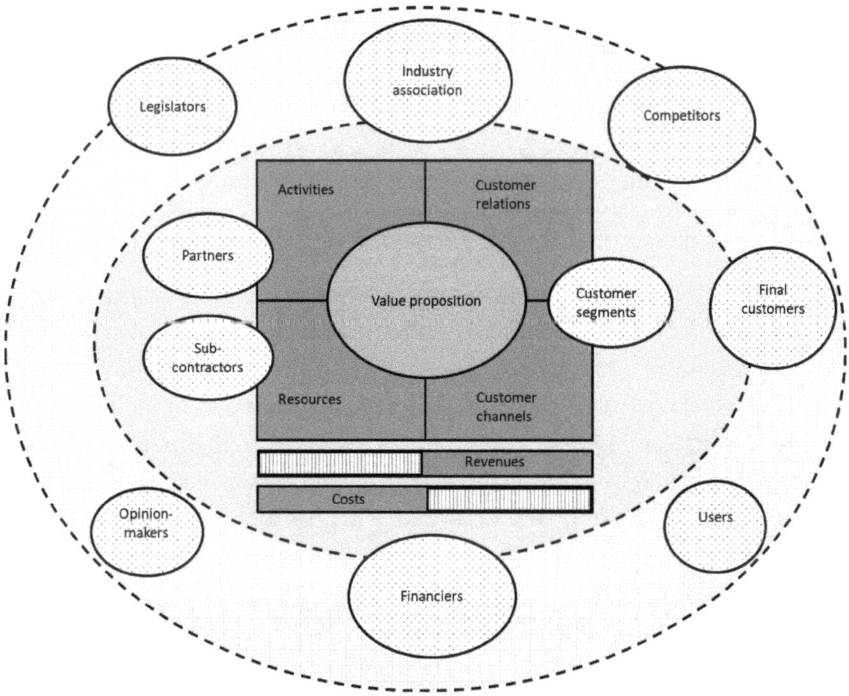

Figure 3.2. The components of a business model and possible actors within the business ecology of which the organisation is a part.

The organisation is represented by a square with four fields and the dashed circles are the business ecology of which the organisation is a part. "Business ecology" is a metaphor for the outside world or market in which the organisation operates. Business ecologies accommodate a number of actors. Some are foreground actors with whom the organisation interacts directly, such as customers, partners and suppliers, reducing joints (those inside the inner circle). Others are considered background actors; that is, they affect the organisation's ecology, but the organisation does not interact directly with them, e.g., legislators, opinion makers, and final customers. Some background actors may periodically become foreground actors, as represented in Figure 3.2 by financiers, industry associations, and final customers (the end customers of a chain of linked business activities). The concept of business ecology is used for an organisation's external analysis because it is a dynamic system. Over time (as in a real ecosystem) some actors may have a reduced significance or disappear completely, while others will grow in importance and affect the organisation and the ecology to a higher degree. Some background actors (even at a distance from the organisation) may come to wield considerable influence over its business, for example by serving as role models. We will not delve further into the business ecology concept here, but will return to it in Chapter 11.

In the middle of Figure 3.2 we see what constitutes the very essence of the business model: the value proposition. An organisation carries out certain activities and has certain resources so as to arrive at a value proposition. These activities and resources may be more or less dependent on partners and subcontractors. Another part of the business model is the customers, who are categorised and divided into different customer segments. Relationships with customers are determined by this categorisation, and an important purpose of customer relations is to help understand customer needs and communicate the value proposition.

At the bottom of the figure are a revenue and a cost stack. The darker part of the bars mark where the main business model revenues and costs are often generated. The largest revenue streams normally come from sales to customers, but can also arise if the organisation is part of an offer from one of its partners. Similarly, in production-heavy organisations, most of the costs come from the activities and resources needed to realise a particular value proposition, but some costs arise in customer relationships and customer channels, and in some organisations, these are even the dominating costs. In the following section, we will take a closer look at each part of the business model and discuss how they are affected by digitisation. We start with the value offering.

3.3. Business Model Digitisation

3.3.1. Value Proposition

Simply put, one can say that a value proposition is the value that can be associated with a particular product. (A product could be something physical, a service or a combination of physical goods and services.) In the business model, value does not simply mean monetary value, even if there is ultimately a price on a product. Instead, the value as expressed in the business model addresses how a product satisfies a customer need. It is also important that the value proposition reflects the strategies an organisation has chosen via their goals to realise, and that the strategies themselves contribute to the realisation of the value proposition.

For some products,. it is pretty obvious at first glance what the value proposition is, but if you think about it, there are often several dimensions to associate with it. Take, for example, the value of foods such as cheese, cereals, and bread (and even those which are lactose-free, gluten-free, or made from alternative ingredients). Their obvious value is that they are fuel for our bodies because they provide us with energy and vital building blocks for muscle, bone, and more. If the value is obvious, however, then why do food producers and grocery stores bother to design packaging and advertise their products? They do so largely because they want customers to choose their products over those of their competitors. Here, the value proposition is crucial. How it is defined—and communicated—makes a difference. Food is much more than fuel, it is also enjoyment, community, and cultural expression (why else would holiday meals involve special dishes?). This type of analysis can be applied to most products, so a value proposition needs to undergo a thorough analysis before it can be formulated and communicated.

For example, consider the car as a product. A common value of all cars is that they enable us to transport ourselves from Point A to Point B. This is such a basic and expected value, however, that car manufacturers do not promote it in communications regarding why we should choose *their* car. Instead, they emphasise other tangible or intangible features, such as safety, speed, reliability, and accessibility, as well as more subtle qualities, such as a sense of exclusivity (you can become part of a small, select crowd of happy owners) and/or wisdom (you are a sensible driver).

IT and digitisation have a major impact on value propositions. The carmaker is a good example. The safety systems in a car are in part purely physical, such as bodywork and brake discs. But just as the design and production of a car's security systems are accomplished through IT, the systems themselves are also controlled largely by digital technology. Sensors that perceive a risk of collision can activate automatic braking and if a crash occurs, then a digitally controlled belt tensioner and airbags are activated to relieve its effects (security). Similarly, a car's digital systems contribute to more efficient fuel injection (acceleration and speed as part of the driving experience) and the optimal utilisation of drive systems (operational safety, performance, and accessibility). Digitisation contributes in a crucial way to enabling the value proposition of modern cars.

The digitisation of business models also adds another dimension: value propositions these days tend to have a greater service content. For the car manufacturer, this could be digital navigation systems (GPS) or the fact that a mobile phone wirelessly connects to the car's audio system and is controlled through a few keystrokes on the steering wheel. GPS features can also be used to enable traceability as part of theft protection, or so that in the event of a collision, a signal to an alarm centre is triggered automatically. When abroad, a help desk function can assist with the remote entry of destinations into the navigation system. Within the not-too-distant future, the sound system may be controlled by eye movements via a head-up display accessed through a pair of glasses included in the car's equipment.

When 6G data communication technology and the Internet of Things are fully operational, they will enable us to consume the car as a service, and the majority of us may rent or lease a vehicle instead of owning it. The price model, and how we pay for the service, can then be differentiated according to vehicle data (speed, mileage, braking wear and other aspects of driving style, climatic conditions, etc.) that is communicated to the service provider. Someone who drives without care will have to pay for it, but for someone who applies eco-driving, the cost will be significantly lower. We could all be part of a carpool, where self-driving, electric vehicles can be ordered via an app for collection at any address within a certain geographic area. This, in turn, would require substantial development of the value proposition, along with the digital, physical, and organisational systems that would enable it.

3.3.2. Partners, Subcontractors, Activities, and Resources

The left side of the business model (Figure 3.2) contains the parts that are necessary when creating a product to which a certain value is attached. Partners and suppliers do not always have to be separate roles, and can be the same actor. The difference between the roles is the way in which the organisation interacts with the actor. It is not relevant to include all subcontractors that sell to us, because in its business model, an organisation should identify the subcontractors whose products are necessary to create the value proposition. A partner may sell something to us as well as being more involved in the business model activities and thus becoming an important part of the resources. Partnerships can take different forms, such as strategic alliances with non-competitors, partnerships with competitors, joint ventures, and so on. The difference between subcontractors and partners is also that a supplier can be replaced relatively easily, while the relationship with a partner is more long-term and extensive, and involves more mutual adaptation.

For the car manufacturer, the manufacturer of seats or airbags is an important subcontractor. Without these products, there is no car and thus no value proposition. However, if the products are relatively standardised, then the subcontractor can be changed, for example, to reduce purchasing costs. A car manufacturer, on the other hand, could be in a strategic long-term alliance with a consultant specialising in software development for controlling car engines. This requires in-depth knowledge of different car models, with the consultant being involved at a fairly early stage of the research and development phase.

The organisation's activities create a value proposition. It is also common to consider the activities as parts of a process: that is, within the organisation there is a network of activities that have a definite start and end, and their combination in the process creates customer value. The activities are intimately associated with the resources, and without the resources there are no activities. Resources can be physical, intangible, human, or financial. As well as partners and suppliers, the business model should highlight the activities and resources necessary to achieve the value proposition. The delimitation of activities can be quite difficult to achieve, depending on the complexity of the product.

Digitisation clearly affects the activities of the business model. When a car manufacturer purchases car parts such as seats and airbags, it is important that they are delivered at the same rate as the cars in which they are mounted. One of many ways to reduce the cost of resources is to have as little stock as possible, which is usually referred to as just-in-time production. To schedule deliveries with production, an enterprise resource planning system (ERP) at the car manufacturer can keep track of stock levels through radio frequency identification (RFID) tags, barcodes, and similar digital reading techniques. When they reach a certain critical point, an automatic order is made to their subcontractors. More proactively, the orders will be based on the actual production plan. If the subcontractor is also a partner, it is probably connected and logged into the ERP system, which enables it to access the necessary information and take both long-term and current plans and deviations into account. This type of seamless information flow between the subcontractors and manufacturers within manufacturing is also known as Industry 4.0. Here too, 6G technology and the development of the Internet of Things play an important role, as they enable every product in the production chain to carry with it information about where to go and how. The goal is a production chain with shorter conversion and lead times, fewer errors, greater flexibility, and less time-consuming programming.

It is not only cooperation in production processes that is affected, however. Digitisation also enables brand-new collaborative relationships. For example, millions of camera-equipped cars on the roads, which will give drivers support, can also be used to provide information about road conditions to those responsible for road maintenance on an ongoing basis. GPS data can, in aggregate, provide up-to-date images of traffic flow that enable better control of rush-hour traffic in metropolitan regions.

For our example, the car manufacturer, all internal activities to achieve a value proposition are dependent on resources in the form of various IT solutions. Design is achieved using computer-aided design (CAD). The testing of bodies, braking systems, motors, and so on, is conducted with the support of digital technology: first simulations, and then, in physical tests, different types of sensors collect measurement data for evaluation. Similarly, computer-controlled industrial robots have long been an important part of production, where they ensure quality and maintain time-efficient production. People are, in the car industry as well as in other industries, still an important resource for providing a value proposition, but they increasingly interact with IT in performing their roles.

3.3.3. Customers, Customer Relations, and Customer Channels

At the far right of the business model (Figure 3.2) we find the customers, to whom the value proposition is aimed. They are rarely a homogeneous mass and therefore can usefully be categorised. One might divide them into customer groups or customer segments, such as age- or lifestyle-related categories, or according to how the customer consumes the value proposition. Car manufacturers usually categorise private customers based on lifestyle, i.e., according to whether they are families with children or young adults without children. "Urban and successful" is a common customer category, as is "adventurous". Willingness and ability to pay should also be assessed in customer segmentation.

Customer relationships and customer channels, as well as activities and resources, are intimately associated with each other. Relationships can be developed in various media, such as by direct contact, websites, or news email—perhaps even through member club discounts. Here, digitisation can enable orchestrated use of multiple channels, a so-called omnichannel approach. Digital channels typically provide organisations with data on their customers' behaviour. Systematic analysis of all available data on customers can allow organisations to better tailor customer offerings. An omnichannel approach provides coordinated communication with customers across channels, which fruitfully combines the various characteristics of the available channels, rather than using multiple channels in parallel. Customer channels are the means through which the value proposition is conveyed to customers, which in turn affects customer relationships. Traditionally, the dealer is an important partner for the car manufacturer, as it is on their premises that many final customer relationships arise, and through them that the car is delivered to the customer. It is through the dealer's brand workshops that a car manufacturer's original spare parts are sold with high profit margins.

Car dealers are an example of a business model that is not necessarily represented by a single organisation. Many car dealers are independent organisations who, through an agreement with the car manufacturer, have the right to convey the car manufacturer's deals. In a way, therefore, the reseller becomes a customer, because they buy the car from the manufacturer. At the same time, it is a partner, because good dealers are an important resource that benefits from long-term collaboration. The car manufacturer's value proposition is not primarily formulated for the dealer, but for the final customer, that is, the car buyer. Of course, there is a proposition from car manufacturers to dealers and vice versa—why else would they do business with each other?—but central to the car manufacturer's business model is the value proposition for the car customer. This is an example of how an actor (the car dealer) can have multiple roles within a business model. This may indicate that the actor is of special strategic importance to the organisation.

Digitisation also affects customer relationships and channels. We found above that these are often divided into groups or segments. Such grouping/segmentation does not depend directly on IT; however, digital technology can be a great support for analysing lifestyle patterns. To achieve such an analysis, you often need to combine several extensive data sources, which is known as big data analysis. In our car example, big data analysis requires access to data and skills that the car manufacturer may be lacking but that some other partner may have.

IT can enable an organisation to manage customer relationships via several media. As we mentioned above, the customers of dealers who meet on-site in a car showroom are probably meeting in the most important customer channel for the traditional car manufacturer. Before the customer decides to visit, they will most certainly have sought out information about different car models. The websites of the car manufacturer and dealer, via price comparison sites and discussion groups on social media, allow potential customers to find documentation on equipment packages, properties, prices, and price models (e.g., buy or private lease). Both the car manufacturer and the dealer should therefore determine which digital channels they can affect either directly (their own websites) or indirectly (e.g., where do they appear in Internet search engines?)

There are also several examples of how digitisation enables new methods of meeting customers. Customer databases are important for creating additional sales, for example, through regular emails or post about service and upgrades to the car system. Car sensors refine the opportunities for additional, situationally tailored sales announcements, and instrument and communication systems in the cars enable new ways to present such offers. Tesla, the electric-car manufacturer, offers the consumer cars directly from the car manufacturer. Not having an existing dealership relation to cultivate and protect, and not seeing any existing dealers with extensive knowledge of the type of offering Tesla provides, their decision to break with the dealership tradition is less complicated than it would be for an established car brand.

Both car manufacturers and dealers can personalise customer relationships to a greater extent with the help of all embedded IT. This is already happening in the sales of commercial vehicles. Data legislation and/or customer reactions might prevent it (owing to privacy issues), but digital technology makes it possible. If the car, as we pointed out above when describing the value proposition, is connected to the Internet of Things, then data on mileage and driving patterns (acceleration, braking, speeds, and more) are regularly transferred to a database held by the manufacturer. This data is then sorted and analysed based on the fact that each car has a digital unique identity in the database. This means, for example, that service intervals can be adjusted to actual driving style and to the climate the car has mainly been used in, rather than simply to distance or time. The provision of customised preventive maintenance is well within reach. Furthermore, companies can communicate with the driver of the car and deliver weekly or monthly reports about how their driving affects the car and tips about how their driving style can be developed to tax the car less (although this may not be appreciated by all drivers).

3.3.4. Revenues and Costs

When a customer buys a product (the value proposition), an income is generated. The summary of incomes that refers to a certain period of time becomes the revenue for that period. The same applies to costs, which are the same period's summary of the monetary value of resource consumption. Only the expenses that have been used (directly or indirectly) to produce the value proposition are counted. For a car manufacturer, some of the purchases may have ended up in a warehouse and therefore should not be counted as a cost for the period. Some have been investments that will last for a long time, and then, only the part "consumed" in the present period counts as cost for that period. This accounting-based information on costs and revenues can be found in an organisation's financial statement. It provides us with some financial information, but an analysis of the business model can assist with complementary perspectives on what actually creates the financial information. The bulk of the business model's revenue is generated by sales (the dark grey part of the revenue stack in Figure 3.2). How the revenue streams look depends on the type of product and the price model, that is, on how the agreed price is tied to what is delivered, including the rights and responsibilities for delivery. In addition to the price model, the size of the revenue is also affected by sales volume and price. As pointed out at the beginning of the chapter, revenue may also arise on the left-hand side of the business model figure. The partners from whom an organisation buys products contribute as resources enabling a value proposition, and may in turn have a sale where the organisation assists with resources for them. In that case, they can choose to define an actor as both/either a partner (cost source) and/or customer (revenue source). This choice depends on how the business model contributes to a comprehensive representation of the organisation's activities.

In the business model, costs arise when purchasing products from subcontractors and partners (the dark grey part of the cost stack in Figure 3.2). In addition, there are activities and resources that are cost drivers, and (often substantial) costs also arise when customer relationships and customer channels are maintained. The business model clearly shows that costs should be regarded not only as a burden on the organisation, which can easily be concluded if only an income statement is considered, but also as an enabler for value creation; the costs arise because the organisation purchases and uses services and other resources to create the value proposition. That is not to say that an organisation should not strive to reduce its costs and use existing resources more efficiently (as successfully done by the HR manager in the previous chapter's example. Different calculation models are of great help to support analyses of how to reduce costs and improve efficiency.

Digitisation has a major impact on business model costs. For example, the direct costs of production tend to decrease continuously as IT enables more efficient processes, including extensive automation and standardisation. Costs for many other activities and resources tend instead to increase. Research and development in the automotive industry, as in other industries, draws increasingly higher costs. Here,

IT can play a role in increasing or decreasing costs, as the technology enables more extensive analyses and tests of the complex digital systems found in today's cars. This can, on the one hand, encourage more testing, increasing testing costs. On the other hand, testing via simulation can be cost-efficient and time-saving compared with physical testing, thus helping reduce testing costs.

It is more difficult to assess how digitisation affects revenue. This depends, among other things, on the fact that some IT is considered infrastructural. This means that it is a prerequisite, such as websites and certain IT systems embedded in cars. Without it, an organisation has no value proposition to convey and thus no revenue whatsoever. Digitisation that can affect revenue tends to make the value proposition different from that of an organisation's competitors. It enables product development that provides a competitive advantage. This can in turn be a combination of different digital techniques, such as the security system we mentioned earlier, or a product with expanded digital service content that makes the car "feel" right, or, as in one of the examples above, new pricing models that change the value proposition and the revenue streams. However, the IT aspect of digitisation is typically easier to copy than the organisational aspect, so advantages based mainly on hardware or software will probably be short-lived; if they are indeed appreciated and profitable, other organisations will soon start offering the same or something similar. A competitive advantage thus rests on the ability to keep improving faster than one's competitors.

The above examples of how digitisation can affect different parts of a business model apply to many industries and organisations whose business models are derived from a more analogue time, but today there are also examples of business models that originated in the digital age and are thus the result of digitisation. In the next section, we will therefore discuss the characteristics of these digital business models.

3.4. Digital Business Models

As more and more individuals have access to various digital communication platforms (desktop, laptop, tablet, and smartphone), business models that are entirely based on digital information flows have emerged. Without IT, they would not exist in their current form.

3.4.1. The Roots of Digital Innovations

Products offered and delivered by digital business models are not rare, nor are they new or unique. On the contrary, they are often the next step (or leap!) in a long-term development based on the emergence of a number of innovations over time, refined and brought together. In other words, the roots of digital innovators often extend far back in time. Take, for example, the gadget that you probably spend most of your time with—the mobile phone. Its origins can be traced back to the nineteenth century, and the then-up-and-coming electric telegraph. Techniques for communicating over longer distances when telegraphs were emerging included optical signal systems in the form of semaphores, or physical devices in the form of human dispatch riders and pigeons. The revelation that electrical impulses travelled at very high speed and that with the help of a binary code (the Morse Alphabet) and Telegraph Keys (Switch) a person could transmit data between two interconnected units over large geographical distances, revolutionised the way to communicate. The technology that enabled electric telegraphy was the platform for the next innovation in the late-nineteenth century, the telephone. The telephone dominated person-to-person communication at a distance in the twentieth century, but it was still wired. The capacities of wired systems gradually increased, thanks in part to innovations such as automatic switches.

In parallel with wired communication technology, the first steps toward wireless communication were taken. Innovations like the use of electromagnetic waves enabled the development of radio transmissions for one-way communication, often broadcast, and for communication between two units, for example via so-called "radio comms". However, it took until the mid-1980s before the mobile phone, a combination of the innovations of the telephone and radio, was launched on the consumer market. At the time this market was quite small (among other things because the phones weighed about 3.5 kilos, had limited capacity and cost in current monetary value about ten times more than a standard smartphone does today) and the telephones were used to make voice calls. The mobile phone innovation developed rapidly in parallel with wireless technologies for data transmission and communication via the Internet. The most obvious leap for mobile phones was to smartphones, where the big breakthrough was Apple's iPhone, which in 2007 was the first to successfully rely entirely on touch-screen technology, with fingers used as pointing devices (although touch screens of different types had then been around as user interfaces on different devices for over forty years). This brings us up to today, and to the emergence and growth of digital business models. We will now categorise and give examples of some of these business models.

3.4.2. Digital Intermediaries and Network Builders

As we noted above, few, if any, digital business models are entirely new. What causes them to emerge and be successful is that they either develop existing, or create entirely new, value propositions. Metaphorically, what these value offerings have in common is their character as bridging joints.

3.4.2.1. Bridging Joints

A passenger riding on an older train can, at some passages, feel the joints in the rails as they are crossed. They are there as a result of a great number of rails that have been linked together over a long distance, and that allow the passenger to move from location A to B. In older wagons and on older tracks the joints feel very distinct, but they are rarely felt in a high-speed train that is running on continuous welded rails built solely for purpose. Similarities may be drawn between innovations that are joined together in order to move us from Demand A, through Supply B, to the final station, gratification. A common denominator for digital business models is that they exist because they help to reduce, and sometimes make almost invisible, the 'joints' in a customer's trip. Let us clarify by studying the example of business models which make music available as their value proposition. These business models are characterised over time by reducing 'joints' in terms of both availability and time.

Listening to music was, for a long time (until the late 1970s and early 1980s), mostly a stationary experience, as the listener had to be in a certain place, where a record player or a tape recorder was available: availability was very limited. Cassette tapes and portable cassette players enabled music consumption to become more portable and thus increased accessibility. Listening was also individualised, as listeners were able to choose which songs a cassette tape would contain by recording a so-called "mixtape". This analogue technology to some extent reduced the joints in the value offering, however, they remained in place because they represented the three separate business models involved in making the music portable: the record label (which offered the predefined products LP disc and pre-recorded cassette tapes), the manufacturers of recordable cassette tapes, and the manufacturers of portable cassette players. This made it necessary to spend a great deal of time in order to put together a music selection that was adapted to your own tastes.

Music consumption started becoming digitised with the introduction of the compact disc (CD), but joints remained, in the form of availability and time, although they decreased somewhat in scope. There were still three actors involved, however: music publishers, the producers of recordable CDs, and the manufacturers of portable CD players. The next digital innovation that further reduced the joints was the mp3 format and the mp3 player. Portable CD players disappeared and were replaced by mp3 players with a completely different capacity to store music, and accessibility increased with the ability to create an individual playlist on a simple laptop computer.

The joint of time remained, however, although it decreased slightly. In order to create playlists and download music to the mp3 player, one had to copy music from CDs to a playback program on a computer (for example, Windows Media Player), which could take considerable time. Another option was to use Internet-based sites that made music available. At first, sharing sites and so-called pirate sites (illegal downloads) appeared, but eventually, niche commercial services, such as iTunes, also emerged. The ability to download music from the web further reduced the joints, as supply and accessibility vastly improved. Music still needed to be downloaded to a computer before it could be transferred to the particular platform—the mp3 player—which made it portable, however, and this was something that still took some time.

When smartphones were successfully introduced in 2007, the need for mp3 players gradually disappeared, because the music player was now on the phone. In combination with the improved ability to transmit data over the Internet (4G communication technology was being introduced), opportunities were created to both increase accessibility and reduce download time (streaming), to organise and listen. Spotify identified this opportunity as a music intermediary, and that is central to its value proposition. Today, the joints of *availability* and *time* are, thanks to Internet-based music intermediary services and smartphones, by and large non-existent. Certainly, there are still three vendors involved—the music service, the Internet operator, and the telephone provider—but in such a way that the tripartite structure is not a problem for listeners. Today, we can listen to what we want, when we want, without delay, and without being tied to a dedicated music or audio platform. Another important contribution in this context is the fact that from the music consumer's perspective, the physical borders between the actors, music publishers, and platform-makers that previously needed to be overcome, are largely non-existent. This is very different from the conditions during the era of the vinyl LP disc and cassette-tape recorder.

One way of further identifying what characterises digital business models is to divide them into categories. Examples of two such categories might be intermediaries and network builders (see Table 3.1). In the text that follows, these categories are illustrated through examples of companies that are not unique in themselves; instead, they have been selected because they can be seen as representatives of digital business models in various industries.

Table 3.1 Examples of companies and industries where digital business models in the form of mediators or network builders are represented.

Mediators		**Network builders**	
Company	***Industry***	***Company***	***Industry***
Spotify	Music	Facebook	Communication/ Entertainment
Uber	Transportation	YouTube	Entertainment
Zalando	Commerce	Crowdfunding	Finance

3.4.2.2. Mediators

Digital business models are based on bringing together individuals in need of a particular product and the suppliers of the product in question. Brokers are found in many industries and existed long before society was digitised, but they were also more geographically limited. Record labels, record stores, records in a department store, and mail-order vendors are all examples of music mediators.

Thanks to their digital brokerage service, companies like Spotify can design a business model that differs from these earlier intermediaries on several key points. In the section above, we described changes in the value proposition achieved by Spotify. Even customer segments are changing because Spotify is not geographically limited, except by intellectual-property-rights restrictions, and can offer a range that appeals to many categories of music consumers. Customer relationships change when their offers are personalised and the customer channel is completely digital. Revenue streams come via advertising revenues and fixed subscription fees, which allows, among other things, a more even flow of payments. The service they offer also means that their agreements with music publisher partners differ from the business models of traditional music intermediaries. For Spotify and its direct competitors, the ability to offer (close to) the world's supply of music is of central importance. Instead of a narrow selection of music, the norm is now that users should be able to find anything in the catalogue. As a result, the activities and resources of the business model differ substantially from previous music intermediaries. Skilled programmers and proprietary software are now key resources that cannot be easily replaced. Without them, there would be no Spotify.

Uber is an example of a transport service that links customers in need of transport with drivers who are interested in earning an income. This has also previously existed (and still does) in the form of taxi companies with a telephone exchange. What is new in Uber's digital business model is that if the availability of vacant cars increases, then consequently the time it takes to get hold of one decreases—at least in a metropolitan region. The service also develops the value proposition by simplifying payment (deducted from a registered credit card) and makes the connection between driver and rider safer, since both can see each other's rating before closing the deal. The customer knows what the trip will cost, roughly, and where cars are available before the order is completed. This creates added value for the customer, in the transparency of availability and cost, and possibly in the knowledge that the cab will accept the prearranged mode of payment. Uber offers fast, flexible, safe, and accessible transport. New conditions are thus created because there are new customer segments. Customers that may have been hesitant about hailing a regular taxi directly from the street can now use Uber's services. As in the case of Spotify, customer relations are also altered. To become a customer, people have to register, and as a result, their orders are entered into a database, enabling Uber to analyse their travel patterns over time (and thus also convey more customised offers) and the aggregate travel patterns in real-time, to help direct cars to where customers are or can be expected to appear. The customer-channel aspect of the business model is concentrated on one channel, the app. Anyone who wants to join as a driver is a partner, which is reminiscent of how some taxi companies are organised. Uber cooperates fully with individuals, however, while some taxi companies collaborate with taxi owners, who in turn hire drivers. There are relatively few resources and activities required by the business model, but these are nevertheless absolutely crucial for operations. Without the software to mediate the service, and developers to optimise it, there would be no Uber.

Zalando is in many ways a traditional mail-order merchant in clothes and accessories, but its business model is mainly digital. The business is based on digital interfaces that offer products from other companies, and they do not produce or offer any product of their own. They therefore associate with a large number of suppliers and partners, and Zalando's internal activities and digital resources are focused on optimising customer offers. Unlike the two examples above, however, Zalando's business model also relies on physical resources, such as their central warehouses where goods are stored whilst awaiting transportation to customers. No matter what size and what brand, Zalando wants to be able to pass it on to the customer. They also compete on price by partnering with price comparison sites. This develops the value proposition as it increases accessibility and reduces the time required by a customer to find an item, and it may also enable the customer to buy it at a lower price. Like the other service providers, Zalando's digital business model enables them to build knowledge of their customers, and thereby develop relationships with them on a seemingly individual basis. There are many customer segments, and the customer channel is largely Internet-based, although physical delivery—and returns—are also important.

Accessibility is fundamental to the value propositions of smaller, focused e-retailers who, unlike Zalando, specialise in one or a few products. No matter where a customer is located, they can (as long as there is Internet access, they have a functioning communication platform, and—for physical goods—can take delivery of shipments), find exactly what they are looking for and have it delivered, even if the retailer is currently on the other side of the planet.

3.4.2.3. Network Builders

The common denominator for business models in the category of network builders is that they provide a platform for individuals with common interests. Network builders existed even before society was digitised, and different types of associations attest to that, but just like the mediator category in Table 3.1, network builders were often more geographically limited. Digitisation has significantly changed the way we communicate. Businesses like Facebook have developed value propositions that increase accessibility to various people and decrease the time it takes to build different types of networks. Table 3.1 shows that they belong to the communications industry, but they are just as much a platform for entertainment, because, for example, they allow links to many different channels to be shared. Their customer segments are both individuals and businesses. For smaller organisations, Facebook may be an alternative to creating a full website. Facebook pages can be used to advertise opening hours, special offers, or whatever is relevant at the time. There could be pictures showing a daily offering, or new products that are now available for purchase. For more established organisations, which already have a website, Facebook can serve as a more dynamic channel of communication: news and offers will be pushed to followers, opinion polls can be implemented, and customers and other stakeholders can comment, ask questions, and receive answers. All of this can be achieved with a website and email account, too, but in Facebook, it is handled through standard functionality and through the customs of using the application that have developed in society. In addition, the network structure of Facebook can facilitate the spread of news and opinions regarding a company and its offerings, for better or worse. Again, digitisation as a catalyst can help fuel the spread of both appreciative and negative comments and opinions.

It is not organisations that make up the majority of Facebook users. The largest customer segment comprises individuals with their own Facebook accounts (and for many, probably also accounts on other social media) where they can share their opinions, positive and negative. Today's widespread use of smartphones also means that people effectively always have access to various communication channels—not just when sitting in front of a computer. Smartphones have also enabled so-called geotagging, which can highlight preferences and opinions based on geographical location. A very important resource for Facebook's business model is therefore the availability of the large volumes of data that are continuously generated. This data can be analysed to offer paying customers access to targeted advertising channels. It is characteristic of network-builder business models that many actors tend to appear in different parts. The customer who posts information, the core of the value proposition, is at the same time a partner and a key resource. The value of network platforms therefore grows when the number of active users increases. Analyses of this type of digital business model therefore tend to become multidimensional. How do we meet a customer's (an individual's or a company's) need for a communication platform and at the same time make them available for other businesses advertising? It is a delicate balance for companies like Facebook not to overuse and blend its data in ways that users find unethical or provoking, because without users, a network platform like Facebook has zero value.

The same conditions apply to more purely entertainment-oriented networks such as YouTube. It is a channel for both entertainment (for example, a whole line of music videos with the band that meant a lot to you when you grew up) and fact-finding (for example, how best to drill into concrete walls to put up a shelf). The content is entirely user-generated—it is not YouTube that creates and posts the content—and the customer segment is wide. It is possible to talk of companies and individuals here as well, but discussion can be even more nuanced. There are certain individuals who just consume content, and those who consume and also produce it. The latter become important partners and resources, as they are the ones who create and contribute to the value proposition. If no one uploaded films to YouTube, there would be no content available, and thus no value generated.

Unlike previous examples in this section, there are so far within crowdfunding no equally dominant players. Briefly, crowdfunding is a platform for financing services. The value proposition here comprises an offer of access to a marketplace for ideas that need funding. The idea can be described in text, image, and/or video, and the financial contributions can be secured in both directions. If, by the closing date, the pledged contributions total at least the amount required by the idea holder, the contributors will be charged via payment intermediaries connected to the platform, and the sum that has been promised is, after deduction of the platform's commission, transferred to the idea holder. The expectation is then that the idea holder realises the idea and, if this has been promised, distributes the product that the financiers have funded. If the requested sum is not reached, then no prospective financiers are charged, and no one will expect the idea to be realised. The value proposition also contains additional dimensions for those seeking funding. The crowdfunding platform works as a form of market research "for real". Previously, anyone wondering about the viability of an idea had to rely on their own or others' judgment, or just ask people directly whether they would be interested in a product, and if so at what price. The problem with that approach is that judgments are uncertain, and statements of willingness to pay are in no way binding.

Just as in the other examples of digital business models, crowdfunding companies are not linear, and do not have clear supplier and customer roles. They offer a brokerage service (for a fee, which is usually a percentage of the funds raised). Anyone who wants financing buys exposure to conceivable financiers and those who are willing to finance fun ideas or sell products that have not yet been developed have an opportunity. But which of them are really the customers, and who is the supplier in the deal? In some respects, both sides are crowdfunding platform customers, and in some ways, they are subcontractors of the service that the crowdfunding platform offers.

3.4.3. Some Common Denominators for Digital Business Models

We chose to highlight six examples in the section above, but of course there are many more out there, as well as additional dimensions of the impact of digitisation on business models. Our categorisation and our examples may be seen as narrow. Companies like Spotify, Uber, and Zalando also share network-building features, and the Facebook, YouTube and crowdfunding services are also mediators of information and financial resources. Such definitions depend on the perspective taken, and our starting point in the examples above was how the organisation is primarily seen.

An important point of our categorisation, connected to the examples of industries, is showing that digital business models generally belong to a traditional industry that has been around for a long time. With their digital business models, however, the above examples have clearly come to influence their respective industries in different ways. Spotify has changed the way we consume music, Uber our view of what a taxi service is, and Zalando has set a standard of accessibility that is difficult for many retailers to live up to. Facebook has largely removed the geographical boundaries of social networks. YouTube has had a particular impact on younger consumers, with many people foreseeing the death of traditional linear television, and with it a number of today's dominant media companies who may soon no longer receive sufficient advertising revenue. Crowdfunding opens doors to private financing that few have otherwise been granted.

Regardless of the category of digital business model, there are still some basic common denominators worth mentioning. These have arisen because they significantly affect the experience of customers/consumers in their apprehension of time and availability. They also, unlike our initial car manufacturer example, have a non-linear character. This means, among other things, that an actor affects several different parts of the business model by being a customer at the same time as being a supplier, and participating in activities that create the value proposition itself.

3.5. Chapter Summary

This chapter introduced the business model concept and its relation to an organisation's goals and strategies. With that as a starting point, we offered examples of how digitisation affects existing business models, from the content of the value proposition to partners, activities and resources. We illustrated the possibilities for new customer segmentation and development of customer relationships and customer channels, as well as how this affects revenue streams and cost structures.

We also discussed digital business models, which have emerged thanks to the ongoing digitisation of society. These have some common features, including the fact that they help to reduce the 'joints' of life through increased ease of access to products by reducing the time spent on accessing them. They can also be understood as mediators of products and/or as network builders.

The first three chapters of this book show that, regardless of the business, digital technologies often play a crucial role. However, it is important to remember that digitisation does not automatically contribute to creating competitive advantages. Some are of a purely infrastructural nature; an organisation sometimes has to choose to digitise, adopting the infrastructure of existing standards, if it wants to continue to exist at all (as in the banking example in Chapter 2). That kind of IT utilisation can hardly be considered a strategic asset (although the lack of it would be a strategic liability). Not adopting commonly used infrastructure will typically become a strategic obstacle. Then there is digitisation as central to developing existing, or creating entirely new, value propositions. That type of digitisation can be of great strategic importance. Companies like Spotify, Uber, and YouTube have become large and successful with business models for which digitisation is absolutely crucial to the value proposition.

It is important to remember that the two roles played by digitisation—digitised infrastructure and digitisation as a central part of the value proposition—are not permanent. Digitisation that is today considered infrastructural was often central to a new value proposition when it was initially introduced. Existing digital infrastructure can, if combined in new ways and/or with new technology, gain increased strategic importance. Organising is ongoing. This means that the organisation's business models and the influence of digitisation on them constantly need to be evaluated. Digitisation *per se* has no intrinsic value; only if it actually generates value does it attain great and sometimes decisive importance. A question that arises in connection with this is: How can we work to detect new opportunities to develop the value proposition through digitisation, and how can we then act to realise them? In the next chapter of this book, we consider this question. We start by discussing organising, how organisations can divide and coordinate work tasks and decision-making when digitising, either within a single organisation or between organisations. Which organisational roles are important for capturing and realising the potential of digitisation? Which role-holders are allowed to have an input in decisions, and who makes the decisions? Which competencies are important for understanding the role of digitisation in a business and how can these competencies be secured? How can different people's experiences and competencies come together in a fruitful way, avoiding conflict, in organisational work on digitisation? We address these issues as we move into Chapter 4.

3.6. Reading Tips

There are three articles that define and categorise what distinguishes the business model concept:

- DaSilva, Carlos M. and Trkman, Peter (2014). Business model: What it is and what it is not. *Long Range Planning* 47 (6), pp. 379–389, https://doi.org/10.1016/j.lrp.2013.08.004.
- Massa, Lorenzo; Tucci, Christopher L. and Afuah, Allan (2017). A critical assessment of business model research. *Academy of Management Annals* 11 (1), pp. 73–104, https://doi.org/10.5465/annals.2014.0072.
- Wirtz, Bernd W.; Pistoia, Adriano; Ullrich, Sebastian and Göttel, Vincent (2015). Business models: Origin, development and future research. *Long Range Planning* 49 (1), pp. 36–54, https://doi.org/10.1016/j.lrp.2015.04.001.

The business model canvas is a concept for understanding and identifying the different elements of a business model, and has received a lot of attention. Its authors have published two manuals for those who wish to identify and visualise business model content:

- Osterwalder, Alexander and Pigneur, Yves (2012). *Business Model Generation: A Guide for Visionaries, Pioneers and Challengers*. New Jersey: Wiley.

- Osterwalder, Alexander; Pigneur, Yves and Bernarda, Gregory (2014). *Value Proposition Design: How to Create Products and Services Customers Want*. New Jersey: Wiley.

An important part of both strategic development and the operationalisation of the business model is to identify how customers should pay and how the organisation should charge for their products. The following articles and book discuss the concepts of business ecology, business model and price model, and how they relate to each other.

- Cöster, Mathias; Iveroth, Einar; Olve, Nils-Göran; Petri, Carl-Johan and Westelius, Alf (2019). Conceptualising innovative price models: The RITE framework. *Baltic Journal of Management* 14 (4), pp. 540–558, https://doi.org/10.1108/BJM-06-2018-0216.
- Cöster, Mathias; Iveroth, Einar; Olve, Nils-Göran; Petri, Carl-Johan and Westelius, Alf (2020). *Strategic and Innovative Pricing: Price Models for a Digital Economy*. New York: Routledge, https://doi-org.ezproxy.its.uu.se/10.4324/9780429053696.
- Iveroth, Einar; Westelius, Alf; Olve, Nils-Göran; Petri, Carl-Johan and Cöster, Mathias (2013). How to differentiate by price: Proposal for a five-dimensional model. *European Management Journal* 31(2), pp. 109–123, https://doi.org/10.1016/j.emj.2012.06.007.

As noted, IT can have various functions in developing a value proposition. A rough but classic distinction is that between IT's streamlining function and IT's function for contributing new insights about the business, such as customer preferences and profitability. An in-depth look at these two features is available in Shoshana Zuboff's well-quoted 1988 book. A shorter overview is given in her 1985 article.

- Zuboff, Shoshana (1988). *In the Age of the Smart Machine: The Future of Work and Power*. New York: Basic Books.
- Zuboff, Shoshana (1985). Automate/lnformate: The two faces of intelligent Technology. *Organisational Dynamics* 14 (2), pp. 5–18, https://doi.org/10.1016/0090-2616(85)90033-6.

The term "crowdsourcing" is said to have been coined by Jeff Howe in a number of articles and blog posts from 2006. An overview is given in this article.

- Howe, Jeff (2006). The rise of crowdsourcing. *Wired* 14 (06), www.wired.com/2006/06/crowds/.

Innovation and product development are common areas for crowdsourcing. This article provides a good overview of those areas and the challenges they can bring.

- Majchrzak, Ann and Malhotra, Arvind (2013). Towards an information systems perspective and research agenda on crowdsourcing for innovation. *Journal of Strategic Information Systems* 22 (4), pp. 257–268, https://doi.org/10.1016/j.jsis.2013.07.004.

4. The Organisation of Digitisation

Ultimately, organising can be said to involve the division and coordination of work within and between organisations: the people, roles, departments, and/or external partners with which one will work, the skills each partner should have, and the mechanisms required to coordinate the work and ideas of each party so that they harmonise with the organisation's goals, strategy and business model.

There is a high degree of specialisation in certain contexts, such as in a fast-food restaurant or on the assembly line at a car manufacturer, where each person is responsible for a narrow work role: frying burgers, taking an order from a customer, or installing a tow hitch on a car. In others, such as a relatively new accounting firm with a few employees, the degree of specialisation is low and every employee may be responsible for performing accounting assignments for individual clients, working with sales, buying computers, and cleaning the office. Most organisations have something roughly called the "IT Department" and/or the "IT Manager". These kinds of designations say something about the prevailing attitude to IT in many organisations: that IT is a specialist area that is managed primarily by a specific department, just as sales are managed by the sales department and consolidation and analysis of financial performance are managed by the accounting department. This division of an organisation is usually based on the aim of achieving specialisation and becoming expert and efficient in a specific area.

There are also numerous tasks that are important to a business, but which the organisation may choose not to perform itself ("outsourcing"). Manufacturing companies have always faced the "make or buy" dilemma: Should car manufacturers make the parts for their cars, or buy them from

 https://doi.org/10.11647/OBP.0350.04

other companies specialised in making each part? Should steelmakers buy iron ore and coal to produce their steel, or should they own their own mines? Services are also prime targets for such decisions; it is not unusual for reception, accounting, cleaning, and building maintenance to be managed by other companies. As mentioned in the introductory chapter, the trend towards XaaS (everything as standardised services for sale) means that product development, recruitment, and executive management can also be purchased or outsourced. This also applies to IT-related goods and services.

Regardless of how an organisation chooses to divide its work, the question of coordination remains. A relatively specialised role or department can impede a more general view of the organisation and the understanding of how one person's actions are intertwined with others', and how individuals contribute to the organisation's goals and strategies. Even if there is an understanding between roles and departments and overall objectives, there may still be dependencies that must be managed. The sales department, for example, is dependent upon the people who produce the goods or services sold by the organisation and on the people who analyse profitability, to name just a few. The parts, in other words, must be coordinated into a whole. Here again, there are various degrees: Should the parts be coordinated by allowing those highest up in the organisation to decide, or should employees slightly lower down also be allowed to make decisions? Should there be many and detailed rules, goals, and contracts for how activities should be performed, or will the organisation rely on employees and/or partners working in a manner that promotes the organisation's goals and strategies without excessive management? How can interaction between various parties be facilitated? Should the organisation expect it to happen by itself, or does it need to be encouraged?

As discussed in preceding chapters, digitisation is today a fundamental element of running a business or other organisation. There is much to indicate that digitisation issues have penetrated many different levels of organisations and have to some extent become "everyone's responsibility", or at least something that multiple employees can be expected to have ideas about. It is thus perhaps more difficult than ever to limit and allocate them to specific departments and/or roles. In the banking example provided in Chapter 2, the bank's IT department was responsible for only part of its IT deliveries, and some departments managed such issues independently. Customer patterns and other events inside and outside the organisation can now be tracked in different ways, and input information is often richer, available much more quickly, and to more employees than before. Communications between employees or between employees and outsiders are typically faster and accomplished through a wide range of digital channels. Increased servitisation has also made it easier to bring in digital resources from outside; software and related packages can now be bought as services, which has both advantages and drawbacks. As a result, the way organisations determine what should be done internally and what should be purchased is changing.

So, how should an organisation organise itself to realise the benefits of digitisation? How are issues related to digitisation allocated among different parties? How are the parties' needs and ideas related to digitisation coordinated so that they harmonise with goals, strategies, and business models? Who is allowed to present decision input and who is allowed to be involved and actually make decisions about implementation? Who will finance an initiative and who will be responsible for the final result? All of this is part of something called "IT governance". We have chosen to use the relatively everyday terms of "organising", "division of work" and "coordination" to describe this phenomenon. To paint a backdrop against which organising can be understood, the chapter begins with illustrations of a few issues related to digitisation that may arise in an organisation. Internal organisation will be covered next: who works with digitisation, various approaches to digitisation and the social aspects of coordinating business operations and IT. Finally, organising in partnership with external parties is addressed: what is outsourcing, the arguments for and against it, and how such relationships can be managed.

4.1. Background: A Few Questions surrounding Digitisation

Organisations have numerous questions about digitisation. Those we have chosen to highlight here are: 'Projects: Go or no-go?', 'Design of the project portfolio', 'The role of IT in goals, strategies, and business models', 'Balance between standardisation and freedom', and 'Level of reliability and security'.

Projects: Go or no-go? The implementation of specific systems, modules and applications entails numerous decisions. Should a new customer data system be deployed? Which supplier should be selected? What are the main benefits that such an investment should generate? For whom? What is the budget? What is the time horizon, i.e. for how many years can it be used? What implementation method should be used? Chapter 9 covers project decisions and management in greater detail.

Design of the project portfolio. There may be several parallel digitisation initiatives in an organisation, in which case the organisation will have to determine whether all of them should be run simultaneously or whether something needs to be postponed. This was illustrated in Chapter 2, where an IT manager at a bank described around seventy digitisation projects taking place simultaneously, and how continuous decisions as to whether all intended projects could in fact be started needed to be made (see also Chapter 8 on project portfolios). Ensuring that benefits from several projects at the same time are realised may be difficult, especially if those projects are large.

On the other hand, different initiatives may be related, meaning that the organisation will have to ask whether one project can generate benefits in another project. During an enterprise systems project carried out by BT, an international manufacturer of forklift and warehouse trucks, the common data management platform they implemented led (a few years later) to the company beginning to supply technicians who travelled to service customers' trucks with hand-held computers for tasks such as billing and registering the withdrawal of spare parts. This rather successful digitisation effort resulted in a reduction of back-office administration of truck service, an increased amount of service per service technician, better spare-part control, and increased status for the service technician role. The digitisation of service administration would not have been possible had BT not conducted the project on common-data-management platforms years earlier. It is not easy to predict what a project may lead to a few years down the line, but it is important to attempt to consider the long-term perspective.

The role of IT in goals, strategies, and business models: now and in the future. In addition to specific projects and any potential conflicts or synergies, there are more general questions about the role of IT in an organisation (as discussed in Chapter 3 on the digitisation of business models): How much in general should be invested in IT? Which parts of the organisation should be supported or developed via IT? How should this be accomplished? Does the organisation want to streamline and save money, or is there an opportunity to use IT more strategically? Is it necessary to generate new information about one part of the organisation? Can IT be used to enhance interaction with customers? With suppliers? What are the latest technological developments and how digitised are the competitors? Naturally, an organisation has to ask these questions when specific projects are discussed, but they can also arise in more general discussions. As noted, using IT to generate business benefit is not only a matter of supporting existing goals, strategies, and business models through specific projects; it also involves picking up on new ideas that may change the future direction of the organisation.

Balance between standardisation and freedom. Another question is whether the same IT solutions should be used throughout the organisation or whether there should be scope for local choices and adaptations, for instance in data definitions and standards. If different definitions of data are used by different departments of an organisation, it will make it harder to compare information between departments. Common standards and definitions, on the other hand, will reduce the flexibility of various departments, which may be important for meeting the myriad needs of, for instance, local markets. In the enterprise systems project at BT, mentioned above, the initial ambition was to achieve common definitions to increase transparency and comparability between the sales companies in various European countries. BT eventually had to modify this ambition because it met with tremendous resistance: the local companies were unwilling to change their definitions and put their operations on display. Numerous modifications were made so that the business system would be more closely aligned with local conditions. The end result was a common platform, but one that screened the local companies from each other.

Level of reliability and security. How reliable and secure digital resources should be is another question. As discussed earlier, IT plays different roles in different organisations. For some, like airlines and stock exchanges, IT is critical and must be immediately restored to service if there is a breakdown. That level of preparedness comes at a price, of course—a price that other organisations, where IT is not as business-critical, might not think is worth paying. Similar balancing can be seen in organisations that want to give customers and clients access to data, such as bank customers, patients in a regional health system, and users of tax agency services. There is no doubt that having access to their data via their own computers is valuable to customers and clients, but it also places an organisation at greater risk of hacking.

A high level of public access may be an obvious need that is not questioned—and not secured against unlikely risks. In connection with a widespread breakdown in 2016 in the data centre of a supplier operating the systems of many public organisations, the e-prescription function at the Swedish pharmacy chain Apoteket and the booking information system at Bilprovningen, the Swedish motor vehicle inspection service, were disabled. Some fifty business customers were affected by the breakdown. Those who had not paid for storage and operation at more than one geographical site were down for a week, and some lost business data. Questions, such as how customers and clients will be affected by an IT breakdown, and whether specific customer groups will be affected or a few specific parts of the organisation, must be discussed when the organisation is deciding the level of reliability and security. Reliability and security come at a cost.

4.2. Who Works with Digitisation?

As seen in the examples above, digitisation involves matters related to benefit, risk, flexibility, and transparency among other things—aspects that can be viewed differently depending on a person's place and role in the organisation and experience with, for example, past IT projects. People working in an IT department, which typically receives much of the blame for breakdowns, hacking, and data losses, may be more inclined to a high level of backup and security. They also tend to favour standardisation, since local deviations and quirks lead to additional work in purchasing, operations, maintenance, and user support. People who work directly with customers, on the other hand, are probably more inclined to give them access to various types of services and data and to push for customisation options and special solutions. Executives in the organisation probably think that uniform definitions of data are more important than middle managers do—the former want an overall picture that allows different parts of the organisation to be properly compared (see also Chapter 2 on how goals may vary between different levels and departments of an organisation).

One thing is clear: the question of who is involved in IT-related issues matters. Like other operational decisions, IT-related issues should be dealt with by a mix of people with an overall view of the organisation, a good understanding of the wider technical issues, detailed operational knowledge, detailed insight into technical matters, and good standing in the organisation. If decisions are to be accepted and complied with, the people involved in the decisions must have the respect of those employees who are most directly impacted. There is thus reason to think carefully about which departments and which levels will contribute their perspectives, where the decisions will be made, who will finance initiatives, and who will be responsible for them. There are, naturally, numerous differences in how IT issues are organised, depending on the type of IT decision (architecture versus decisions that will have a heavy impact on operations) and the type of organisation (with regard to size and strategy, for example). As organisations change and new IT issues arise, the organisation surrounding the IT issues may take on various forms, consciously or unconsciously, rapidly or cautiously. We do not believe that the organisation of IT is always necessarily the most rational for the specific situation. Consequently, we do not want to generalise to any great extent, but instead to present a few patterns that have been observed in studies, and provide a few concrete examples of the organisation surrounding IT issues in a few different businesses.

4.2.1. Who Decides?

According to some studies involving IT managers from various sectors and countries, the IT department is mainly responsible for decisions about IT architecture and IT infrastructure, although those decisions may be shaped by input from operations. This suggests that many managers believe that architecture and infrastructure are primarily technical issues and something they cannot or do not need to be involved in to any extent. In more clearly operations-related issues, it is more common for cross-functional groups to make the decisions, either unilaterally or taking into account views from individual departments. Operations-related decisions are made solely by IT managers in only a few organisations, which indicates an understanding that IT questions often involve the organisation itself, how it should be run, methods, allocation of roles, responsibilities, and so on. Apart from the austerity measures in the wake of the dot-com crash of 2000 and the financial crisis of 2008, when decisions about IT matters tended to be centralised around IT managers, the current trend is that more people are involved in IT-related decisions and local operations managers are more involved in strategic IT initiatives. The wider selection of IT suppliers, not least through the cloud, is sometimes cited as one important reason for this. Business managers describe cloud services as a way of liberating themselves from the IT department because cloud services are easy to buy and maintain (read more about cloud services in Section 4.5.1). It is perhaps not terribly surprising that operational employees have proven to be more positive about this increased decentralisation than IT employees (see also Chapter 5 on representing different parts of the organisation when making IT-related decisions).

When scholars have sought to identify successful approaches to organisation, they have looked at factors including how companies that are profit or growth leaders in their sectors have organised themselves around IT issues. Top financial performers tend to have more centralised IT decision-making. They may aspire to a more centralised IT environment in order to achieve synergies and cost efficiency; in that case, decision-making should also be centralised to a certain extent so that the IT environment does not grow into a jungle of disparate systems. Companies that have delivered the best growth tend instead to have more decentralised decision-making, where local units are given great latitude to initiate and run IT projects. The aim is to encourage innovation and alignment with external parties; if a company is to be able to rapidly respond to changes in customer preferences or the competitive landscape, it will not want to risk delaying critical decisions on IT investments because they must be filtered through a large group of representatives from various departments and levels of the organisation. This applies particularly to multinational organisations, where it is rarely reasonable to manage IT-related issues from a head office in another country when there are most likely skilled personnel and suppliers available on site.

These results should be interpreted circumspectly, as there are numerous other factors that can affect profitability and growth. It can be said, however, that these patterns are consistent with several studies that have shown how governance, whether or not it has to do with IT, should be designed according to a company's situation. Governance should be tighter, or looser, depending on how dynamic the environment is with regard to customer preferences, competitor actions, technological advances, the availability of substitute products, and political decisions. A more dynamic environment demands greater flexibility and independence among employees, usually characterised by a greater authority to make local decisions and greater scope to diverge from set budgets and goals (loose governance). In a more stable environment, success is not found to the same extent in rapid local response to external changes, but in delivering products efficiently. In such a situation, there is often more to be gained by coordinating the organisation, by means, for example, of more centralised decision-making, more detailed rules, and firmer demands to meet budgets and goals (tight governance). Adjusting governance mechanisms to the situation creates better conditions for the organisation to perform well.

Naturally, there is a greyscale between the two extremes of a "stable" environment and a "dynamic" one, and between "tight" and "loose" governance. An organisation aiming to achieve a cost-effective IT environment, and which has therefore centralised its IT decisions, also needs a structured approach to managing departures from this stance. A modification or investment that requires additions to the infrastructure that do not harmonise with the existing infrastructure might generate so much benefit that it is still considered worth implementing. There should thus be a process for evaluating such proposals. Accordingly, it is difficult to find any exact formula for how IT-related issues should be governed. Understanding that there are different types of situations and different types of governance and that these may harmonise with one another to a greater or lesser degree, is crucial.

4.2.2. Combining Perspectives from IT and Operations

According to a survey conducted in 2016 by the magazine *CIO Sweden*, about 60% of organisations have a formal IT advisory board that deals with IT-related issues on an ongoing basis. Just like formally established structures elsewhere, IT advisory boards seem to be most prevalent in larger organisations. The IT manager seems to have a relatively obvious role on these boards, as do business area directors in 86% of cases. The CFO is included a little over half the time, while the CEO is included in 44% of cases. The IT manager often presides over the board. A few illustrations will follow.

The multinational conglomerate Siemens has an IT advisory board at the corporate level and one for each business division. The boards at the division level include employees from both operations and IT, meet quarterly, and discuss which projects should be prioritised and how much money should be spent on IT, according to the needs of the division. Matters related to things like infrastructure and suppliers, however, are dealt with by the corporate-level board. Considering the size of Siemens and the breadth of its business, it is difficult to manage IT-related issues only at the central level.

Itab, a mail-order company that sells outdoor clothing via a number of subsidiaries in Europe, also has a combination of local and central decision-making, albeit not quite as formalised. The company wanted its subsidiaries to actively pursue IT issues, but they were not doing so, so the CIO now convenes meetings several times a year at each subsidiary, bringing together the local controller, head of accounting, managing director, and IT personnel. The subsidiaries vary in size, have varying needs when it comes to customer service, and there are numerous local systems, so the CIO therefore attempts to gather information about the needs of each subsidiary. They take certain matters further with the group CFO. In addition, they bring together representatives from all of the subsidiaries once a year to discuss matters related to infrastructure and integration.

The IT Advisory Board at Stokab, the dark-fibre provider owned by the City of Stockholm, Sweden, consists of the executive team, apart from the CEO, and meets about once a month. The various operations representatives are permitted to submit business that they want to be addressed at the meetings in advance, and the board usually also gives the various system owners a few minutes to talk about any ongoing changes. In general, the board discusses strategy, system administration, and system development and prepares input for upcoming investment decisions. The IT Advisory Board also has a budget to finance IT projects it has assessed as capable of generating value, and that need to be implemented quickly to respond to external changes. Without such a budget, there is a risk that projects will not be carried out because each operation is locked into its ordinary budget and thus does not have the budgetary space for more spontaneous projects.

The question of who should finance IT initiatives is not only a matter of flexibility in relation to emerging needs, but also concerns responsibility. The previously mentioned enterprise system project at the forklift truck manufacturer BT was centrally financed, and that caused difficulties in getting local units to accept responsibility for the project. The implementation of hand-held computers for service technicians a few years later was locally financed, but centrally monitored, and was characterised by stronger local responsibility. The degree of responsibility probably depends on several things, such as who was involved in initiating and deciding to carry out a project, but the source of financing is likely to play a major role.

In addition to advisory boards that regularly deal with IT-related issues, advisory boards, often called steering groups, are usually appointed for specific projects aimed at making decisions about supplier selection, the implementation method, and organisational changes that are within the framework of that specific project. These steering groups should also reflect a balance between operations and IT and between the central and local levels that aligns with the organisation's ambitions for IT utilisation.

Integration between IT and operations also takes place in a day-to-day context. The IT department at the Swedish Parks and Resorts entertainment group has recruited one person from the accounting department and another from marketing. They are meant to provide support for each function, so that the marketing department, for example, can manage much of the website itself. The weather report supplier AccuWeather has also loosened up the boundaries between IT and other operations in its day-to-day work. The company has an innovation team, for example, comprised mainly of former technicians from the IT department, who offer analyses to customers. Some of the tasks previously assigned to the sales department have been transferred to IT, because technical issues often arise in dealings with customers. For that reason, the technicians have also undergone training in listening and providing customer service by telephone. The Schools and Education Division of the City of Stockholm, Sweden, has created an

ICT department staffed by educators and IT personnel because the city wanted an environment in which multiple perspectives could contribute to further developing the organisation.

Even if IT has become more integrated with operations, and skills from various parts of the organisation are needed to understand how IT can be used, the CIO and the IT department still play a key coordinating role. Allowing the organisation to run IT projects any which way can be risky; different systems and cloud solutions need, at least sometimes, to be connected into some kind of whole. In addition, cost advantages in purchasing and maintenance should be possible if purchasing, at least to some extent, is made more centralised, provided that the standardisation does not complicate the work of users. As mentioned before, the point is to strike a balance between centralisation and decentralisation according to the organisation's situation. In a particular organisation, it might not matter that employees choose different ways of storing and sharing their documents, as long as it is done with a reasonable measure of care. Certain decisions, especially those related to IT architecture, are still often made by central IT departments, precisely because architecture is a matter that demands an overall approach. As an example of who works with digitisation, and how digitisation initiatives may develop over time depending on conditions in the organisation, we now present the case of a school that implemented an information system for planning and grading.

A primary school implemented an IT platform designed for planning and grading. The platform was initially perceived as burdensome and user-unfriendly. Planning had previously been done on computers or even written by hand, and shared with others at the individual teacher's discretion. Following the implementation of the new system, teachers were required to enter their planning, both short-term and long-term, into the system, according to pre-set menus. Assessment and grading were to be done in accordance with a matrix where different goals and criteria from the curriculum were stipulated. Planning and grading were now more automatically shared with colleagues, headmasters, pupils and their parents.

Not only did this require a new way of structuring planning and assessments, but it also became evident that additional measures, aside from the platform *per se*, were needed. When made visible to a larger audience, it became evident that formulations of plans and assessments varied a great deal among teachers, despite certain guidance from the pre-set menus. This raised discussions about the need to streamline formulations. Such discussions largely departed from the teachers' own experiences and wishes. Although headmasters organised meetings where teachers were meant to discuss these matters, teachers also organised their own meetings in smaller groups, often based on subjects or year-groups. Those teachers who already collaborated closely in their day-to-day work typically also gathered to discuss the meaning of certain criteria and content, and how planning and assessments could be formulated accordingly.

Another issue that arose during the implementation was the question of how planning and assessments were understood by the external audience, the pupils and parents. Teachers were of the opinion that parents in general did not bother to read lengthy formulations, and that formulations must not contain bureaucratic vocabulary that would obscure the basic message.

After about a year, many teachers were significantly more positive about the system. The shared storage of content between colleagues over the years was deemed to save a lot of time; the initial heavy workload had ultimately, it seemed, paid off. The system was also perceived to facilitate work, as it provided guidance, both through its features and the collegial discussions that had taken place over the year. Teachers now felt that the system helped them to obtain an overview and to ensure that they covered all parts of the curriculum when doing their planning and grading. Both teachers and headmasters furthermore believed that the discussions that had arisen in conjunction with the system's implementation were refreshing, as they directed attention to important pedagogical issues, such as how to interpret certain knowledge criteria and what to include in the planning of a certain theme in a certain grade. However, there was still variation in how teachers formulated their planning and assessments, and some teachers expressed a wish for clearer guidelines from headmasters.

We learn several things from the above case that need to be considered by those who are responsible for, or work with, digitisation in organisations:

- How the use of an IT tool unfolds depends on existing structures in the organisation, such as division of work and habits of collaborating.
- Involving those who are deeply involved in day-to-day work and who will be affected most by an IT tool enables the implementation to be more suited to their needs and ultimately more positively perceived.
- Documenting and storing data not only requires the appropriate technology but also comes with costs in the form of the users' time: time that not everyone may be willing to devote.
- Documenting and storing data therefore requires some sort of guidance and/or incentive. This could include agreed-upon standards, sanctions, rewards or, not least, internal motivation, whereby users see the value of documenting and storing data, for themselves as well as for others.

4.3. What Does Working with Digitisation Entail?

In addition to allocating joint responsibility for digitisation issues across central and local levels and between IT personnel and other employees, it may also be useful to think about the nature of digitisation issues and how an organisation wants to distribute and balance various types of issues. We previously mentioned architecture as a distinct category that should be managed by the people responsible for IT at the central level, but IT issues may also be differentiated in terms of routine work and innovative work. It is easy to get the impression that digitisation is all about innovation and creating change in an organisation, but as mentioned in Chapter 3, innovative approaches to using IT eventually become established approaches, and some organisations jump on trends much later than others. On the one hand, digitisation can thus be considered a potential tool for finding new ways of working and new products to offer, thus justifying expenditure of time and energy on it. On the other hand, existing digitisation needs to be taken care of, systems upgraded, and users supported, which means that people are required to work more regularly on IT-related issues. The first may involve projects that last a few months and must quickly generate value for the client, while the other may involve a temporal horizon of several years.

In IT contexts, this balance between different tasks has been called "bimodal IT" (a term reportedly coined by the research firm Gartner). In management research, the phenomenon has been noted more generally, and has been called "ambidexterity". Some would argue that it is more efficient to have employees specialise in one thing or another and that the innovative part of the IT department should in such cases work in the organisation to get closer to the needs of those outside the department (as discussed in the previous section). Others would argue that it is difficult to draw a hard and fast line between innovative and administrative employees, and that such a division risks creating an unfortunate alienation—perhaps of the administrative group above all. First, the two types of work are not entirely clear-cut; new ideas can improve the operation of existing systems and innovations are meant to eventually become part of day-to-day operations. Secondly, system expertise is spread more evenly among IT personnel if everyone works on both innovative and administrative aspects; otherwise, there is a risk that valuable knowledge essential to systems administration will be lost.

This brings us to the many different roles with links to digitisation that can currently be found in organisations. As mentioned in the previous section, the C-suite roles of CEO, CFO, and CIO are often members of an advisory board. It is perhaps unsurprising that the CEO is included, as they are ultimately responsible for the business. Nor does the presence of the CFO raise any eyebrows; accounting and finance functions have a long tradition of using IT to support transaction management, and to consolidate input. The chief marketing officer and the head of communications can also be key roles in digitisation; nowadays, identifying the opinions and preferences of customers and other stakeholders, or communicating messages to stakeholders often involves the use of a full palette of digital channels. There are actually no limits to the roles in an organisation that may be important in creating value through digitisation: it depends on the organisation's focus. The Chief Information Officer (CIO) is often emphasised as an important role. Most recently, one might have heard of roles such as Chief Digital Officer, Chief Data Officer, and Business Information Officer (BIO).

The latter is found, for example, on the staff of a Swedish bank, where the BIO is described as a sort of "sub-CIO". The CIO is a member of the corporate executive management team, while the BIO is a member of the executive team for their particular business area. The BIO is responsible for the business area's IT budget and reports to the business area manager. Depending on the organisation, the same title may cover fairly disparate tasks and areas of responsibility, and the various titles may also overlap. Consequently, we do not believe there to be any point in defining what all these titles entail. We can only say that digitisation has led to several of the more established roles having to manage such issues and to the emergence of new roles entirely, and we will leave it at that. Here, we will be focusing on the role of the CIO, which has been studied quite extensively and is often brought up when talking about the need to work bimodally.

Some researchers, such as Mark Chun and John Mooney, discuss the role of the CIO in two dimensions: the organisation's information systems (IS) strategy and information systems infrastructure. The first applies to the level of forward-thinking and risk-taking and the second to how systematic and coordinated the organisation's technologies and processes are. Based on this, four types of roles emerge in a CIO typology:

Triage Nurse/Firefighter. In an organisation with a risk-averse IS strategy combined with a fragmented infrastructure, the CIO's main focus is to keep costs down and make the best of existing technology. As the name suggests, the role involves prioritising urgent cases and putting out fires, rather than taking a long-term, big-picture approach. The role requires considerable technical expertise, as much of it has to do with fixing what does not work.

Landscape Cultivator. In an organisation with a risk-averse IS strategy but a more systematised infrastructure, the CIO focuses on the ongoing maintenance and integration of various applications and processes. The connection between IS and operations is more distinct than in the first role and the CIO thus needs to be skilled at tasks such as project management, change processes, and training. The emphasis, however, is on technical issues and the CIO does not intervene in strategy.

Opportunity Seeker. In an organisation with a risk-tolerant IS strategy and a non-systematised IS infrastructure, the CIO must work to identify gaps where processes can be improved with new technology.

Problem-solving and relationship-building are key skills in this role. There is thus an opportunity here to use IS to develop the organisation, but in the form of isolated initiatives rather than from an overall perspective.

Innovator and Creator. In an organisation with a risk-tolerant IS strategy and a systematised IS infrastructure, the CIO can concentrate on innovation and driving new revenues through new ways of using IS. Unlike the Opportunity Seeker role, this type of CIO is more engaged in the organisation's strategy and the role that IS should play in the organisation. Insight into the business strategy and the capacity to negotiate and build relationships are especially important in this role.

In Chun and Mooney's study, there were roughly the same number of respondents in each role, but many wanted to move toward the more innovative role. In simple terms, the CIO could be called either the "IT manager" who seeks to keep infrastructure alive and make sure the organisation gets as much benefit as possible for the money it invests, or the "Chief Innovation Officer", who is more visionary and tries to find new ways to generate revenue through IS organisation-wide. The latter typically had a business background rather than a technical background. Some scholars point to the general trend that it is becoming more common for the CIO to come from a business background. The opportunity for a CIO to move towards a more innovative role also seems to depend largely on whether the infrastructure is stable (in which case less energy needs to be spent on technical problems and on training employees and persuading them of the value of IS) and the extent of IS integration with the organisation's strategies and processes (for example, IS may be considered a more integrated part of the business in a data analysis firm than in a construction company). A more recent study of Swedish CIOs (Magnusson et al., 2019), claims that CIOs tend to take fewer risks, partly due to IT governance models, and that such a defensive stance will diminish the role of CIOs in the digitisation of the organisation.

It has long been said that the CIO role should act as a bridge between IS and business, but the CIO's tasks and place in the organisational hierarchy vary, as indicated above. Many would argue that the CIO naturally belongs on the executive team, but some still report to the CFO, for example. While some have received support from an assistant CIO in order to become more involved in the organisation's processes and strategies and less involved in technical details, others argue that the CIO role is going to become redundant or be reallocated elsewhere in the organisation as the utilisation of IS becomes more integrated. The point here is that there are many and partially overlapping labels for IS-related roles and that their content probably depends on both organisational conditions and interactions with others, and the personal characteristics of the individual in the role. Studies have specifically focused on the interaction between IT managers and business managers and have found it to be important to the development of common goals regarding how IT creates value in an organisation. This will be addressed in the next section.

4.4. Social Aspects of Coordinating IT Specialists and Operations

So far, this chapter has mainly discussed more structural aspects of the division of work and coordination of IT-related issues, such as roles, tasks, and representation in decision-making fora, planning processes, and project teams. As noted numerous times in management research, structure and planning form only one dimension of running a business. The everyday actions and attitudes of employees can also have a profound impact on which initiatives are prioritised and realised, and the results of those initiatives. Ultimately, people will fill the roles, take on the tasks and represent their organisational home, and it is therefore equally important to understand what knowledge, attitudes, and values people may be carrying and how those affect the relationship between IT units and wider operations. The following section addresses how employees from different groups can approach each other and create good relationships.

First and foremost, we must ask what characterises a good relationship between IT units and operations. Some observers, such as Blaize Reich and Izak Benbasat, argue that this is characterised in the short term by business managers and IT managers understanding and supporting the respective unit's plans and goal setting and, in the long term, by a shared vision about the way that digitisation will contribute to the business. Their study is based on interviews with managers from Canadian insurance organisations, where IT was assessed as having a strategic role (defined according to the size of the IT budget and the hierarchical distance between the IT manager and the CEO). To achieve this kind of relationship, it is important to consider at least four factors.

Shared IT knowledge. This requires certain knowledge to be shared between business managers and IT managers. Business managers, for example, should be up-to-date with new technology and have experience participating in, or leading, IT projects. Why should only IT managers attend technology conferences? IT managers should have experience as line managers and should understand the industry, as well as the history and current situation of various business units. It goes without saying that other top management should keep track of the organisation's business environment, its goals and strategies, and what makes it successful (as discussed in Chapter 2) and the IT manager should thus be no exception. In so doing, the respective managers will not only better understand how IT can create value, how the other managers contribute, and the challenges that they (not least the IT manager) are facing, but can also personally participate in and feel a sense of responsibility for their counterparts' work, instead of looking out only for the performance of their own unit. This applies regardless of whether digitisation is used to solve a problem, improve an existing process, or transform the business and create new types of revenue. Depending on the hierarchical structure of the organisation, it may of course also be relevant for people other than managers to have insight.

IT experience. This refers to an organisation's previous IT-related projects. If past projects were successful, business managers may see more potential and value in digitisation and consequently involve IT managers in planning to a greater extent. Unfortunately, this logic also works in the reverse: there is a risk that a history of failed IT projects will damage the confidence of business managers and their willingness to collaborate.

Communication. This encompasses several forms of interaction between business managers and IT managers, ranging from informal meetings and emails to more formally designed interactions, such as project teams, committees, and cross-functional roles. There is much to indicate that more frequent communication promotes mutual understanding. *How* you communicate matters, of course: IT personnel may have to tone down their technical jargon and try instead to express themselves in terms with which the other party is familiar, which may differ between the various business units.

Links between business and IT planning. This refers to whether activities in the IT units and business units are planned separately or jointly, and whether the IT side is planned subordinately to operations, or whether it affects business planning. If business and IT are planned in a more integrated way, it is more likely that the parties will understand each other. Meetings at which both IT-related and non-IT-related project proposals are evaluated, and where space is allowed for continuous dialogue about priorities in the organisation, are important to integrated business and IT planning. Certainly, such meetings can lead to conflicts, but some scholars argue that cross-functional discussions with broader participation are more important than tight governance of the planning process from the top down (unless the organisation has very clear and stable goals, in which case there may be advantages to a top-down planning process).

Chapter 8 delves deeper into the prioritisation of projects based on the benefit they can generate and how well they align with other projects in the organisation. In some organisations, the prevailing idea is that IT should be delivered with a clearly identified buyer and seller, i.e., the IT department delivers a customer data management system ordered by the marketing department. The transaction may be regulated by a contract. Could such a strict division lead to difficulties in integrating the activities of IT units and business operations as recommended above? Or could it provide more reasons for communication between the parties since preferences, specifications, and conditions must be made explicit? It is not clear-cut that one solution is better than the other to achieve good relationships between IT and business operations. The success of organisations is not only dependent on structures, but also on people's actions within those structures.

The above factors, interacting with each other, can promote or inhibit the emergence of common goals and visions. For example, an IT manager who has experience with both IT and business may be highly successful at implementing a project, which helps create trust in the IT department. Such trust may be critical to whether a manager is asked to participate in cross-functional contexts, such as an IT committee, or to act in integrative roles. This creates multiple networks and facilitates more frequent communication and more integrated planning. Under these circumstances, it is possible that business managers and IT managers will develop a body of shared knowledge. When an IT manager is very familiar with business plans and goals, the chances that other IT personnel will also become familiar with them increase. Some organisations insist that IT personnel should regularly visit operations and that everyone must work with user support, and this knowledge can promote even better collaboration in the next IT project. This is, of course, something of an ideal scenario; naturally, the absence of any of the factors mentioned above may lead to shortcomings in other factors and thus a lack of shared goals and visions. Shared knowledge seems particularly important, as it helps to bridge difficulties in the relationship between IT and operations which may have arisen during less successful IT projects.

In more concrete terms, this means that organisations intent on improving integration between IT and business operations should think about how they recruit, train, organise, and reward their employees, e.g. by encouraging participation in courses and conferences, physically placing people from different departments together (the amount of information that can be spread and exchanged in an open-plan office or on the same floor of the building should not be underestimated), letting IT people manage parts of the business and vice versa, rewarding breadth of experience, and carefully discussing recent IT projects to learn lessons from any setbacks.

These integration mechanisms may be equally pertinent between groups other than IT and business, and have over the years often been brought up in management research, perhaps so much so that they sound obvious today. Nevertheless, they have often proven difficult to implement. For example, it has been determined that the social mechanisms mentioned above mainly promote more short-term harmonisation between IT and operations, which is indicative of the difficulty of creating enduring attitudes in an organisation. It has also been established that organisations that demonstrate good short-term harmonisation may also have a fairly long history—of perhaps ten years—of communication, successful projects, and job rotation. One possible reason for these difficulties is that all forms of specialisation lead to a specific vocabulary and a specific approach. Very extensive and frequent job rotation may be necessary to prevent this from taking root, and the situation may differ in various parts of the world. A study of digitisation in Japan found that it was common for business managers to have worked in the IT department for a few years and for IT managers to be responsible for other functions, often finance or planning, as well. Employee turnover is another possible reason. Regardless of how accepting and integrated existing employees are, the same attitudes are not automatically transferred to new employees, and may need to be learned, depending on their previous experience.

Whether harmonisation between IT and business operations is always a good thing is also open to discussion. There has been some talk of productive friction, which may be needed when the business environment is changing rapidly. If different parts of an organisation do not thoroughly understand each other's work and share goals and visions about how IT should be able to promote the health of the business, there is a risk that the organisation will be unable to respond to change as fast as necessary due to excessively one-sided perspectives and contentment with the status quo.

A case about e-government in municipalities is included below as an example of social aspects of coordinating IT specialists and operations. E-government—IT-supported initiatives to develop public operations, such as through the provision of services and information to citizens—has been developed widely in Sweden during the last decade. There are various forms of e-government: examples include new channels for communication between a municipality and its citizens, such as Facebook pages, chat forums, and YouTube clips, as a supplement to printed material and personal meetings, apps for reporting things that need to be repaired or addressed in different places, and portals where citizens can log in and obtain an overview of school, childcare, leisure activities and the like, all in one place, for example, when choosing a school. But what is the essence of e-government, and is it primarily a matter of technology or operations? Based on Gabriella Jansson's study of e-government, the case below describes two municipalities, A and B, both considered pioneers in e-government. Both municipalities have had a stable political government and clear operational goals for a long time.

Municipality A is characterised by far-reaching marketisation where services such as schools, eldercare and leisure activities are offered by both private and municipal actors, based on individual preferences. Municipality B has a long tradition of so-called citizen offices; places where citizens can obtain information and speak with both officials and politicians. This has been considered important in light of the large proportion of citizens with limited knowledge of the Swedish language.

The politicians in Municipality A have a clear vision of how IT should be used to generate benefits in the municipality, both for citizens and for employees. An example of the link between IT and political visions is the replacement of the previous IT portal, to which only municipal providers of welfare services had access, as it was considered important that it also be available to private actors. IT has thus been a means of supporting prevailing values. Some projects have been implemented quickly, with a lack of support from, for example, school principals as a result, but the advantage highlighted by officials is that the goals and vision of the IT projects have been marked by great clarity, which has helped to guide and legitimise the projects. The municipality has no separate strategy for IT, but instead takes as its point of departure the operations and what it wants to achieve.

In Municipality B, it is to a large extent the officials who have driven the development of e-government. The role of the politicians has mainly been to approve the officials' proposals for IT projects and to set budgetary frames. Costs and investments related to IT are also managed within the budget of each entity, which tends to reinforce fragmentation and short-term orientation. Projects have been added one at a time, leading to the feeling that no one has a complete grip on the various projects and how to prioritise them when financial resources are insufficient. There is an IT strategy, but it is perceived by some as too technically oriented. There is also the perception that IT projects are run by the IT department, despite an opinion among officials that IT is an organisational matter rather than a technical one. Even though the politicians are considered to be very committed and visionary with regard to the citizen offices, they seem to view e-government as a technical initiative rather than something that interacts with operations to any large extent.

The case above illustrates a couple of things to consider regarding coordination between IT specialists and operations:

- Depending on which actors are involved in IT-related decisions, those decisions will enjoy varying degrees of legitimacy and be more (or less) clearly related to operations.
- Previous IT projects can influence the attitudes of the different actors.

4.5. Outsourcing and Partnership with Suppliers

Our discussion of who participates in an organisation's digitisation, and how, and how various initiatives are coordinated, continues in this section, but the focus will now shift to situations of "outsourcing", in which digitisation is managed by external actors. The section begins with an account of what outsourcing entails and the possible reasons for and against outsourcing an organisation's digitisation. This is followed by a discussion about how outsourced operations are managed to align with the needs of the organisation.

4.5.1. What Does the Outsourcing of IT Entail?

Narrowly defined, outsourcing entails transferring something the organisation previously did for itself to an external supplier. The actual purchasing of such a service is merely sourcing, and could take place when a business is started or when a business switches from one supplier to another. In ordinary parlance, however, these have come to be known as outsourced services, rather than just the step from internally managed operations to contracting the job to an external party. It is in this wider sense that we address the phenomenon of outsourcing in this section.

IT support can involve both goods and services. Back when computers were still large and costly, companies commonly rented hardware rather than buying it themselves. After the breakthrough of the PC, it became more common for an organisation's computing power to come from PCs that it owned. At that point, outsourcing began instead to involve systems integration, networks, and telecommunications, the use of temporary contract workers instead of hiring people with the required expertise, or contracting for transmission capacity instead of trying to build and own the lines for transmission to the target audience. Since then, the pendulum has swung back and forth between owning and leasing computer capacity and between providing services of various kinds internally or buying them externally. Today, outsourcing is common in numerous areas of business, from computing capacity to systems development and operation, and even tasks that utilise computerised systems.

According to a 2019 US survey, application development is the most commonly outsourced service, and some of the fastest growing areas for outsourcing are network operations and IT security. Help-desk support and disaster recovery are particularly popular outsourcing areas for organisations intending to reduce costs, but as we shall see in Section 4.5.2, there may be several other reasons for choosing to outsource. Although it does occur, the outsourcing of entire processes is unusual. An example of outsourcing an entire process would be when Sweden Post redesigned its entire office network and, instead of only running its own post offices, began to partner with Swedish retail stores, such as ICA and Pressbyrån. For this to be possible, Sweden Post needed new systems that could be used by retail companies, whose employee turnover was high, and where employees were given only minimal training in handling mail and using systems. They also needed to install relevant systems in the partner stores and provide some training for store employees. Contracts were also required to specify what services the stores would perform and on what terms. In addition, Sweden Post chose to outsource much of the development and implementation work to consultant firms.

Markets for IT-related services are still developing. One prediction, based on a 2016 study carried out in the Nordic countries by Whitelane Research in partnership with PA Consulting, is that outsourcing is set to grow, especially in the areas of application development, maintenance, and testing. This scenario is not limited to the futures of large IT departments. As more goods and services are digitised, product and business development will increasingly become a matter of software and hardware development. As the total scope of such activities expands, companies naturally take advantage of the potential for specialisation and the development of markets for specialised services. Who does what may change over time, and going forward, some organisations will probably choose to conduct jobs that they previously outsourced internally, but, in general, the growth in outsourcing IT-related services is expected to continue.

Before we take a closer look at the reasons for outsourcing and how it can be managed, we will discuss a few types of outsourcing that have demonstrated particular growth in recent years.

Offshoring. One tendency is for companies to outsource certain operations abroad, for instance to India and the Baltic countries. This is usually called offshoring or nearshoring, depending on how far away the supplier is. This approach is commonly driven by cost-cutting, and it thus makes sense that the focus is on countries with a lower cost profile. According to a 2015 survey conducted by the magazine *CIO Sweden*, about 60% of survey respondents had outsourced part of their IT operations abroad, primarily to India, but also to the Baltic countries and the Czech Republic. Internationally, rather than being replaced by IT support, customer service, telephone sales, and other human support services are increasingly becoming the objects of offshoring. Language is important in interactions with customers, and Filipino companies are now competing successfully with Indian companies to become outsourcing partners for English-language services. Nearshoring and offshoring do not always result in cost reductions and efficiency. Language barriers, cultural differences, and differences in time zones can make it more difficult to make these partnerships work than it would be if they were outsourced within the same country or indeed if the services were performed internally.

Captive. Governance and coordination problems may cause an organisation to outsource IT-related operations abroad while still retaining control over them. This is known as a "captive solution". In a narrow sense, this is thus not a matter of outsourcing, but it is still distinct from having an IT or customer service department within the same building as other departments, which is why we mention it here. Companies including Danske Bank, AstraZeneca, and Volkswagen have taken this route. After having engaged an Indian IT company for a few years, Danske Bank decided in 2014 to establish its own IT centre in Bangalore, India, and have them handle everything from major development projects to minor services of a simpler nature. EF, a company providing language-learning travel and exchange, has made a similar move, from previously having engaged an Indian consultancy to creating its own centre in Bangalore, the city sometimes called the "Silicon Valley of India".

Cloud services. "Cloud services" are another form of IT outsourcing that has grown in recent years and is expected to continue to do so. Cloud services involve the delivery of IT-related services over the Internet—which is sometimes depicted as a cloud in illustrations—instead of their being physically installed or performed at the purchasing organisation. Subscription is the most common form of contract, whereby the subscriber has access to the cloud for a finite period and often the option to adjust capacity upwards or downwards as needed. It has been possible to buy various forms of service from service agencies ever since the use of computers began in the twentieth century, but with the development of the Internet and the advent of increasingly faster and cheaper broadband, market opportunities are constantly expanding. Terms such as IaaS (Infrastructure-as-a-Service, i.e., the provision of storage space and computing power as a service), PaaS (Platform-as-a-Service, i.e., the provision of a platform for systems development), and SaaS (Software-as-a-Service, i.e., the provision of use of an online program) have been coined to describe the various types of standardised services available over the Internet. As the types of services—and their acronyms—multiplied, the all-encompassing XaaS (Everything-as-a-Service) was coined. These days, we are used to being able to get hold of everything under the sun as standardised services via the Internet, even as consumers. This might involve simpler services, such as document storage, email, and videoconferencing, but also survey instruments, business systems, databases, tools for accounting, billing, payment monitoring, etc. To some extent, programs from established software vendors are moving into the cloud. Office 365, the Microsoft Office package with an email program, word processing, document storage and sharing, is one example. Consumers have been using this type of IT via the Internet for a long time and organisations are increasingly choosing to manage these services through the Microsoft cloud, for example, instead of through their own infrastructure. There are also firms in other industries that have seen business opportunities in offering cloud services via their own extensive infrastructure. Amazon is now a leading supplier of cloud services and is challenging traditional vendors like Oracle and IBM. The traditional vendors are also taking action: IBM, for example, has sold parts of its hardware operations to concentrate more on cloud services.

Ultimately, outsourcing—in any form—can be said to involve striking a balance between control and flexibility. It can free up resources and thus enable more flexible action, but also entails fewer avenues through which to control how the specific aspect of operations is performed and how it fits into the rest of the organisation. Instead of direct management, it becomes a contractual matter. It is common to try and achieve clarity through specifications or service level agreements (SLA), in which the content and agreed quality of the service delivery are set out. This type of clear specification works better for a familiar, standardised service than for one that is flexible and changeable in terms of the access agreed between parties, response times, and so on, but things start to get tricky even with a helpdesk. What types of issues should the buyer expect to get help with? When is an issue actually resolved? What is the quality of the help? How should support for new products be dealt with? Is a new contract necessary or can the parties identify procedures for how soon the helpdesk must be able to provide (efficient and competent) support?

As we discussed in the introductory chapter, an organisation should be able to essentially build a Lego structure from purchased (cloud) services, integrated via systems that are either shared, or at least communicate with each other. In reality, however, standardisation is not quite that seamless, and the interface is not as clear and simple as the stacking of Lego bricks. The shape of the bricks and how they are combined may require both continuous contact and discussion. What kind of feedback do we have about the service execution and its suitability? What needs for development and adaptation exist now or will arise over time, and how should they be managed? What assurances does the organisation require before leaving a current and familiar service provider for a new one that seems promising but is as yet untried?

We will return to matters of governance and governability, but will first take a closer look at the reasons for and against outsourcing. Some of these are listed in Table 4.1 and will be further discussed in the following section.

Table 4.1 Reasons for and against outsourcing an organisation's IT.

Reasons for outsourcing	Reasons against outsourcing
Cost efficiency improvement	Cost of maintaining insight and monitoring
Focus on core business	Loss of skills
Flexibility	Data exposure
Development and improvement	

4.5.2. Reasons for Outsourcing

Cost efficiency improvement. As said, reducing costs is a key reason for outsourcing. A number of studies indicate that organisations that choose to outsource large parts of their IT management are often struggling with falling profits, high operating costs, high debt, and low liquidity. Studies that more explicitly studied reasons for outsourcing also clearly show that the potential to control and reduce costs is highly significant. Outsourcing can certainly contribute to lower costs; a supplier that has specialised in providing large-scale IT support can potentially deliver cost advantages (but also quality advantages, more on which later in this section) compared with providing support internally. When the airline company Scandinavian Airlines (SAS) decided in 2015 to weed its fragmented system flora and hand over a large part of IT operations to external partners, the airline's choice was an Indian firm, Tata Consulting. The CIO at SAS expressed the hope that costs in particular would be reduced, through several changes including shrinking the company's own IT department and digitising additional processes.

The cost argument is even more prominent in connection with the choice to outsource IT operations abroad, as there is a huge gap in wage levels between, for example, India and European countries. The choice to buy IT as cloud services is also usually characterised by cost savings arguments. In 2015, the Scandinavian grocery chain ICA moved parts of its IT operations to the cloud. After less than a year, they estimated that they had recouped the investment thanks to lower costs of administering databases and application servers. When the National Property Board of Sweden chose Microsoft Office 365 instead of continuing to run Office (including email) internally, the agency estimated that it would be about 40% cheaper. A government inquiry was conducted in 2015 that determined that Swedish government agencies generally needed to take better advantage of the opportunities provided by cloud solutions. The committee of inquiry estimated that large cost savings were possible, in part because the buyer of a cloud service can share operational personnel, software, and hardware with others instead of buying resources dimensioned to handle peak loads separately. When the usage of users in different organisations is aggregated, the peak loads of some will coincide with the off-peak usage of others, so that the combined capacity requirement will be much lower than the sum of everyone's peak loads.

Naturally, the savings are greater for organisations requiring either investment or new hires than they are for those that have already made the investments and hired the employees, because once resources have been spent, they can only be recovered to a certain extent. Outsourcing can thus be particularly economical for new organisations that have not yet had time to build up their own IT environments, customer service, accounting units, or whatever they are considering buying as a cloud service. Buyers of outsourced services often pay only for the capacity and storage space they actually use as opposed to paying for a peak load capacity that goes largely unused, which is typical for in-house operations. In turn, the supplier achieves economies of scale through the sharing of resources among customers. Upgrades are processed more often, but in smaller stages, which is thought to save the buyer a great deal of effort. It should be noted, however, that cloud services are not necessarily cheaper; after cost/benefit analysis, the location data company Foursquare concluded that it was more economical for them to rent space in a data centre and use their own hardware than to use a cloud-based database. If an organisation has highly specific systems developed in-house that still serve their purpose and an operating environment that is tried, tested, and efficient, the transition to cloud services, which are standardised to fit many, may require compromises, changes in working methods, or new learning and relearning, all of which make continued internal operations seem preferable.

The coordination gains that can be obtained through cloud services can instead be considered a special case of outsourcing. In traditional outsourcing, many of the potential cost advantages are based on efficiency gains related to the sharing of resources, such as premises, equipment, software, employees, and knowledge production. Although there is potential in many cases to improve cost efficiency through outsourcing, the underlying reasons are increasingly more strategic. We will now shift our focus to these.

Focus on core business. One more strategic reason for outsourcing is the opportunity to free up resources to focus on core business. It is a common view that IT which is not critical to the delivery of the value proposition can be outsourced. Email, intranet, accounting systems, and electronic billing are all examples of IT applications that fulfil a vital function in the day-to-day work of many, but which are established tools that do not in themselves constitute a way of further developing the unique selling points of an organisation's value proposition. That which constitutes the core of the value proposition varies. For a trading company, the logistics of delivering goods to customers can be a key component and its IT support must then be seen as strategic. In a high-tech firm, the main concern is instead the design and development of new products, in which case such IT support is of greater strategic significance. It is increasingly common for digital elements to be central product features: the logistics company's route planning, the battery charger manufacturer's charge management, the billing company's credit rating algorithm, the heat pump company's temperature control, or the car manufacturer's automated driving system. There may be a good reason to maintain control over such central components, which are strategically important to the business, by developing and managing them in-house or possibly in collaboration with a trusted partner.

The non-profit organisation NACE International argued in the above terms for a focus on core business when they chose to outsource their maintenance of infrastructure, as well as their cybersecurity activities, while keeping the development of their customer-facing applications in-house. The choice was based on the idea that back-office activities should be outsourced and that activities related to customers (i.e. activities that constitute the core business) should be conducted within the organisation. A Northern European social insurance agency cited the same reasons when they decided in 2015 to outsource systems development and certain parts of systems administration. The truck and bus manufacturer Scania has both outsourced and insourced system development and operation based on different assessments of the advantages and drawbacks of the respective alternative. British

Petroleum (BP) concentrated on forging alliances with other companies in the energy industry to encourage the growth of independent standard-systems developers so that it became possible to outsource systems development and operation to external parties. Different organisations come to different conclusions and the same organisation may change its position over time, so it is impossible to say in general that it is always wise to outsource one part of the chain.

Flexibility. The previously mentioned approach of varying usage according to the organisation's changing needs is another strategic reason for outsourcing. In 2015, the Swedish Transport Agency entered into a contract with IBM for the management of their data centres, worth nearly SEK 1 billion (EUR 100 million) over five years. The plan was to have IBM initially operate the data centres and eventually take them over entirely. As the need for a large data centre will vary, an ability to scale either up or down according to immediate requirements was considered important. Dimensioning to ensure the capacity to manage every conceivable peak load would be a waste of resources if the potential variations in needs are large and a cost-effective solution can be achieved through outsourcing. The Swedish Council for Higher Education knows there is a huge peak load a couple of times a year when eager prospective students who have just taken the national university aptitude test want to see the correct answers. This can be easily managed by outsourcing operations to a specialised supplier. There is even more reason to choose outsourcing instead of internal management if the type of resource requirement also varies in a way that cannot be satisfied by the organisation's own multi-skilled employees or other internal resources.

Cloud solutions, which are sometimes described as "IT on tap", usually entail tremendous flexibility. The European hotel chain Scandic started a project in 2015 to put its IT operations related to the website and the market into the cloud. A primary reason for this was the ability to scale up and down as needed, for example, when there was heavy traffic on the website in connection with events. The push for flexibility is not limited to existing IT use, and also applies to the development of new forms of IT use. Scandic wanted to offer cutting-edge solutions to their customers, and they concluded that they would not be able to develop tools fast enough on their own if they wanted to get a jump on the next big thing, for example within social media. Because the payment model for cloud solutions is typically tied to use of existing services—unlike purchased software or in-house/purchased development, where full payment is required before the company can begin to use it, and before it knows whether and to what extent it will be used—cloud services provide greater opportunities both to try competing services and (as long as the term of the cloud services contract is not too long) to switch suppliers. There is a drawback in flexibility, however, as often only standard solutions are on offer.

Development and improvement. A related strategic justification for outsourcing is the opportunity to leverage external skills and technology to learn new things and improve internal processes. This may apply to both strategic and less strategic aspects of a business. Although the argument above—that outsourcing should only be considered for things that do not make a critical contribution to the value proposition—is common, there are those who choose to outsource strategically important aspects precisely to gain access to high-level, up-to-date skills that can promote new ways of working. According to Deloitte's 2018 global outsourcing survey, one third of respondents were in fact willing to pay more for cloud services, if those services contributed to improved performance and innovative capabilities. Similarly, the choice to have outsourced activities managed abroad through either an offshoring or captive solution is not necessarily a matter of cost-cutting alone, but may also be made with a view to gaining access to a large number of highly educated software developers. The CIO at EF, a global language education company, has praised the skilled and dedicated personnel at the IT centre in Bangalore, who actively contribute suggestions for how operations can be developed. But it is by no means a given that access to high-level skills will lead to successful development. A manufacturer of smart electricity meters decided after a while to reverse the development of the function logic in the meters from a collaboration with a highly specialised development consultancy because the process of developing new functionality required more continuous dialogue and collaboration than the consultancy's contract model allowed for.

Thus, there may be several reasons behind outsourcing. Consultant reports in recent years have indicated that organisations in general are interested in outsourcing more of their IT, and that they increasingly regard outsourcing as a potential source of business development and innovation. Many argue, however, from both the buyer's and the supplier's side, that business development and innovation are not given much scope in connection with the outsourcing of ongoing operations. One reason for this may be a strong focus on costs in the contract and in ongoing management (more about this later in the chapter). One reason might be that it is more difficult to get feedback on needs and opportunities for development from a partner than from the organisation's own employees. First, it is thought that provisions concerning such feedback, for example from an outsourced helpdesk or customer service, need to be expressed in the contract. Secondly, outsourcing is based on the premise that the partner's employees will perform the tasks that have been outsourced in parallel with equivalent tasks for other customer organisations, and that standardisation across customers is what makes them efficient. The scope for the partner to contribute to the development of a specific business is thus limited. Another reason might be that the partner does not feel comfortable to allow an external party, such as the IT supplier, to work closely with the end customer, which is often required in order to develop operations in a relevant way. There may thus be good reasons to reject outsourcing, which we will now delve into further.

4.5.3. Reasons against Outsourcing

Cost of maintaining insight and monitoring. Letting an external actor manage parts of an organisation's operations presents a risk that the organisation will have less insight into how they are run than if operations were run by internal personnel. First, the organisation does not have the same physical opportunities for insight and monitoring when it is not on the same premises, or even in the same country (if the organisation has chosen an offshoring or captive solution). Secondly, buyers and suppliers may have different cultures and different approaches to communicating (which can of course also be the case between an internal unit within an organisation and the rest of the organisation), which can impede insight and monitoring. If the supplier is completely independent of the organisation, it also has its own incentives, which may not be fully aligned with those of the buyer, while an in-house department is likely to be more cognisant of, and concerned with, the organisation's goals and needs, for instance when the supplier must be chosen and the contract drafted, as well as in the ongoing relationship as progress is discussed and adjustments made. Travel, sometimes long-haul, is required when operations are outsourced abroad. Add to this any cultural conflicts and language barriers, and a relatively complex picture of the buyer/supplier relationship emerges.

Beijer Bygg, a Swedish chain of builders' merchants, has chosen not to outsource its IT to any significant extent, explaining that it is difficult to assure things like quality and development by means of a contract. By handling operations in-house, they believe they will be better equipped to ensure that they are sufficiently up-to-date with any development projects. For other, mainly large, organisations, it has instead been popular to try and create a version of the buyer/seller relationship internally, for example to ensure the quality of development and operations in IT through variations of the ITIL governance model. In such cases, the organisation prepares a service catalogue—a definition of the services to be delivered and specification of the parties responsible for ordering and executing each service—and reaches an agreement on the level of service delivery in scope and quality (SLA and OLA, service-level agreement, operational-level agreement). The value of proximity versus distance, and of informal dialogue versus formal contract drafting to establish the content of deliveries thus varies among organisations and, to an extent, over time. While some argue that quality-enhancing professionalisation requires formalisation, others argue that close and trusting dialogue is the foundation of quality and efficiency.

Loss of skills. One argument for retaining a sub-operation within the organisation is that there is otherwise a risk that the organisation will lose valuable skills. Even skilled buyers of services need to understand what they are trying to buy. First, it is not clear if someone who is only a buyer will be able to maintain that skill and secondly, it is not certain that skilled employees will stay with the organisation and transition to an exclusive buyer role. To be a skilled supplier, the supplier may need to understand the business or organisation to which it is delivering services. It may seem tempting to reduce the workforce through outsourcing, but the challenge is to retain a sufficient skills base. If, for example, an organisation shuts down the IT department and outsources its operations, what happens when employees leave? In an initial step, the organisation's employees may be transferred to the outsourcing partner and take their knowledge about the organisation and internal relationships with them, but as time passes, there is a risk that this knowledge will fade, and if the organisation switches suppliers, the training of the supplier will have to start from scratch.

As discussed earlier in this chapter and elsewhere, the IT department should cooperate closely with the rest of the organisation (if there is a separate IT department) to ensure that the use of IT will create value. If IT personnel exit an organisation, there is also a risk that valuable skills in the intersection between IT and operations will be lost. This has been argued in the banking industry, for instance, which has for a long time avoided outsourcing IT that supports its core business. This can become a problem in the event that an organisation no longer wants to work with its IT supplier. It might have been bought out and transformed into a supplier that no longer fits the needs of the organisation, and in that case, the organisation cannot quickly bring that part of its IT operations in-house. Any loss of skills can also constitute a problem even in a supplier relationship that is working well. As mentioned in the previous section, the relationship must be managed. What happens when things change externally and the organisation needs to review its value proposition? Should digitisation play a more prominent role in how the organisation competes? Or could there be better ways to use existing IT that the organisation should adopt? When essential parts of IT operations are contracted out to a supplier, there is a risk that the organisation will lack the skills necessary to respond rapidly to such changes.

Data exposure. Another fear sometimes expressed about outsourcing is that the organisation's data will be more exposed. This applies not least to cloud solutions, where data is processed in a public cloud via the Internet. In some contracts with public cloud suppliers, it is not even certain that the buyer will be given insight into how its own data is processed. As mentioned above, there are hopes that Swedish government agencies will be able to achieve significant savings by putting parts of their IT in the cloud, but the National Defence Radio Establishment of Sweden has recommended that the agencies join together and create a private cloud, specifically for data security. There are also legal requirements in the EU for how customer data must be handled from a security perspective. This affects where cloud service providers choose to locate their data centres. IBM works with local firms to create data centres that are situated in the country where the buyer wants to keep their data. The company also has its own networks, so that data traffic between data centres is free and more predictable than via the Internet's best-effort delivery. HL, a company that supplies retail stores with solutions for the placement and display of merchandise, manages its infrastructure and operations through the Amazon cloud. The servers are in Ireland and are thus covered by relevant EU legislation. Outsourcing outside the cloud can of course also involve risks. The agreement between the Swedish Transport Agency and IBM, mentioned in Section 4.5.2, has been intensively covered in the Swedish media. This is because of the emergence of information that sensitive data was possibly exposed to IBM employees who had not been authorised by the Swedish Transport Agency.

Another question that can arise is that of who owns the data circulating in the cloud, especially once a subscription has ended. In the light of these problems and risks, many organisations have doubts about the extensive use of cloud services. As we have previously discussed, however, it is highly possible that some organisations are already using them. In these contexts, there is discussion of "shadow IT" and "bring your own device", the phenomenon whereby employees choose their own IT tools, which the central organisation may not have approved or even know about. The pricing structure for cloud services means that they can be used without a big budget. To a certain extent, they can even be financed by other means, so that the extent of use is not associated with the price. Applications like Dropbox and Google Docs may generate commercial and legal risks if employees store business-critical data there and, for example, unauthorised individuals gain access to the documents. Services like Facebook can also put users in a subordinate position *vis-à-vis* the supplier, which decides what can be posted and can choose to impose new requirements on the user before providing continued access to existing data. This may be regarded as similar to the risk that, for example, service providers delivering outsourced customer service, who have learned an organisation's business and products and are in contact with its customers, could choose to end the relationship or impose new demands on the business in order to continue acting as an outsourcing partner for it.

The above reasons for and against outsourcing are often related to the ability to manage whatever product or service is outsourced. This topic will be discussed in the next section.

4.6. Management of Outsourcing

If an organisation chooses to outsource, the activities that are outsourced need to be managed so that they contribute to the goals of the organisation. Such management roughly concerns two things: first, procurement competence, the initial stage when a relationship is to be established, and second, the ongoing management when the relationship has been established.

4.6.1. Procurement Competence

As we noted in the previous section, it is important to understand what is purchased, so that price and quality are reasonable and there are favourable conditions for continued delivery during the intended period of outsourcing. If systems development is outsourced, there must not only be a well-founded idea of the desired functionality now and in the future; but also an ability to assess the extent to which the developed application can be adapted to the future needs of the organisation. Is the development taking place on a platform that several suppliers can handle, and that can be expected to last for the foreseeable future? Do systems architecture and coding allow for future adjustments, or will such adjustments be very complicated to implement? To some extent, assessments on these questions can be made by third parties, but a certain degree of insight on the area is necessary in order to be able to determine whether such an assessment is credible and competently carried out. The less that a buyer knows and understands, the greater their risk of becoming completely dependent on a counterpart whose competence cannot be judged.

Procurement competence is a difficult area, as the basis for deciding to outsource activities to external suppliers is often the notion that your own organisation should devote its resources to something else. This can make it difficult both to maintain procurement competence within the organisation, and to persuade those employees who possess important insights to participate in the procurement process. Recommendations usually include gathering a wide range of people in procurement projects. There should be people with a management perspective on what is to be purchased, as well as people with practical experience of the activities that are to be affected by the procurement. If the area is of strategic importance, people from the management team should be more than marginally involved. Furthermore, those involved should have a standing in the organisation that the other parties concerned will accept and in whose judgments and decisions they will have confidence. A proper market survey should be conducted, with potential suppliers roughly sorted according to relevant criteria, and two or more thoroughly evaluated in order to assess their ability to deliver the desired services both in the short term and in the longer term. If possible, the evaluation process should also follow a standardised model. See Chapters 5 and 6 on structured decisions and procurement.

Of course, such a recommendation is sound from the perspective of making as well-grounded a decision as possible, but if there are competent and knowledgeable people within the organisation, they probably have other tasks on which they should spend their time and which they, or their managers, see as more of a priority. Recommendations generally advocate long-term, strategic thinking. In both organisational and private life, it is easy to find examples of how more long-term considerations are sidelined in favour of short-term issues. Applying these recommendations in practice is therefore difficult. The better the procurement, the more favourable the conditions for the outsourcing to work well. The less insightful the procurement process, the more important it is to follow up and try to control the supply of resources or services. We now turn our attention to the continuous monitoring and management of outsourcing.

4.6.2. Continuous Monitoring and Management

Few or many suppliers? One question is how many suppliers are required. Having few strategic partners can provide opportunities for long-term cooperation and mutual adjustment. At the same time, it can make it difficult to judge whether the partner is competitive, and it becomes problematic to change suppliers. Having many alternative suppliers makes comparability easier, but in that position no counterpart will see any reason to try to adapt long-term, as there is too great a risk that they will be replaced or will not receive large order volumes. The general view of a balance between a few close collaborations and several at arm's length varies. Trends are not unambiguous and ideals are not consistent with practice. The CIO of the Northern European insurance firm IF reports that in the past decade they have gone from one to nine suppliers, primarily in infrastructure. They did this to obtain better prices and to increase their skills base. On the other hand, some would argue that there is a trend, among both private and public organisations, to reduce the number of suppliers so as to gain a better overview and to avoid escalating costs. In recent years, the Swedish Social Insurance Agency has reduced its IT suppliers from over forty to three.

Short-term or long-term contracts? This is a question that is in part related to the issue above: the length of a contract with a supplier. Ten-year contracts were once not uncommon, but nowadays outsourcing contracts are typically shorter. More long-term contracts seem to increase the risk of the supplier not maintaining a good level of service. Long-term contracts can also "lock in" the customer, so that the changing needs that arise as an organisation develops and technology changes cannot be met within the scope of the existing agreement. In short-term contracts, on the other hand, the responsibility for development relies largely on market-driven competition; a supplier with only a short-term contract will find it difficult to motivate long-term investments to adapt to the buyer. Long-term contracts make it more reasonable for the organisation to try to develop alongside the counterpart, and may therefore be important for organisations resorting to outsourcing to transform the product or service that is being outsourced. Having said that, it is wise to incorporate some amount of flexibility in a long-term contract.

Hard or soft governance? As discussed earlier in the chapter, there are different forms of outsourcing, and outsourcing may involve different aspects of IT-related operations. The governance mechanisms that are most suitable therefore depend on the situation. A study by Jérôme Barthélemy shows that outsourcing handled through detailed contracts tends to be of the simpler kind, such as a data centre, where the supplier has the potential for economies of scale. Outsourcing that is governed by such contracts also tends to generate cost efficiency, but not other types of benefits. In contrast, outsourcing relationships where governance is based on trust rather than strict formalisation often include complex projects, such as development. The use of soft, trust-based governance tends to be related to benefits such as goal attainment. These patterns are in line with the reasoning in Section 4.2 that the suitability of hard and soft governance depends on how dynamic an organisation's environment is, however the Barthélemy study is not sufficient to establish causal relationships between governance and outcomes.

Complex exchanges are difficult to formulate in a detailed contract; it is difficult to anticipate everything that will happen in the relationship, and questions about what should and should not be included can more easily arise. In such a relationship, the softer side of governance becomes important. The combination of both detailed contracts and softer governance seems advantageous, as it has been shown to provide both cost efficiency and goal attainment. It is used in both simpler and more complex outsourcing arrangements. For example, it is possible to specify in a contract that "new technology" is to be used and that a certain amount of money should be spent on technology development every year. It is difficult to be more detailed than this when it comes to technology development, and this is where soft, trust-based governance plays an important role. According to Deloitte's 2018 global outsourcing survey, purchasing organisations are also increasingly incorporating incentives for innovation in their outsourcing contracts, not only in the form of compensation, but also by moving additional services to the supplier as they innovate. As mentioned earlier, many IT buyers now want their supplier not only to deliver something predetermined but also to deliver improvements and innovations. Studies of the procurement of innovations in general indicate that there are risks to being overly detailed as a buyer, because new thinking can be stifled.

Contracts can be useful in the beginning, so that trust can develop over time, and in the same way, a contract that is not fulfilled will probably result in a lack of trust. There have been some studies on buyer-supplier relationships that were initially governed by detailed contracts. These have suggested that only when the contract management is abandoned and a person responsible for the relationship with each party is introduced, do buyers and suppliers get to know each other better and more clearly understand how they might mutually gain from the relationship. For example, loosely formulated incentives were created for possible development and innovations implemented by the supplier. One conclusion is that even fairly simple exchanges need relationship management to some extent.

As previously mentioned, it is unlikely that a seemingly standardised service can easily be purchased and integrated like a Lego brick into our own operations without any maintenance. Outsourcing tends to be a learning journey, sometimes termed an "experience good"; what defines quality and value for money only becomes evident during the journey, and is difficult to determine before the contract is signed. It is therefore important to continually follow up and try to get an idea of how well the outsourced activities are functioning. If users of the services are internal to the organisation, it is possible to evaluate, although obviously not easy. If users are external, for example, if the outsourced activities relate to customer service or a webpage, the contract may need to be supplemented with specific types of feedback required from customers or the supplier's interactions with them. Can they (easily) find what they are looking for? Are their questions answered adequately? Do they perceive the supplier's services as part of the business, or does it appear to be a separate, independent element? Contracts can be comprehensive, however. The supplier and the staff working on behalf of the organisation need to understand the role of such feedback in operations if the business is to maintain good quality. Just as in internally managed activities, trust-based collaboration is necessary, as well as insight into how the activities fit in with the rest of the organisation.

Ongoing collaboration and operations may be full of small decisions, but these will to a large extent be guided by the routines and habits that are developing gradually over time. The standardisation of routines is often considered as something leading to good work outcomes, but this is far from certain. Only certain tasks are so naturally standardisable that it makes sense to use routines to produce quality-assured results. Often, the performers' insights on what constitutes a successful result are what enable them to utilise their judgment and opportunities for feedback so as to deliver good quality. It is no coincidence that agile methods have become popular in systems development; fundamental element of agile methods is the close dialogue between supplier and customer. This close dialogue allows for prioritising and re-prioritising future development in the light of current insights into successes and challenges. In more complex types of outsourcing and in new outsourcing relationships, such close collaboration between clients and suppliers is extremely valuable.

4.7. Chapter Summary

In this chapter, we have described different ways of allocating work and responsibilities related to digitisation. A clear trend is that employees from many parts of an organisation are taking increased responsibility for questions related to digitisation. This is in line with the idea that digitisation is no longer just a technical issue, but above all an organisational issue. Depending on the size and type of strategy of the organisation, the responsibility and involvement of operations—and IT specialists—may be either at the management level or at the local level. Employee involvement can include everything from discovering new ways to digitise operations to effectively managing established IT use. The view on how digitisation can strategically contribute to operations will probably vary depending on where in the organisation someone is located, so coordination between different employees should be characterised by, for example, shared knowledge, positive experiences of previous joint projects, and regular communication without overly specialised jargon. In this chapter, we have also presented various ways of allocating an organisation's digitisation to external actors, the advantages and disadvantages associated with doing so, and how such buyer-seller relationships can be governed in terms of, for example, a balance between detailed contracts and a more flexible, trust-based attitude.

This chapter has dealt with the organisational aspects of digitisation, and the next chapter will focus more on how specific digitisation decisions can be handled. Regardless of who is involved in the organisation's digitisation and in what forms, decisions will have to be made, for example when choosing a supplier for outsourcing or evaluating whether to invest in a project. One part of such decision-making is the weighting of different preferences; preferences that may differ depending on who is involved in the decision. We will therefore now shift focus from the issues of roles, competencies, and skills, and how these relate to each other, to how decisions can be structured according to processes, criteria, and the weighting of criteria. This also entails a shift from what can be considered feasible, and even from current practices, to a more ideal world that many organisations are still nowhere near.

4.8. Reading Tips

Below are two examples of large digitisation projects with differing governance approaches briefly discussed in this chapter. The first is a drawn-out, rather painful project, in which ambitions regarding business aspects are gradually diminished in order to get a technically functioning system in place. The second is a highly business-focused project, where the learnings from the first contribute to a different governance approach, and to a digitisation effort where organisational and technical development are more in line with one another.

- Westelius, Alf (2006). Muddling through: The life of a multinational, strategic enterprise systems venture at BT Industries. *Linköping Electronic Articles in Computer and Information Science* 10 (1), 46 pages, http://liu.diva-portal.org/smash/get/diva2:256674/FULLTEXT01.pdf.
- Valiente, Pablo and Westelius, Alf (2007). Sustainable Value of Wireless ICT in Communication with Mobile Employees. In: Per Andersson, Ulf Essler and Bertil Thorngren (eds), *Beyond Mobility*. Lund/Stockholm: Studentlitteratur/EFI, pp. 175–206.

For broad empirical studies on the interaction between IT and operations, see Weill's article and Andriole's more recent article. A more in-depth study of the relationship between IT and operations is found in Jansson's article on e-government in municipalities. Practitioner-oriented journals, such as *CIO*, have also presented surveys on the theme.

- Weill, Peter (2004). Don't just lead, govern: How top-performing firms govern IT. *MIS Quarterly Executive* 3 (1), pp. 1–17.
- Andriole, Stephen J. (2015). Who owns IT? *Communications of the ACM* 58 (3), pp. 50–57, http://dx.doi.org/10.1145/2660765.
- Jansson, Gabriella (2013). Politikens betydelse för e-förvaltning: Om lokala IT-projekt och det demokratiska ansvarsutkrävandet [The importance of politics for e-governance: On local IT projects and democratic accountability, in Swedish]. *Scandinavian Journal of Public Administration* 17 (2), pp. 103–125, https://ojs.ub.gu.se/index.php/sjpa/article/view/2480/2210.

- CIO Sweden (2016). En ny, digitalare governance. [A new, more digital governance, in Swedish]. 5, pp. 16–19.

For those who want to know more about the balance between centralised and decentralised governance in general, and how it can be adapted to an organisation's strategic focus, we recommend the following anthology, which contains examples from many industries.

- Jannesson, Erik; Nilsson, Fredrik and Rapp, Birger (eds) (2014). *Strategy, Control and Competitive Advantage: Case Study Evidence.* Berlin/Heidelberg: Springer, https://doi.org/10.1007/978-3-642-39134-7.

A nice overview of the development of the CIO role and its different possible foci in terms of innovation and management is given in Chun's and Mooney's article. A paper by Magnusson and colleagues provides more recent insight into the role in the Swedish context.

- Chun, Mark and Mooney, John (2009). CIO roles and responsibilities: 25 years of evolution and change. *Information & Management* 46 (6), pp. 323–334, https://doi.org/10.1016/j.im.2009.05.005.
- Magnusson, Johan; Högberg, Erik and Sjöman, Hampus (2019). How the West was lost: Chief Information Officers and the battle of jurisdictional control. In: *Proceedings of the 52nd Hawaii International Conference on Information Science*, Grand Wailea, Maui, January 8-11, 2019, https://doi.org/10.24251/hicss.2019.746.

For a more general understanding of what it means to combine innovation and novel thinking on the one hand, and more repetitive, maintenance-related tasks on the other hand, and how such a combination of tasks can be supported within an organisation, the following article describes the phenomenon of ambidexterity.

- Adler, Paul S.; Goldoftas, Barbara and Levine, David I. (1999). Flexibility versus efficiency? A case study of model changeovers in the Toyota production system. *Organization Science* 10 (1), pp. 43–68, https://doi.org/10.1287/orsc.10.1.43.

The phenomenon has been studied from many perspectives, however, and the journal *Organization Science* devoted an entire issue to it: 2009, 20(4).

If you want to know more about the social dimension of the relationship between IT and operations managers, or how the mutual understanding and knowledge between these parties can be deepened, Reich and Benbasat's study of Canadian insurance companies is recommended, as well as Bensaou and Earl's study in the Japanese context.

- Reich, Blaize H. and Benbasat, Izak (2003). Measuring the information systems business strategy relationship: Factors that influence the social dimension or alignment between business and information technology objectives. In: Galliers, Robert D. and Leidner, Dorothy E. (eds), *Strategic Information Management: Challenges and Strategies in Managing Information Systems*. Rochester: Butterworth-Heinemann, pp. 265–310, https://doi.org/10.4324/9780080481135-19.
- Bensaou, Ben M. and Earl, Michael (1998). The right mind-set for managing information technology. *Harvard Business Review* 76 (5), pp. 119–128.

For a more general understanding of the challenges of integrating different parts of an organisation, we recommend the following two seminal articles.

- Daft, Richard and Lengel, Robert (1986). Organizational information requirements, media richness and structural design. *Management Science* 32 (5), pp. 554–571, https://doi.org/10.1287/mnsc.32.5.554.
- Galbraith, Jay R. (1974). Organization design: An information processing view. *Interfaces* 4 (3), pp. 28–36, https://doi.org/10.1287/inte.4.3.28.

If you want to read more about IT outsourcing, underlying motives and how outsourcing relationships can be governed, we recommend Blaskovich and Mintchik's review article, as well as Barthélemy's and Kern et al.'s empirical studies on how different control mechanisms function in different outsourcing situations. *CIO* and various consulting firms have also published surveys and investigations on IT outsourcing.

- Blaskovich, Jennifer and Mintchik, Natalia (2011). Information technology outsourcing: A taxonomy of prior studies and directions for future research. *Journal of Information Systems* 25 (1), pp. 1–36, https://doi.org/10.2308/jis.2011.25.1.1.
- Barthélemy, Jérôme (2003). The hard and soft sides of IT outsourcing management. *European Management Journal* 21 (5), pp. 539–548, https://doi.org/10.1016/s0263-2373(03)00103-8.
- Kern, Thomas; Kreijger, Jeroen and Willcocks, Leslie (2002). Exploring ASP as sourcing strategy: Theoretical perspectives, propositions for practice. *Journal of Strategic Information Systems* 11 (2), pp. 153–177, https://doi.org/10.1016/s0963-8687(02)00004-5.
- Whitelane Research and PA Consulting Group (2016). *IT Outsourcing Study 2016 Nordics*. Report published in collaboration between Whitelane Research and PA Consulting Group.
- CIO Sweden (2015). Trenden går mot multimiljö: Så IT-sourcar svenska CIOer 2015 [The trend is moving towards multi-environments: How Swedish CIOs source IT 2015, in Swedish]. http://cio.idg.se/2.1782/1.630340/sa-sourcar-svenska-cio-er-2015.

Standardised routines have many advocates, but this seminal article illustrates how such routines may conflict with professional knowledge and development:

- Brown, John S. and Duguid, Paul (1991). Organizational learning and communities-of-Practice: Toward a unified view of working, learning, and innovation. *Organization Science* 2 (1), Special issue: Organizational learning: Papers in honour of (and by) James G. March, pp. 40–57, https://doi.org/10.1287/orsc.2.1.40.

5. Structured Decisions and Decision Processes

So far we have seen how important it is to have adequate business models and business strategies in an organisation. The point is to orient organisations towards concrete targets and to have well-deliberated strategies to drive them towards their goals.

Central components include the decisions that must be made, which are to be aligned with plans and objectives. However, decisions are unfortunately often handled far too frivolously and many organisations believe that it is enough to introduce strict regulatory structures that are somewhat harmonised with the business models in order to achieve an adequate organisational setup, or to try to realise the strategy work in some kind of intuitive sense, which usually leads to underperformance. Instead, well-founded decision-making, where the various priorities are clearly defined, is an important component in achieving quality in strategy work and goal fulfilment.

The value of good decision-making in an organisation cannot be underestimated. Not taking decision-making seriously can become expensive, and there are lots of activities that must be considered. Firstly, it is important to clarify the context, that is, the preparations for the decisions and the organisational decision-making structures since decisions are always made in a context. Secondly, it is important to have appropriate methods and tools for compiling and evaluating the information and to understand the existing strategies and their advantages and disadvantages based on established targets. Thirdly, there should preferably exist an overall decision-making process. In summary, to achieve good decision-making, we must have a proper decision-making structure, access to adequate models and methods, and a process for managing our decision-making in the organisation.

 https:doi.org10.11647OBP.0350.05

The decision structure may look different depending on the conditions and the nature of the business. Informal decision-making needs to be identified and clarified. Likewise, responsibilities and power relations must be made clear, which helps to reduce conflicts and dissatisfaction that can easily result otherwise. The necessary models and methods also depend on the nature of the business, but one important component of the decision-making is about collecting and interpreting facts and deciding what is relevant and what is not. This creates a decision basis to which some deliberated method can then be applied for the actual decision evaluation. However, it seldom helps to stare at an Excel spreadsheet if you really want to get a picture of the possibilities and options. We will return to this later.

One of the most important things is thus that the organisation has a proper decision-making process. Here, we often see large but unnecessary shortcomings; we often underestimate the real complexity of compiling a decision basis and the decision situation when enforcing the decision. An efficient, coordinated process is needed to manage decisions. This applies both to the organisation's various parts and to the organisation as a whole. This may seem difficult, especially where experience is lacking. At least at an abstract level, however, this is quite straightforward.

First, you determine who will do what in upcoming work, then what you want to achieve (the target), and thereafter you identify the strategies that can possibly realise this target. This means that you formulate the process and identify partial decisions, the strategy and its properties, and the criteria on the basis of which you will assess the strategy. The criteria and priorities should, of course, express the objectives of the business. Furthermore, you must analyse the properties of possible outcomes and other variables as well as how they might affect the result. Thereafter, you can evaluate the decision.

The overall decision-making process is not necessarily a linear process. Sometimes, we have to go back and forth as roles change, new people enter the process, unexpected information pops up, implementation becomes difficult, compromises become necessary, groups oppose one another, and so on. We simply have to be open to changing circumstances and the need to adjust. Models only represent aspects of reality and yet they are the basis for our analyses.

The components of decision-making are basically as follows. First, the roles should be determined. Thereafter, a rough analysis of the problem must be carried out. After that, opportunities for improvement of the business should be examined, and those requiring closer examination should be identified. It is important to reconcile the results of this examination with the overall goals of the business. Then comes the detailed decision-making process. When the process is completed, it must be documented and, where applicable, presented to the decision-makers, and sometimes to larger sections of the organisation. As with all thorough processes, the process should be evaluated in order to assess what could be improved in subsequent strategy work.

After the above, the actual implementation of the selected alternative commences. This step sometimes also contains decision-making processes, especially when the decisions mean radical changes. Decisions should be firm and timetables should be kept. Many new issues may arise when it comes to major decisions. The process description that we will go through here works well for decisions that will occur during the implementation phase. The decision-making process also requires a clear structure. Employees who feel involved in decisions will perform better, thereby avoiding many conflicts.

5.1. Rough Analysis and Improvement Potential

The first phase is a review of how decisions of relevance are made in the organisation. Then one must look to understand what can be improved. During this rough analysis, the following questions should be posed.

- What is the decision basis? How does the collection of information take place? Is there anything of relevance documented by previous decision-making processes?
- How do the strategies relate to the organisation's goals and how are the overall objectives affected?
- Which sub-decisions are involved in the decision? What types of decision should be made during the various decision-making processes? Only long-term strategic ones? Or quick ones? Are all relevant criteria covered by the different decision types?

- Which decisions are repetitive? Which components of the strategy can be used in future decisions? Can parts of the information be reused, and if so, which parts and when?
- Which methods are used today? Are there elements that make these methods structured? Or do most things just happen?
- Who makes strategic decisions? Is it primarily the CEO, management group, board, or IT manager? Or are there other decision-makers who make important decisions affecting the business as a whole and impacting the strategy?
- Is there a documented process for implementing the strategy? Which decision components should be employed? Which informal processes can be formalised?
- What are the experiences and outcomes of previous decisions? How do the organisational structure and delegations look? What are the responsibilities and reporting paths?
- Are there adequate information systems and other information management processes?
- Are there well-specified quality assurance and rules of procedures for different staff categories as well as for the board and management groups?
- Who should be in the groups that will be involved in the different phases of the project, and how should they be involved?

The final point is very important for the result of the decision-making process. Developing well-composed groups that are anchored in the business will have a major impact on the decision quality and implementation. It is also fundamental that multiple end users are involved. A well-composed group of active and interested members who feel involved and have representative views is integral to the analysis.

Finally, the conditions for structured processes and the potential for improvement are examined during the strategy work. Often, there is much to be done to address risk analyses, transparency, dependence on individuals, and how fact-based the decisions usually are.

In the analysis of the improvement potential, the following questions should be posed.

- Is there enough potential for implementing and introducing a structured process at all, or is significant preparatory work required? What should be included in the analysis? What boundaries should be defined?
- How can we learn from different experiences in the organisation?
- Who is perceived as beneficial to the organisation?
- What are the qualitative and quantitative goals of the organisation?
- What are the risks and conditions of managing new strategies that appear during the process?
- Are all of the above sufficiently documented?

After the rough analysis, a more formalised decision-making process should be carried out. It is normally advisable to start with a few select decision problems that are particularly important to the organisation.

5.2. The Decision Process

A decision-making process should constitute a complete process of data collection, investigation, analysis, and recommendation. It may look different, but a common one would look as follows:

- Identification of the decision problem (or problems), so one knows what to do
- Structuring the problem so that the decision components and their relationships are clearly visible
- Information collection resulting in a detailed information basis
- Modelling the problem around the information basis
- Evaluation of the model whereby existing information is aggregated and analysed
- If necessary, feedback on and repetition of previous steps
- Creation of a decision basis consisting of instructions and recommendations

5.2.1. Identification and Structuring

It is surprising how often the identification of the problem itself is missing, even though it is central to reasonably tackling the decision problems. In this step, we must clarify the purpose of the decision, what it should include, and what it should omit. The problem can often be seen from several perspectives, and assigning values to different strategies thus depends on the perspectives from which they are considered. The perspectives are represented by various criteria. All of this should be documented in a project specification based on the rough analysis outlined above.

The structuring of an actual decision problem involves specifying the relevant criteria and possible strategies for obtaining a more precise problem formulation to support the collection of information. After this, one should have a rough summary of the criteria based on the specified objectives and a list of the strategies that are considered feasible along with descriptions of what they mean at different levels.

To make the discussion more concrete, we will consider an example of how an organisation might develop an efficient and secure physical IT infrastructure with high transmission capacity nationwide, granting people easy access to interactive public e-services.

After the process described above, the most important criteria are believed to be security, efficiency, availability, and transmission capacity (throughput). There are also three main strategies: i) to outsource the entire development and operation, ii) to develop the necessary services in-house as needed, and iii) to develop more qualified services in-house and outsource simpler services.

Financial aspects are generally central to both the investment itself and the continuation of the operation. Personnel satisfaction and development, as well as changes to work tasks, are further perspectives to consider. We will soon proceed with this example, but first we must explain how to model the information involved.

5.2.2. Information Capture and Modelling

During this phase, precise criteria are developed and ranked, and the strategies are specified. The criteria must be prioritised. This is usually achieved through the assignment of weights indicating importance to each, but the criteria could also simply be ranked. Thereafter, the consequences of the different strategies are analysed and valued. Finally, scenarios are analysed and the probabilities of different strategy consequences are estimated.

There are several difficulties at play here. The first time one gathers information, it is often difficult to find out what is really required for the analysis, that is, to correctly model the relevant criteria, priorities, and possible strategies with consequences as well as utility values and weights.

Further complications usually appear when trying to estimate the probabilities of the different scenarios. Furthermore, there are often preferences that may conflict with each other, such as maximising the quality and at the same time obtaining a high financial return on investment. Such goal conflicts lead us to make some trade-offs between our goals.

There are thus often contradictions. For example, the strategy with the best economic forecast might entail issues with the work environment. Often, one strategy is the most suitable for the short-term profitability of the operation and another is most suitable for accessibility. In this case, which strategy should be chosen? One way of managing the choice would be to evaluate all strategies solely on the basis of the most important criterion, but this approach ignores the information that other perspectives provide. Taking all perspectives into account can yield somewhat absurd effects, such as one strategy being merely slightly better than another from an economic perspective, but obviously worse from a quality perspective.

In order to progress in the analysis, we must prioritise how different criteria relate to each other and express this so that it can be calculated. This can be achieved by assigning significance weights to the criteria that express their relative importance. The greater the weight, the more important the criterion. Then we can assess the strategies based on the criteria by aggregating everything in an evaluation. This approach, whereby criteria are weighted or ranked according to importance, is called a multi-criteria analysis. We also usually study the effects of any uncertainty in the background information in order to assess the reliability of the solutions.

Some of the prerequisites for successful decision-making are thus a real ability to describe the strategies and also a clear sense of how well they fulfil the different criteria. We also need to understand how important the different criteria are in relation to the operational goals. There are better and worse methods for doing so. We will begin by considering a kind of base case, in which criteria weights and strategy values are numbered precisely.

The range of values assigned to strategies can differ depending on the situation. A scale from 1 to 5, for example, where 1 indicates that a strategy has a very poor rating under that criterion and 5 indicates that it has a very high rating, is not uncommon. We then obtain weighted values for the strategies where the values under the criteria are weighted with the criteria weights. The weights must be greater than or equal to zero and the sum of all weights must add up to 100%.

Suppose that in our e-service example above we consider that *safety* is more important than *efficiency*, which in turn is more important than *accessibility*, which is more important than *transmission capacity*. In order to carry out the analysis, we must formulate this more concretely. Let us specify our criteria preferences on a scale from 0% to 100%, to reflect how important the different criteria are. This is of course impossible to do precisely and reasonably, but let us pretend for the sake of argument that it is actually possible. The importance of:

- Security is 40% (0.4)
- Efficiency is 30% (0.3)
- Availability is 20% (0.2)
- Transmission capacity is 10% (0.1)

The strategies under the criteria are valued in terms of utility (i.e., how "good" they are), represented as numbers. A common method of valuing strategies is, as in Table 5.1, for the lowest possible utility for each criterion to be 0 and the highest 5. Intermediate strategies allow for utility values between 0 and 5. Note that the full utility scale range [0, 5] need not be occupied.

Table 5.1. Development of an e-service structure – valuation of strategies.

Strategy	Security	Efficiency	Availability	Transmission capacity
Outsource the entire development and operation	1	3	4	5
In-house development of the necessary services as required	4	3	5	4
In-house development of more qualified services and outsourcing of less qualified	3	4	4	4

5.2.3. Evaluation

The values of the strategies under the criteria are then weighted together. If plainly unreasonable strategies have already been sifted out, then a fairly simple and well-established method is to weigh together criteria and values using the following formula:

$$V(A_1) = w_1 \cdot v_{11} + w_2 \cdot v_{12} + w_3 \cdot v_{13}.$$

Here, w_j is the importance of criterion *j*, and v_{ij} is the utility value for strategy A_i under criterion *j*. We then look at which strategy is the most suitable by calculating the weighted values for all strategies:

$$V(\text{Outsource}) = 0.4 \cdot 1 + 0.3 \cdot 3 + 0.2 \cdot 4 + 0.1 \cdot 5 = 2.6$$

$$V(\text{In-house}) = 0.4 \cdot 4 + 0.3 \cdot 3 + 0.2 \cdot 5 + 0.1 \cdot 4 = 3.9$$

$$V(\text{Mixture}) = 0.4 \cdot 3 + 0.3 \cdot 4 + 0.2 \cdot 4 + 0.1 \cdot 4 = 3.6$$

We select the option with the highest weighted mean value, which is the strategy of developing the necessary services in-house as requirements arise. See Figure 5.1 which also shows the contribution of each criterion to the total value of each strategy.

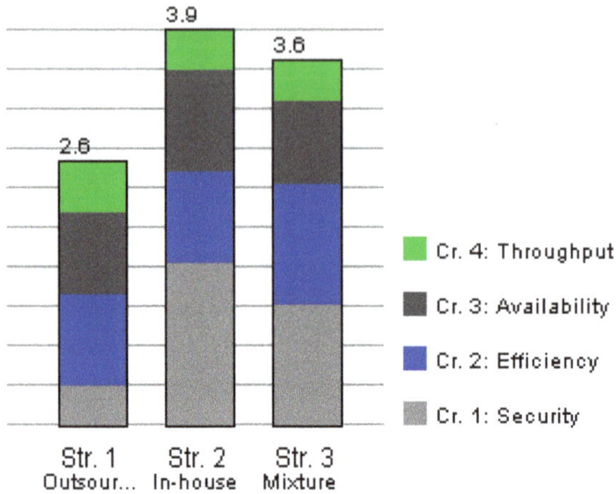

Figure 5.1. Values of strategies using one level of criteria.

Note that it is in reality in most cases very difficult, if not impossible, to produce precise weights and values for the strategies. Instead of expressing utilities or weights as precise numbers, we can instead work with comparisons and intervals. This is especially important when handling qualitative criteria such as those we have discussed here. Even without the requirement for precise values, people often find it difficult to express their preferences and therefore use different methods. Sometimes the criteria are compared to a so-called reference criterion, such as cost, and the decision-maker works out which trade-offs he or she is willing to make on that basis. For example, a cost reduction of EUR 10,000 can be perceived as having as much worth as a certain reduction in quality. Needless to say, this requires that everything is measured on well-defined scales with well-defined units.

Good decision support can be obtained by visualising the differences in weights and values through different graphic tools. Surprisingly, it is often sufficient to use quite inexact weightings with interval weights (or rankings) in order to distinguish between strategies. But again, one needs computer support to calculate the results. We will describe this more closely when discussing procurement (which is actually a type of multi-criteria analysis).

5.2.4. Refinement of the Decision Basis

Once we have obtained a result, we may find that we need more information or that we want to expand the analysis for other reasons. For example, we often need to give a more detailed description of the problem by building so-called criteria hierarchies with additional sub-criteria. This is to further facilitate assessing the goal fulfilment of different strategies. In this way, we can often better capture the structure of the decision problem. Criteria hierarchies are applicable when there may be sub-criteria to some or all of the criteria.

In the example of e-service structure development, we can, for instance, partition the main criterion *efficiency* into the sub-criteria *development efficiency* and *operational efficiency*. In this way, the assessment is facilitated, as the analysis becomes more detailed and we might more easily understand what the criteria entail. When we have sub-criteria in this way, it is usually helpful to model the problem in a tree format as in Figure 5.2. There is no important computational difference, and the calculations essentially look the same, but the trees give a little more visual structure to the problems. In the figure, we have also added weight indications for the two sub-criteria.

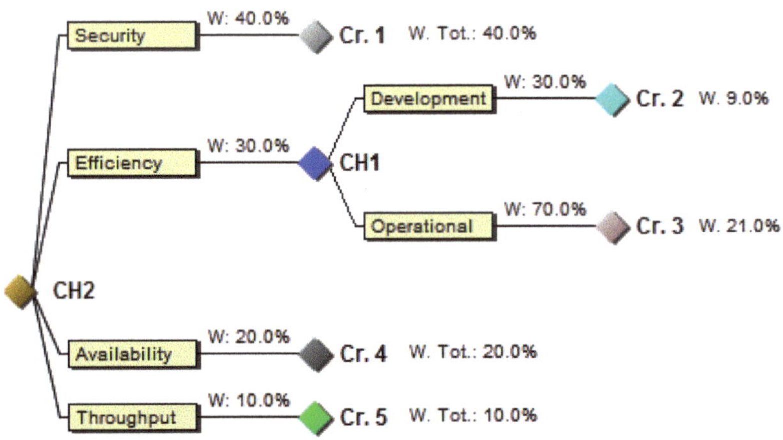

Figure 5.2. A criteria hierarchy – an example of iteration in the decision process.

We now assume that *development efficiency* has a weight of 30% (0.3) and *operational efficiency* a weight of 70% (0.7), and that the values for the respective strategies are as shown in the table below.

We then, again, use weighted averages to obtain the values of the strategies. See Figure 5.3:

$$V(\text{Outsource}) = 0.4 \cdot 1 + 0.3 \cdot (0.3 \cdot 4 + 0.7 \cdot 2) + 0.2 \cdot 4 + 0.1 \cdot 5 = 2.48$$

$$V(\text{In-house}) = 0.4 \cdot 4 + 0.3 \cdot (0.3 \cdot 4 + 0.7 \cdot 2) + 0.2 \cdot 5 + 0.1 \cdot 4 = 3.78$$

$$V(\text{Mixture}) = 0.4 \cdot 3 + 0.3 \cdot (0.3 \cdot 4 + 0.7 \cdot 4) + 0.2 \cdot 4 + 0.1 \cdot 4 = 3.6$$

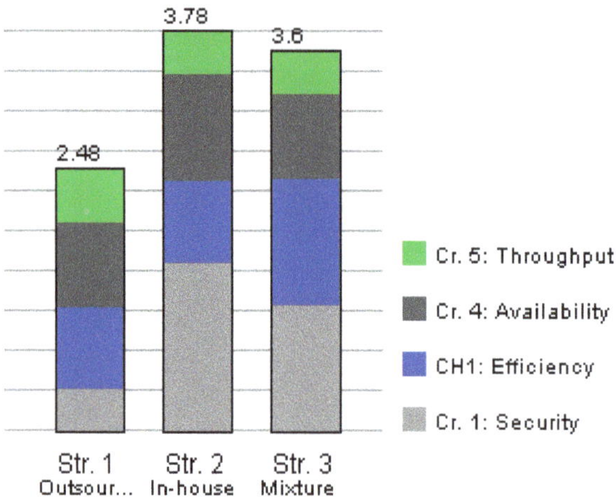

Figure 5.3. Value of strategies using sub-criteria.

When we consider ourselves finished with the analyses, we compile them into a structured decision basis.

Table 5.2. The values of the strategies under the sub-criteria.

Strategy	**Development efficiency**	**Operational efficiency**
Outsourcing of the entire development and operation	4	2
In-house development of the necessary services as needed	4	2
In-house development of more qualified services and outsourcing of less advanced ones	4	4

5.3. Extensions of the Analysis

Once we have come this far, it is possible to deepen the analysis further. Multi-criteria analyses are in this context a good tool for gaining a clearer picture of the decision situation, but do not normally reflect the fact that there is often a great deal of uncertainty involved. When working with risk analyses, which try to assess the probability of various threat scenarios, we must perform more detailed analyses and also estimate the probabilities of the different scenarios, as well as assess how the different consequences of the strategies will affect the situation. We must also work out how to value these consequences in order to get a clearer picture of the characteristics of the possible strategies. The components of a more detailed decision formulation are as follows:

- Criteria weighting, which specifies how important the criteria are in relation to the desired goals. We have explained this above.
- Event description, which specifies the possible events or scenarios and the probability of the occurrence of each. As mentioned, this is particularly important in risk analyses, since we are normally very interested in the likelihood of negative consequences.
- We must also understand the consequences of the different strategies and events and how they are to be valued considering the goals.

During the evaluation phase, we analyse the strategies by, for example, maximising their expected utilities. Sensitivity analysis is often used to investigate robustness (remember that this is the stability of the result considering information changes) and to highlight information that should be clarified or re-evaluated. The evaluation results in a preference scheme for strategies, a risk analysis, a stability analysis, and a specification of any additional information required for the decision. The result is an updated picture of the situation with clearer and more reliable information.

The result of the evaluation forms the basis for the decision, along with other documentation from the decision process and well-founded and well-motivated recommendations regarding development and implementation.

5.4. Chapter Summary

A large part of the total work time in organisations is spent gathering, processing, and compiling information in the light of a set of business goals. The purpose is usually to create a basis for making organisational decisions. Much is gained if the decisions—or at least the important ones—are made in a rational and not intentionally biased manner, and if the decision-maker takes all relevant available information and all reasonable possibilities into account. Unfortunately, this is not usually how it works. People often make decisions on the basis of unclear reasoning, and this chapter has thus provided an introduction to how professional decision-making and quality-assured decision-making processes in companies and authorities should work.

In the next two chapters, we will review and expand on various aspects of decision-making. We will show how decision-making can be applied to procurement processes. Procurements consume a lot of resources every year. Risk management and scenario analyses are also important parts of any organisation's activities. To act sensibly, we need to understand the possible outcomes and form an opinion on the probability of their occurrence.

6. Procurement Competence

The discussion in Chapter 5 easily veers into abstraction, and one might therefore wonder whether the theoretical models really are useful in practice. We will therefore give concrete examples of the models by contextualising the decision analysis and demonstrating how one might apply more developed multi-criteria analyses in practice. We will then expand the decision analysis through a careful review of its components.

As we discussed in Chapter 1, earlier IT strategies were mainly concerned with computer technology. In contrast, IT is now seen as an integral part of the organisation's general strategy and decision-making. IT is thus one of several business-support functions. Purchasing competence and, in particular, procurement competence are therefore becoming increasingly important. Failing to cultivate procurement competence can ultimately be very costly, but good procurement practises require a great deal of work as well as good methods. Considering that the annual turnover of public procurement alone is equal to just under 20% of the European GDP, the importance of a deliberate process should not be underestimated. There is much to consider in the context of procurement. Improved structuring is important, but not sufficient alone. One must also understand some basic problems connected to the analysis phase. Procurement is a complex area and various skills are required:

- Domain competence, i.e., knowledge of the product
- Decision-making skills, i.e., knowledge about, as well as capacity in, processes and support systems
- Process competence, i.e., the capacity to achieve the target image when running projects

 https://doi.org/10.11647/OBP.0350.06

- Adaptation skills, i.e., an understanding of the systems development and what constitute feasible and reasonable time frames
- Organisational competence, i.e., an understanding of the organisation's dynamics and how they work to achieve the stipulated goals
- Social competence, i.e., an understanding of how to use the organisation's human competence to formulate an adequate specification of requirements for the systems.

6.1. The Complexity of Procurement Processes

In general, the abovementioned competences are lacking, even when procurements of large systems are carried out, which often leads to catastrophic results. For example, when organisations have procured *Business Intelligence (BI) systems*, these only consist of an attractive interface, and do not actually provide what they claim to.[1]

When people procure systems or system parts, their needs often are not met. So how can these needs be identified? The simplest analysis is based on a single criterion, which is usually financial. But in general, the issues are far more complex and more complicated analyses must be utilised. At least four preconditions must be met to perform adequate procurement analyses: i) Data must be available, sufficient, accurate, and durable; ii) The procurer must understand the data space representing the organisational needs and resources; iii) The procurer must have adequate analytical competence; and iv) The procurer must have access to adequate tools.

If these criteria are reasonably met, there is hope and we can, in principle, implement a reasonable procurement process. Unfortunately, these requirements are seldom fulfilled, and even if some people really are quite talented, it is impossible to handle complex problems involving large values with a prevailing lack of methods, or with methods that are far too simple. Far too many believe that it is possible to successfully reach goals through group meetings and simple negotiations. It is not. Rather, successful achievement of one's goals requires the following:

1 This is extensively discussed in Kjell Borking, Mats Danielson, Guy Davies, Love Ekenberg, Jim Idefeldt, and Aron Larsson's *Transcending Business Intelligence* (2022). See Reading Tips in Chapter 7.

- Targeting
- Needs analysis
- Modelling and evaluation
- Decision modelling and analysis
- Implementation
- Monitoring

To make reasonable procurements, we must understand the organisation's goals and needs. Moreover, we need a clearly stated target. We need reasonably sophisticated methods that correspond to the complexities involved. And we need adequate evaluation and monitoring methods.

Unfortunately, organisations usually put too few resources into the modelling part of the procurement process. However, we must remember here that the number of decision components that a human being can hold in their head is severely limited, and this is why we need adequate tool support.

6.2. Evaluations of Tenders

Evaluations of tenders are particularly problematic and usually fail in three ways: i) Through using unreasonable precision; ii) Through awkward management of qualitative values; and iii) Through management of value scales without great insight.

However, there are methods for achieving significantly better decision-making. Here we highlight the problems and present a solution that leads to safer procurement decisions of a considerably higher quality. We also discuss how relatively simple modifications of the current evaluation models can contribute to the selection of the most advantageous tender in a procurement process.

As an example, suppose you want to invest in a new business intelligence (BI) system to try to gain better control of your business, and you want to develop this system in collaboration with an established partner. QlikTech, IBM, and SAP have dominated as suppliers of BI systems for a long time, closely followed by players such as Microsoft, SAS, and Oracle, as well as a number of smaller and more niche companies. After some deliberation, you decide on one of the three largest companies as your future vendor. You also consider what is important in your business when it comes to BI, and find that *usability* is the most important criterion, followed by *functionality*, *quality*, *price*, *education*, *reputation*, and the *contact networks* of suppliers. You assess the risks of different suppliers as being equivalent. In the most common procurement methods used today, the criteria weights are directly and precisely quantified. We will discuss how to improve this quantification later.

For now, assume that you have agreed on the following criteria weights:

- Usability: 30% (0.3)
- Functionality: 20% (0.2)
- Quality: 15% (0.15)
- Price: 10% (0.1)
- Training: 10% (0.1)
- Company reputation: 10% (0.1)
- Diversity: 5% (0.05)

As discussed before, it is problematic to assume that precise weights can be determined in this way. Nonetheless, this is usually how it is done, and so we will do it here for the sake of argument.

The different companies are then evaluated on the basis of the criteria, on a scale from 0 (appalling) to 10 (excellent). Let us assume that the valuations result in the table below.

Table 6.1. Criteria and criteria weights for three systems.

	Usability	**Functionality**	**Quality**	**Price**	**Training**	**Reputation**	**Diversity**
QlikTech	6	7	6	4	4	5	5
IBM	7	6	6	6	4	6	6
SAP	7	6	6	5	3	6	7

First of all, note that no supplier dominates across all of the criteria. For example, IBM and SAP seem quite similar, but IBM is expected to have a somewhat better price and training, while SAP has slightly larger diversity in its contact networks. We thus have no strict dominance and must continue the analysis.

When performing the evaluation, the values for the suppliers are weighted together under each criterion and then summarised into a weighted average, where our criteria weights are the weights. In our case, this means:

$$V(\text{QlikTech}) = 0.3 \cdot 6 + 0.2 \cdot 7 + 0.15 \cdot 6 + 0.1 \cdot 4 + 0.1 \cdot 4 + 0.1 \cdot 5 + 0.05 \cdot 5 = 5.65$$

$$V(\text{IBM}) = 0.3 \cdot 7 + 0.2 \cdot 6 + 0.15 \cdot 6 + 0.1 \cdot 6 + 0.1 \cdot 4 + 0.1 \cdot 6 + 0.05 \cdot 6 = 6.10$$

$$V(\text{SAP}) = 0.3 \cdot 7 + 0.2 \cdot 6 + 0.15 \cdot 6 + 0.1 \cdot 5 + 0.1 \cdot 3 + 0.1 \cdot 6 + 0.05 \cdot 7 = 5.95$$

This is also illustrated in Figure 6.1.

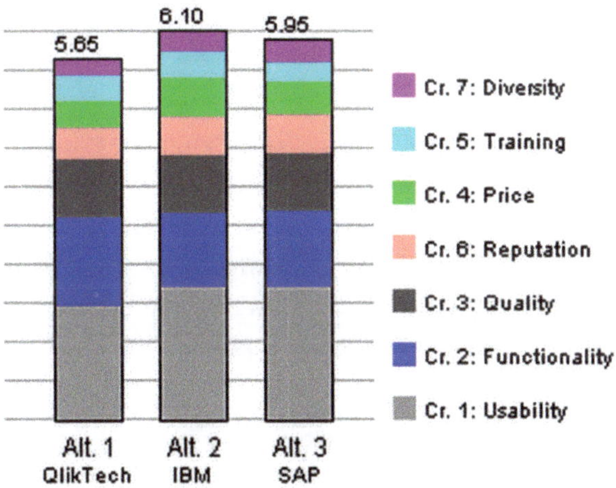

Figure 6.1. Evaluation of BI vendors using fixed numbers.

We should then select the supplier that scores the highest value. We thus consider a procurement process much like a regular decision-making process. In practice, this means that each tender is initially analysed on the basis of how it performs under each of the stated criteria in the tender documentation. The result is then calculated in the same way as in a classic multi-criteria analysis.

This approach is not strange in itself, except for the fact that it does not work. We will now demonstrate why, and what should be done instead.

6.3. Evaluation Criteria

We will now discuss a simplified procurement example. However, the same reasoning will apply to all procurement problems, regardless of their complexity.

A public company must procure a consulting service for the development of an IT system for customer management (CRM). After preliminary work, we identify a number of criteria that we must be able to balance against each other: cost, competence, responsiveness, and design. One common approach is to apply weights to them as in a regular multi-criteria analysis. We assign the following weights:

- Cost: 40% (0.4)
- Competence: 30% (0.3)
- Responsiveness: 20% (0.2)
- Design: 10% (0.1)

There are rules that apply to criteria in the sense that they must be formulated in contract documents or in contract notes so that all tenderers can interpret them in the same manner.

This means that we must try to describe the criteria, so that the tenderers can leave as accurate a bid as possible:

- A cost is usually specified in monetary terms, but it can also be stated more qualitatively, as we do in this case
- Competence means being educated and experienced in the field
- Responsiveness means paying attention to the customer's needs and demonstrating flexibility in the proposed solutions
- Design means showing creativity and being able to create functional, aesthetic, and other values

Point scales are often used for the properties of the bids:

5 – Much better than the basic level of the criterion

4 – Better than the basic level of the criterion

3 – Meets the basic level of the criterion

2 – Slightly worse than the basic level of the criterion

1 – Much worse than the basic level of the criterion

0 – Does not match the basic level of the criterion at all

Following the call, we receive four tenders from suppliers A, B, C, and D, all of whom have submitted well-prepared tenders. We apply the valuation scale to the tenders in a decision matrix.

Table 6.2. A simplified procurement matrix.

	Cost	**Competence**	**Responsiveness**	**Design**
A	5	2	2	4
B	4	4	3	3
C	2	3	5	1
D	1	5	2	5

An immediate observation is that no supplier has at least as much value as any other under all criteria. We therefore cannot directly designate a winner and must continue the analysis.

The values are thus weighted together under each criterion, and the result is then summarised as a weighted average. With calculations analogous to those used before, this means:

$$V(A) = 0.4 \cdot 5 + 0.3 \cdot 2 + 0.2 \cdot 2 + 0.1 \cdot 4 = 3.40$$

$$V(B) = 0.4 \cdot 4 + 0.3 \cdot 4 + 0.2 \cdot 3 + 0.1 \cdot 3 = 3.70$$

$$V(C) = 0.4 \cdot 2 + 0.3 \cdot 3 + 0.2 \cdot 5 + 0.1 \cdot 1 = 2.80$$

$$V(D) = 0.4 \cdot 1 + 0.3 \cdot 5 + 0.2 \cdot 2 + 0.1 \cdot 5 = 2.80$$

Using this method of evaluation, which is also shown in Figure 6.2, we would consequently select supplier B.

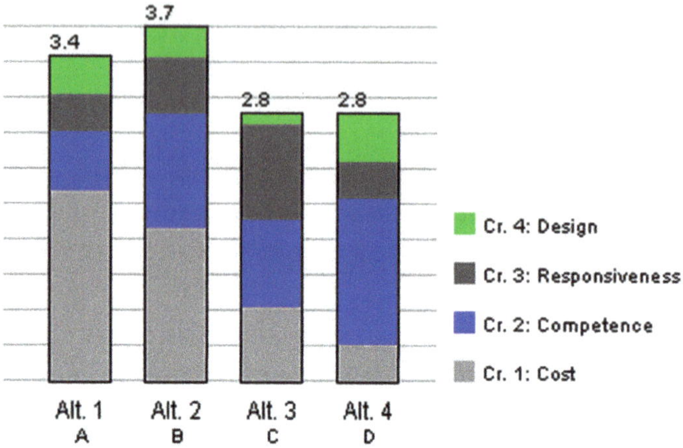

Figure 6.2. Evaluation of CRM consultant using fixed numbers.

Now, of course, the question is whether this would be the right choice, i.e., whether we would really have chosen the best bid. The answer is that we cannot know. The model is not sophisticated enough to determine which bid is the best.

In this chapter's introduction, we suggested that there are at least three fundamental problems with procurement models, and we will begin with the first: unreasonable precision.

6.4. Unreasonable Precision

When making procurement decisions, it is acknowledged that exact weights are not always possible (in fact, they are very rarely possible), and therefore interval estimates are permitted. Thus, in public procurement processes it is possible to set the criteria weights as, for example, 20–40%. In the example above, we had four criteria. Understanding how to handle them with precise values in a satisfying way is not easy. How could we reasonably state that, for example, competence has exactly 30% weight? Or 35%? Or indeed any exact percentage? How could we reasonably say that this is correct? Psychological risk research has shown that most people are normally unable to intuitively distinguish between percentages in estimates, even for example between starkly different ones such as 30% and 70%. Nevertheless, weights are almost always handled and understood as precise statements. Imprecise statements are harder to handle from a calculation point of view, but there are, as we will see, calculation methods that can easily solve this.

So now let us for example assume that the importance of:

- Cost is 30–45%
- Competence is 25–35%
- Responsiveness is 15–25%
- Design is 5–15%

The difficulties of precision also apply to the value indications for the tenders within the criteria. In general, it is perhaps even harder to assign adequate values to qualitative properties with reasonable precision. Thus, as with the criteria weighting, we will assign slightly less precise values to the suppliers for each criterion. For example:

Table 6.3. Introduction of value intervals.

	Cost	Competence	Responsiveness	Design
A	4–5	1–3	1–3	3–5
B	3–4	3–4	2–4	3–4
C	1–3	2–4	4–5	0–2
D	0–2	4–5	1–3	4–5

We then reach the following weighting of the values for each supplier:

V(A) is between 2.40 and 4.00

V(B) is between 2.80 and 4.00

V(C) is between 1.80 and 3.60

V(D) is between 1.80 and 3.40

This is also shown as a visual comparison in Figure 6.3.

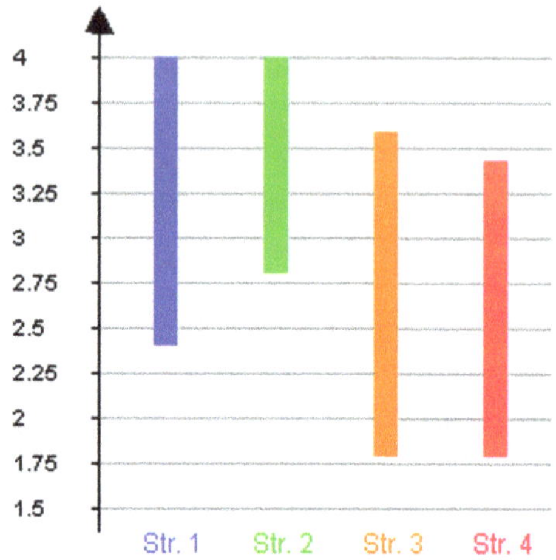

Figure 6.3. Evaluation of CRM consultant using intervals.

We can now see that the situation, perhaps unsurprisingly, is no longer so clear. This reflects the lack of clarity from the outset, and proves that the earlier use of precise numbers only introduced a distorting simplification. In reality, we will probably never have more precision in assessments than in Table 6.3, and indeed we will often have less.

Intervals are also often difficult to estimate, especially when it comes to assessing qualitative criteria. There are also further problems with normalisation and other technicalities that we do not address here. Thus, intervals alone might not be sufficient for selecting the best option, but they do at least provide a more realistic picture of the situation, and we will discuss how to solve the problem of discriminating between alternative actions later on.

6.5. Shortcomings of Handling Value Scales

Introducing point scales to manage values is difficult, as stated above. Nevertheless, it is necessary that we understand the scales that we are using. For example, if we have a five-grade scale, how do we know that it is adequate? On what are our assessments based? And when evaluating suppliers, for example through our weighted average using this five-grade scale, we must assume that the distance between 2 and 3 is as large as that between 3 and 4. In other words, we must assume that we use so-called *interval scales*.

Let us return to the first scale and matrix in Table 6.2. Suppose that we have the following situation:

Table 6.4. The valuation of costs according to Table 6.2.

	Cost	Value
A	200,000	5
B	500,000	4
C	600,000	2
D	800,000	1

However, we could instead use the following scale. It might still be reasonable for our purposes, and very few would be able to tell the difference.

Table 6.5. Revised valuation of costs.

	Cost	Value
A	200,000	5
B	500,000	2
C	600,000	1
D	800,000	0

We would then get the following results (Figure 6.4) if the valuations under the other criteria are the same as in Table 6.2:

$$V(A) = 3.40$$

$$V(B) = 2.90$$

$$V(C) = 2.40$$

$$V(D) = 2.40$$

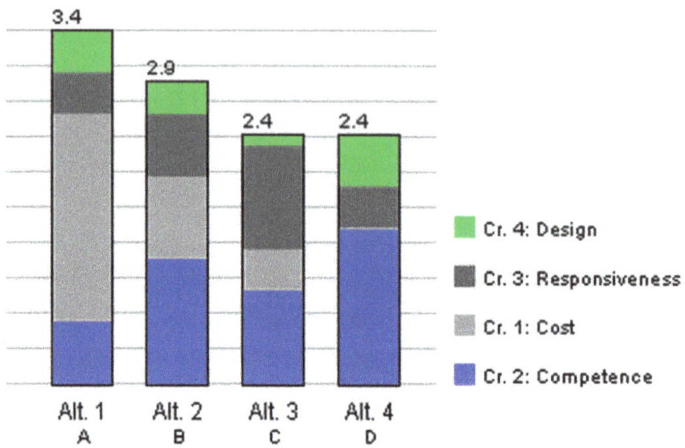

Figure 6.4. Evaluation of CRM consultant using new cost values.

Now A is the best. This example shows the dilemma when dealing with scales without understanding exactly what we are doing. The outcome will probably be even more uncertain when we are dealing with even more qualitative aspects such as competence, responsiveness, or design.

This example further illustrates two parts of the dilemma. We can seldom set precise numbers as qualitative values so that they really make sense. And we rarely have control over our measurement scales.

6.6. Weights and Value Scales

Further problems arise in procurements because people believe they have a clearer idea of the weights than they actually do. However, we must remember that weights (and often values) express purely subjective perceptions that are difficult to quantify.

There are additional difficulties arising not from a lack of information, but rather from negligence. For example, consider a procurement evaluation that only uses two criteria: cost and quality. We might initially consider that cost itself is much more important than quality and ascribe the cost a weight of 95% (0.95). Quality is then weighted at 5% (0.05). Now assume that there are two tenders from suppliers A and B respectively, which are valued on a ten-degree scale, as defined in the tender documentation. Now assume that it turns out that the prices in the tenders hardly differ, and in fact that both are considerably lower than what was initially anticipated, and that price is thus no longer particularly critical in this situation, even if in general it would be. Instead, quality is crucial here. We must therefore be very careful when calibrating scales.

For instance, if the value of tender A for the cost criterion changes from 0 to 1 and if this difference really is perceived as small, the criterion is not important in this particular decision situation, even if we initially believed it to be so. Correspondingly, let us assume that the perceived difference for the quality criterion grows for tender B when the quality increases from 0 to 10. These differences are known as the potentials of the criteria. Numbers have been selected so that the calculations are easier to follow. See Table 6.6.

Table 6.6. The valuations under the criteria.

	Cost	Quality	Calculated value V(X)
A	0	10	$V(A) = w_1 \cdot 0 + w_2 \cdot 10$
B	1	0	$V(B) = w_1 \cdot 1 + w_2 \cdot 0$

Now suppose (for argument's sake) that we perceive a quality increase from 0 to 10 as five times better than an increase from 0 to 1 for the cost criterion. That is, the potential of the quality criterion is five times as great as the potential of the cost criterion. Then $V(A) = 5 \cdot V(B)$, which is the same as $w_1 \cdot 0 + w_2 \cdot 10 = 5 \cdot (w_1 \cdot 1 + w_2 \cdot 0)$ where w_1 is the weight of the cost criterion and w_2 is the weight of the quality criterion. The calculation then yields $w_1 = 2 \cdot w_2$. That is, w_1 should be 2/3 and w_2 should be 1/3 in our weight assignments.

Table 6.7. Assigning the weights.

	Cost (2/3)	Quality (1/3)	Calculated value V(X)
A	0	10	$V(A) = 2/3 \cdot 0 + 1/3 \cdot 10 = 10/3$
B	1	0	$V(B) = 2/3 \cdot 1 + 1/3 \cdot 0 = 2/3$

Now comes the dilemma. There are fundamental difficulties in measuring completely different criteria with the same scale. We can express the same relationships either by changing the weights or by changing the scales. It is therefore problematic if we allow the value scales to vary without interacting with the weights (the so-called weight/scale dualism). If we are not attentive, our weight assessments become meaningless; as if we are comparing temperatures in Celsius and Fahrenheit without understanding how these scales relate to one another. Thus, even if a legal procurement framework requires criteria weightings, applying an unspecified value scale can significantly impact the outcome.

To demonstrate this, let us assume that we have only two criteria to consider. According to the EU directive 2004/17/EG on public procurement, we must specify how the criteria will be weighted when assessing the tenders. We assume that the weights for cost and quality are both 50% (0.5) in the tender documentation, and we further assume that we receive bids that we value on a ten-point scale according to Table 6.8. The evaluation is thus as in the table and in Figure 6.5.

Table 6.8. The weights are equal.

Tender	Cost (0.5)	Quality (0.5)	Calculated value V(X)
A	6	4	$V(A) = 0.5 \cdot 6 + 0.5 \cdot 4 = 5.0$
B	4	6	$V(B) = 0.5 \cdot 4 + 0.5 \cdot 6 = 5.0$

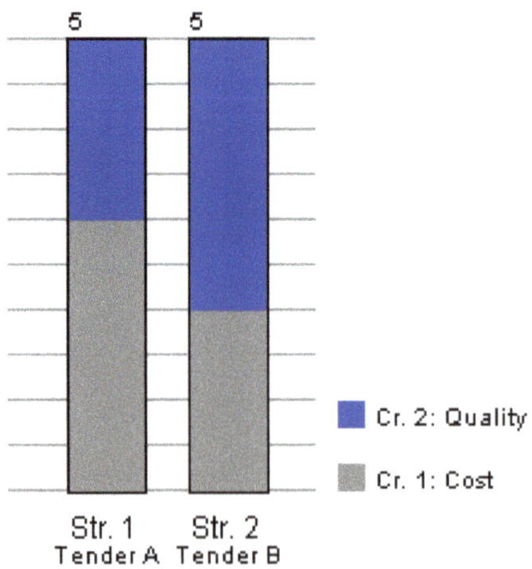

Figure 6.5. Equal weights given to cost and quality.

But then we realise that this is wrong. We want quality to be more important: the weight for this criterion should instead be 75% (0.75) and cost should thus be 25% (0.25), which results in Table 6.9 and Figure 6.6.

Table 6.9. With revised weights.

Tender	Cost (0.25)	Quality (0.75)	Calculated value V(X)
A	6	4	$V(A) = 0.25 \cdot 6 + 0.75 \cdot 4 = 4.50$
B	4	6	$V(B) = 0.25 \cdot 4 + 0.75 \cdot 6 = 5.50$

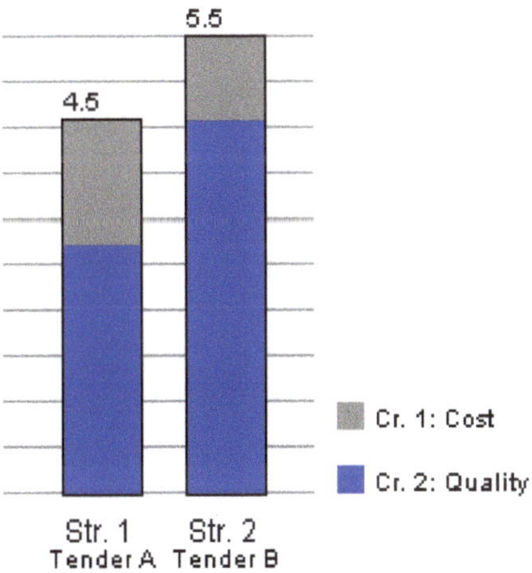

Figure 6.6. Quality is three times that of cost.

We have already specified the weights in the tender documentation and usually cannot change them at a later point. But here, we can utilise the relationship between weights and value scales. We can achieve exactly the same effect without changing the weights (which is not allowed) by instead changing the value scale (curiously, this is allowed, hinting that the legislators do not understand the dualism).

Let us suppose we have weights w_i for each criterion i that are specified in the inquiry data (50% and 50% in our example). We cannot alter those. The weights that we really want are 25% (0.25) and 75% (0.75). But we can instead redefine the scales by calculating scaling factors, i.e., by calculating a factor $z_i = v_i/w_i$ that is used to convert the scales so that the result is consistent with our aims. The scaling factors in our example are 25/50 = 0.5 and 75/50 = 1.5.

Thus, we multiply the values by these scaling factors, and thereby recalculate the resulting values whilst retaining the former weights (in this way, the legal requirement is still fulfilled). We then obtain $z_1 = 0.5$ and $z_2 = 1.5$. If we now multiply the values by these factors and keep the old weights, the legal requirement not to change weights retrospectively is fulfilled, even though we have changed the evaluation conditions dramatically. We can thus "cheat" in any way we like, as can be seen in Table 6.10 and Figure 6.7.

Table 6.10. With new scaling factors.

Tender	Cost (0.5)	Quality (0.5)	Calculated value V(X)
A	3 (6 · 0.5)	6 (4 · 1.5)	V(A) = 0.5 · 3 + 0.5 · 6 = 4.5
B	2 (4 · 0.5)	9 (6 · 1.5)	V(B) = 0.5 · 2 + 0.5 · 9 = 5.5

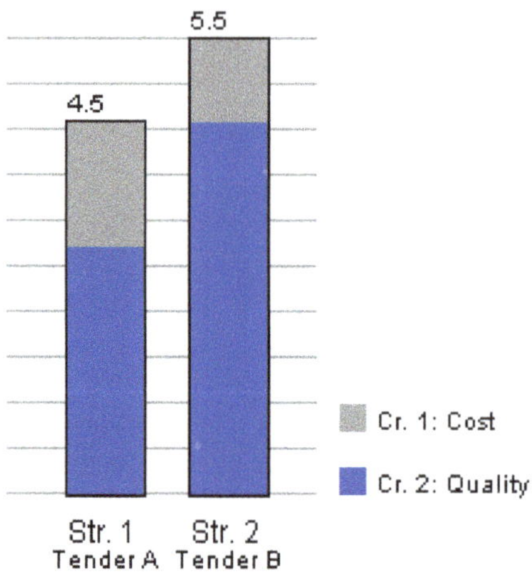

Figure 6.7. Equal weights with modified scales.

We thus obtain our desired result without changing the weights. We have only adjusted the scales from 0–10 to 0–5 and from 0–10 to 0–15, respectively. The weights that we initially stated are thus preserved, but we have shifted the scales so that they correspond to the weights that we actually want. This mechanism leaves room for huge arbitrariness. Problems arising from this arbitrariness may go unnoticed if we do not use a proven method, without any misdirected intention.

The main point is that the scales do not really have any meaning *per se*. They must therefore be pre-calibrated to avoid the situation in the above example. In addition, we must calibrate the value scales for the tender by analysing the interaction between criteria weights and the values of the tenders. If it is allowed, we can of course change the weights, as in Table 6.9. We can also keep them as they are, and instead change the properties of the scale that we use to value the tenders as in Table 6.10, where the scale for cost is 0–5 and the scale for quality is 0–15. This is a consequence of simple arithmetic showing the interaction between weights and value scales (the dualism), which should not be ignored, as is currently the case. The current legal requirements are therefore insufficient in their stipulation of how the valuation should be conducted.

There are, thus, general problems in evaluating tenders in procurements. The most serious is that we usually overestimate our ability to provide correct information. Allowing the use of intervals and comparisons as well as realising the limitations of the different scales is one way forward in these situations, particularly when we are dealing with qualitative values with no objective proxy measurement. Even if the procuring organisation has the best intentions in terms of fairness and transparency, this type of problem can arise and go unnoticed when we simply use our unguided intuition without reflecting on it.

6.7. Rankings

Above, we have seen how to handle interval estimates in procurements, and we will now take a closer look at rankings. Rankings are normally perceived as easier to use since it is often possible to say what is better or worse, or what is more or less important, even if precise values or intervals cannot be provided. To return to the example above, we would therefore use our original criteria and bid data without trying to quantify them.

We will now revisit the example in Section 6.3, where we considered cost as the most important criterion in the procurement, followed by *Competence*, which was somewhat more important than *Responsiveness*, which in turn was clearly more important than *Design*. We then naturally have a ranking of the criteria. The values of the bids can also be ranked using different criteria. Note that no values must be assigned here unless we particularly want to do so. It is quite difficult to mathematically evaluate such situations, particularly when the rankings are mixed with interval estimates, but the DecideIT program[2] can do the work for us. However, in this example, let us assume for simplicity that we have only rankings, as opposed to a mixed problem that also contains intervals or precise values.

Suppose we have the same situation as in Table 6.2, but we now know more about the strengths of the differences between the tenders. Table 6.11 shows these strengths, and uses the following metric to represent them succinctly:

> means "slightly better"
>> means "clearly better"
>>> means "much better"

Cost

A is slightly better than B
B is clearly better than C
C is slightly better than D

Competence

D is slightly better than B
B is slightly better than C
C is slightly better than A

Responsiveness

C is clearly better than B
B is slightly better than D
D is equal to A

Design

D is slightly better than A
A is slightly better than B
B is clearly better than C

2 DecideIT is a software application designed for handling such problems. See the Appendix and Reading Tips section in Chapter 7 for more information.

Table 6.11 Comparisons between suppliers with strength statements.

Cost	Competence	Responsiveness	Design concept
A > B	D > B	C >> B	D > A
B >> C	B > C	B > D	A > B
C > D	C > A	D = A	B >> C

In the next step, we describe how these criteria relate to each other. In order to compare suppliers in a meaningful way, we must, as before, know the scales according to which we are making the assessments.

We will now examine how much better a supplier would be if it had the worst value from the beginning but later obtained the best value for a criterion. This improvement represents the criterion's potential. We do this to obtain a ranking for the importance of each of the criteria outlined in the current tender documentation. Here, we can also specify the strength relationship of this ranking.

Thus, in the calibration, we compare the potentials of the four criteria, i.e., how much a supplier would improve if it had the worst value for the criterion from the beginning but then subsequently the best. In our example, this would mean the following comparisons:

- The potential of the cost criterion: a change from D to A
- The potential of the competence criterion: a change from A to D
- The potential of the responsiveness: a change from A to C
- The potential of the design criterion: a change from C to D

Let us assume that through the above process we obtain the following qualified ranking between the potentials of the criteria in the example:

- Cost is much more important than competence
- Competence is slightly more important than responsiveness
- Responsiveness is clearly more important than design

As a result, we now neither need to specify the criteria weights nor the values for the tenders explicitly. We can handle any scale differences as before, by calibrating the scales to correspond to our conclusions from the above comparisons. The result is considerably more difficult to calculate by hand, especially when mixing qualitative relationships with quantitative estimates, so we use the computer program DecideIT. The result of the calculations is shown in Figure 6.8.

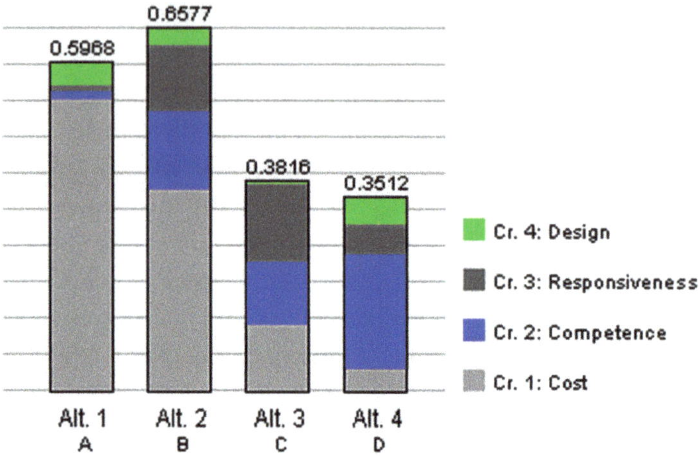

Figure 6.8. Evaluation of the tenders through rankings.

Simplifying somewhat, we can say that the higher the bar, the more favourable the bid. We see that bid B should win the contract, and tender A should come second. The other tenders cannot compete at all with B. The result of this process thus gives us both improved and more natural representation, as well as considerably more information.

But is it not as good to use the first method, which we criticised above? No. We have already shown that the methods used in the previous sections can lead to completely different results depending on how we handle the scales. Unlike in those examples, here we do not translate the tenders' answers into precise, artificial numbers. Instead, we start from the actual answers that are ranked relative to the criteria as a documented basis for the decision. This evaluation method is therefore based on a systematic analysis of the various factors that are present in the valuation. It is not based on artificial estimates, and we can thus investigate what will happen if the decision data change. Furthermore, we can extract more from the graph than from a traditional evaluation using sensitivity analyses, which we will discuss further in Chapter 7.

6.8. Right and Wrong in a Procurement Process

We have now seen that a procurement process is very much like a regular decision-making process. In practice, this means that each tender is initially analysed on the basis of how it responds to the stated criteria in the tender documentation. The result is then calculated as if it were a standard multi-criteria analysis.

But, as we have seen, there are four important observations:

- In order to obtain the tender that offers the best deal, a careful and conscious needs analysis, extraction procedure, modelling, and weighting are needed.
- We should not apply precise values for tenders under different criteria, at least not without knowing exactly what we are doing. This applies particularly to qualitative criteria.
- Criteria weights can be managed in different ways. Exact numbers cannot be realistically assigned, since they come mostly from subjective deliberations. Methods such as interval-scale values or rankings are preferred. Usually, a pure ranking reflects what a decision-maker can confidently accomplish.
- The strong correspondence between weighting and selection of scales can skew the result significantly if it is not handled properly.

6.9. Chapter Summary

In this chapter, we have discussed some fundamental issues with the decision models that are commonly used in procurement processes. Furthermore, we have shown how to systematically improve the quality of the analyses by employing intervals and relations. By using intuitively more natural assessments of the suppliers' tenders, we obtain results that provide more complete analyses. Even if no single tender candidate emerges as clearly better than the others, the analyses still provide a much clearer picture of the decision situation and highlight the critical points, or where further investigation resources should be focused.

We have also described methods for evaluation that lead to significantly better decision-making. All of this also applies to multi-criteria analyses in general. However, we have not yet dealt with those situations where future events might greatly affect the outcomes of our decisions. Therefore, in the next chapter, we will more closely investigate those situations where uncertainty must also be reflected in the analyses.

7. Probability and Risk Management

In Chapters 5 and 6, we went through various decision situations and considered how they might be modelled. However, uncertainty about the future affects most business decisions, since most of the world is simply uncertain. Although it is impossible to know anything about future scenarios with absolute certainty, uncertainty must somehow be modelled and managed because uncertain future events can greatly affect the outcome of a decision, and we will now investigate how to handle this complicating factor.

7.1. Probabilities and Decisions

Let us assume as discussed in the previous chapters that the main goals are defined and clearly communicated within the organisation. Let us also assume that the decision components, including the modelled scenarios, the possible consequences in each separate scenario, and the set of criteria, have been clarified during the decision process. Furthermore, we have a sense of how to prioritise the criteria and the values of the consequences, and we believe that we might know something about the probabilities of the different scenarios' outcomes. What should we do with all of this information? If we have structured the decision situation with all of the relevant components, how do we actually make a decision based on it?

An important aspect that is too rarely considered is how one determines what a correct decision is. So we need some kind of framework based on reasonable principles. One way to begin is to look

 https://doi.org/10.11647/OBP.0350.07

at how much we know about different scenarios and the probabilities that they will occur.

We usually distinguish between three main cases of uncertain decisions, even if most realistic situations reflect different mixtures of these categories:

- Strict uncertainty, where one does not know anything at all about the probabilities
- Uncertainty, where one does not know what will happen but does know the exact probability of each possible scenario
- Certainty, where one knows for sure which scenario will occur

Now assume that our organisation is in the middle of a digital transformation, and that we are considering whether or not we should streamline parts of the system development by introducing a new server platform. We have two strategies: i) to change platforms and ii) to maintain the current platform.

We are uncertain about the effects of a platform change. It is likely that it will take significant time for the staff to adapt to a new platform, which could mean that they experience the change negatively, at least initially. This, in turn, could lead to major reductions in efficiency. However, the members of staff are divided on this issue since a large proportion of them do not want to maintain the current platform. We therefore make the simplified assumption that there are two main scenarios of principal interest (in which we assume that other factors are the same): a) The staff react negatively and b) The staff react positively.

Depending on what we decide, and which scenario then unfolds, different consequences will follow. If we select the strategy of introducing a new platform and the staff reacts negatively, we will experience large efficiency losses. If the staff reacts positively to the platform change, we will have a clear increase in efficiency. Conversely, if we choose to keep the present platform and the staff reacts negatively, we will experience (comparatively small) efficiency losses, and if the staff reacts positively the business will continue as usual but less well than we would like. We can illustrate this via a so-called decision matrix, as in Table 7.1.

Table 7.1. A decision matrix.

	Negative staff	**Positive staff**
Change platforms	Large losses	Large gains
Keep the present	Small losses	Very small losses

Based on this matrix, we can now characterise the decision situation.

- In decisions made with certainty, there is only one state in the matrix. For example, we know for sure that whatever we do, the staff will react negatively.
- With strict uncertainty, we usually do not assign any probabilities at all, because we have no way of predicting them.
- In decisions with risk, we estimate probabilities of different outcomes. For example, we might estimate based on existing information, that the probability of the staff reacting negatively is 35% and that the probability that they will react positively is 65%.

These types of decision situations are solved differently. In decisions under security, the issue is about finding reasonable value estimates and then choosing the strategy with the best consequence. For example, suppose that we, for some reason, know for certain that staff will react negatively to whatever we do. In that case, the best thing is to keep the platform as it is since the losses will be smaller. Similarly, if we know for certain that staff will react positively, it is best to change platforms. In both cases, we only make the choice based on how beneficial the consequences are (and we assume that increased efficiency yields higher consequence values). The choice is thus pretty simple, and we just have to make up our minds.

When we have decisions under strict uncertainty, the situation is of course different. In these cases, we do not know anything about the future at all, so it is rather a matter of our relationship to risk. We sometimes consider the worst values of the consequences and choose the strategy that would yield the best consequence if the worst were to happen. In that case, we would therefore choose not to change the platform because the worst consequence would be a large loss of efficiency, and we would prefer to exclude that strategy. This decision principle is called *maximin* and it is a highly defensive rule that advocates choosing the strategy whose worst consequence is the least bad one of all. We can simply search for the matrix row whose worst consequence is as good as possible. For the more optimistically inclined decision-maker, there is the *maximax* rule, which is instead aggressive: it dictates that we should choose the strategy whose best consequence is the best of all the consequences. There are also mixed forms of these decision rules and several additional suggestions depending on how much we would regret the decision if it turned out that we had chosen the wrong strategy. But it is not really worth dwelling on such details here since they are often only of theoretical interest. In practice, it is not really likely that in a real-life decision situation there would be neither information nor opinions regarding the probabilities available. For our purposes, we can therefore now leave decision rules under strict uncertainty.

Next, we have decisions under risk where we know something about the probabilities of the different consequences. This is often the case in, for example, market decisions and investments (and actually in most decision situations). Decisions under risk can also be modelled with a matrix model, where we then add a new row with probabilities for each state, which is thus assigned a probability (p_i), which is estimated in one way or another. Table 7.2 shows the (precise) probabilities of the scenarios and the (precise) values (v_i) of the consequences. We assume here that the values are on a scale from 0 (the worst) to 1 (the best).

Table 7.2. A decision matrix with values and probabilities.

	Positive staff (p_2 = 65 %)	**Negative staff (p_1 = 35 %)**
Change platforms	Large gains (v_2 = 1.0)	Large losses (v_1 = 0.0)
Keep platform	Very small losses (v_2 = 0.7)	Small losses (v_1 = 0.3)

The information on probabilities is often weighted into an expression that is called the expected value and which is calculated by weighting the values with the probabilities similarly to the multi-criteria analyses in Chapters 5 and 6. In this case, using E to denote the expected value means that we calculate:

$$E(\text{Strategy}) = p_1 \cdot v_1 + p_2 \cdot v_2$$

for each strategy. If we insert our numbers in the expression above, we will obtain the expected values for the strategies. We then choose the strategy with the highest expected value, which according to the calculations and Figure 7.1 is the strategy to change platforms.

$$E(\text{Change platforms}) = 0.65 \cdot 1 + 0.35 \cdot 0 = 0.65$$

$$E(\text{Keep platform}) = 0.65 \cdot 0.7 + 0.35 \cdot 0.3 = 0.56$$

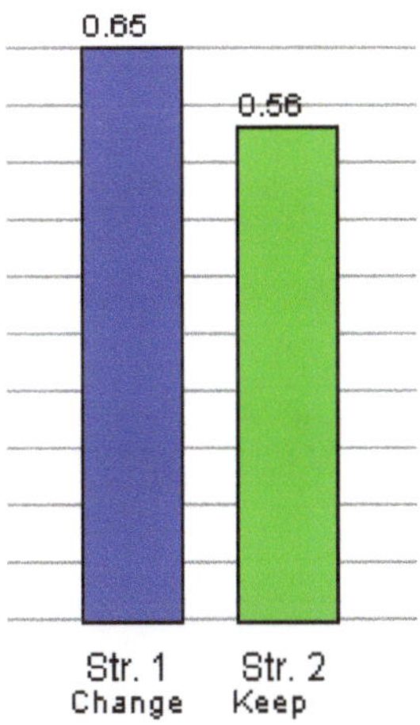

Figure 7.1. Evaluation of decision matrix.

The strategy with the highest expected value is usually perceived as the best. The expected value rule has the great advantage of being clear and easily calculable as long as the probabilities and values are known. The theory of maximising the expected value (or utility) has therefore dominated decision analysis, for instance in financial decision-making when making decisions under risk. It constitutes a so-called normative model of rational choices and is also widespread as a descriptive model of economic behaviour.

7.2. Tree Models

Matrix models are to some extent limiting, and in many situations a tree representation is more transparent because it can represent decisions at several levels, so consequential events and subsequent decisions can also be included. One decision problem often leads to another, and so on; that is, we have decision situations where an event can lead to new events. This is of great importance in, for example, risk analyses.

A decision tree is a structural model that includes the various important components in a decision situation, i.e., the criteria, the strategies, the events, and the consequences, as well as different estimates of the weights of the criteria, the different scenario probabilities, and the values of different consequences. A decision tree thus describes the decision situation more schematically and consists of three types of nodes. In decision nodes (squares), the decision-maker chooses one of several possible strategies. There are then event nodes (circles) where the uncertain outcomes occur, and finally outcome nodes (triangles), which show the outcomes of different paths through the tree. Figure 7.2 shows the same platform example in a tree representation.

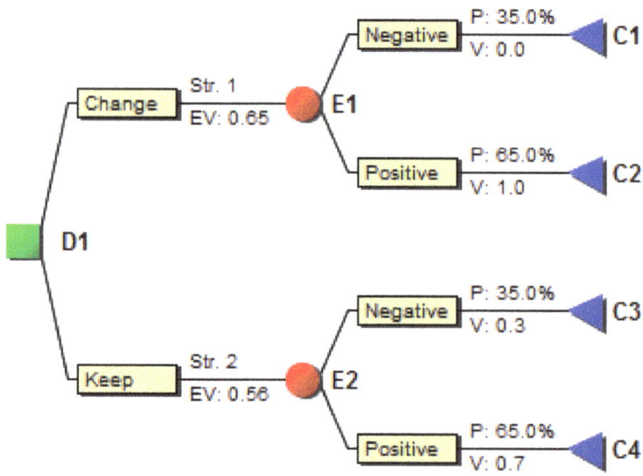

Figure 7.2. Decision tree for decisions under uncertainty.

The strategies are the paths out to the right from the green decision node. In the tree, we assign probability distributions to the event nodes which express the uncertainties of the different possible consequences of the strategies. These are often estimated using numbers to represent the respective probabilities of the events leading to specific outcomes or sequential events. In Figure 7.2, we have two strategies to choose from. Each will lead to different events with varying consequences. The events will occur with differing probabilities, as shown in the tree. The numbers connected to the outcome nodes represent the values of the different consequences.

A decision tree can express more than a matrix is able to. Suppose, in the platform-changing case, that we have sequential consequences, for example that we get consequential effects of reduced efficiency as the profitability decreases. We can also imagine that the probabilities for different staff reactions will be different, since they are likely dependent on the choice. Figure 7.3 shows the model in an expanded decision tree. Note that some of the probabilities have been added and others changed due to new information as it comes in.

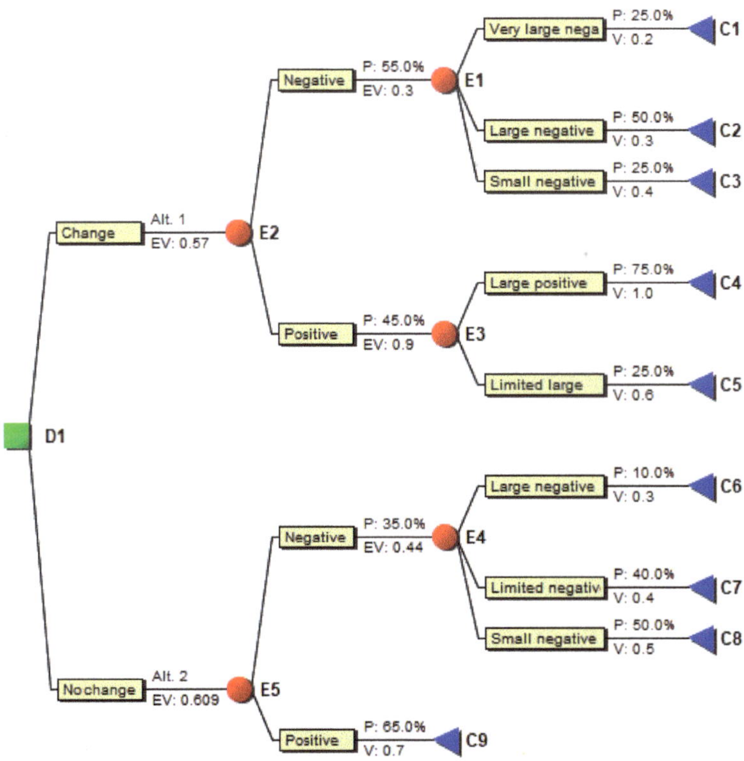

Figure 7.3. Expanded decision tree.

The calculations are similar, but we must consider the partial tree branches:

$$\text{E(Change platforms)} = 0.55 \cdot (0.25 \cdot 0.2 + 0.50 \cdot 0.3 + 0.25 \cdot 0.4) + 0.45 \cdot (0.75 \cdot 1.0 + 0.25 \cdot 0.6) = 0.57$$

$$\text{E(Keep platform)} = 0.65 \cdot 0.7 + 0.35 \cdot (0.10 \cdot 0.3 + 0.40 \cdot 0.4 + 0.50 \cdot 0.5) = 0.609$$

The results can be seen in Figure 7.4.

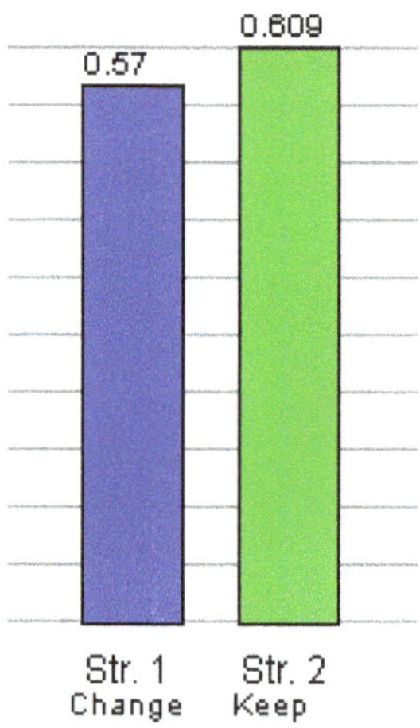

Figure 7.4. Evaluation of two-level decision tree.

Under these conditions, the preferred choice is reversed so that the *keep platform* strategy now has the highest expected value, although only by a slim margin. Through the depiction of the decision tree, it becomes rather straightforward to follow the arcs from a calculated expected value to the underlying probabilities and outcome values, and in the process to derive a sense of the bases of the calculation and the robustness of the differences between expected values.

7.3. Realism in Decision Models

The above model can be useful as a structural component, but keep in mind that it is highly simplified. Always trying to maximise the expected value seems to be a reasonable rule, provided we have the necessary information. It is also important to understand our preferences and how these relate to the risks involved. We usually talk about risk neutrality when a decision-maker believes that, for example, twice as much of a certain amount of money is perceived as twice as desirable. However, this rule is questionable, because such a linear approach to preferences does not always exist—for organisations or individuals. There are often other factors to consider as well. For example, we might be unwilling to take large risks if we could lose a lot of money, even if the expected value is high.

Many decisions are so important that an undesirable outcome cannot be tolerated, even if it has a low probability. It then seems reasonable to require that if the probability of a very poor outcome is too high, the strategy that could lead to it should be disregarded, even if it exhibits a good expected value. We can say that this is a kind of modified maximin principle. Such safety considerations may be of interest to, for example, insurance companies, who do not want to enter into agreements where the profit opportunities are good but there are non-negligible risks that the outcomes may be so disastrous that the entire company is jeopardised. The expected value maximisation does not take this into account and should be modified on that point.

Therefore, we usually speak of a more general concept of utility, and our own methods are expected to handle utility values that are more complex than simpler financial values. Furthermore, it is already difficult to determine the usefulness of different strategies at the individual level, but when it comes to decisions at the group level, it is even more complex.

Another issue is that just as with criteria weights and strategy values in multi-criteria analyses, a difficulty in risk management with uncertainties is that a decision-maker can seldom give precise numbers, as the above calculations require. Again, the decision-maker usually lacks access to such accurate information and (let us hope) wants to say what he or she knows and nothing else. He or she might want to be able to express claims such as that the value of a certain consequence is between 0.3 and 0.5, that the financial value of another consequence is between EUR 250,000 and EUR 400,000, that the value of a consequence is greater than the value of another consequence, that an event is more probable than another, and so on.

We emphasise once again that in real-world decision-making, we rarely have access to precise information on weightings, probabilities, and values. We most often have to rely on probabilities, which are estimated, often on rather unclear grounds. Sometimes we have frequency probabilities based on statistical data of a reasonable size, but these usually come with uncertainty in the form of confidence intervals. Furthermore, our conception obviously lacks adequate precision, making it impossible to specify fixed probabilities or values. Methods based on fixed numbers thus become difficult to use meaningfully.

Different types of uncertainties basically always appear in real-life situations. Over the years, various methods have been proposed for extending decision analyses to account for this complication. They are usually more mathematically demanding and can be quite cumbersome without a good knowledge of mathematics. Sets of probability distributions, so-called upper and lower probabilities, and interval probabilities are examples of methods for expressing uncertainty in the background data. Within such frameworks we can, for instance, state that a probability lies within a confidence interval, instead of specifying it as an exact number. But even then, there are often large difficulties in assessing information. So, despite the huge assets that are sometimes involved, surprisingly little has been done to carry out proper risk and decision analyses in businesses. However, it is possible to handle impreciseness, although the computational effort required for evaluations increases dramatically.

There are thus, on the one hand, methods that completely lack probability estimates and, on the other hand, methods with over-specified probability estimates. There is consequently a large space (and a great need) for methods that at least allow probability intervals and comparisons to avoid forcing values that are erroneously over-specified. You should specify what you know, and nothing else. Maybe surprisingly, there is often still enough information available to gain a good overview of the situation.

We work with expressions such as the probability of an event being between 10% and 35%, the probability of an event being less than 5%, or one event being more likely than another. Such statements can easily be represented by equations that form a so-called *probability base*. Correspondingly, for example, it can be stated that one consequence is more desirable than another or that the value (or utility) of a consequence is between 0.3 and 0.7. The value statements here form a so-called *value base* (or utility base).

Since both the probabilities and the utilities are now variables instead of precise values, the expected value calculations give rise to more complex expressions, so-called multilinear expressions. Figure 7.5 shows what this can look like. In the tree, the probabilities are given as intervals instead of precise numbers.

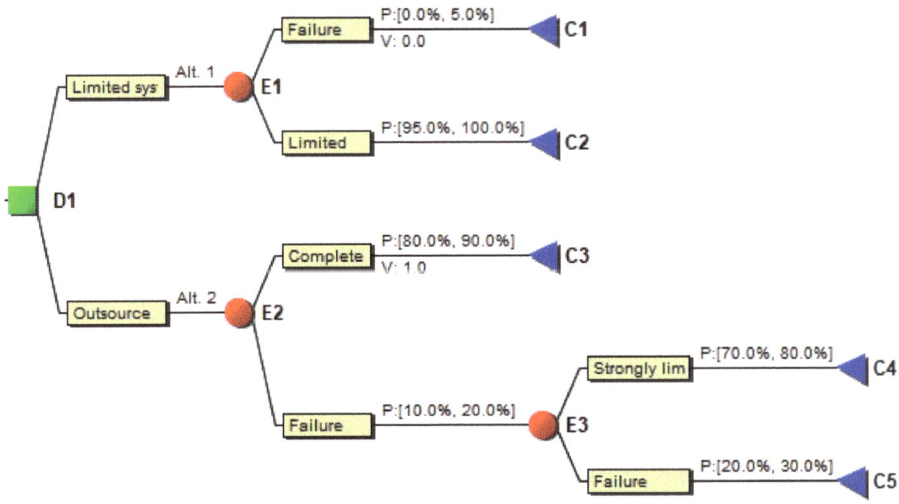

Figure 7.5. A decision tree with intervals.

Now, as before, the expected value is $p_1 \cdot v_1 + ... + p_n \cdot v_n$ although it is no longer a number but a set of numbers, depending on how the variables (p_i and v_i) are assigned numbers. We will briefly explain how this works. It is not at all necessary to understand this in detail, because one should use software to handle these types of calculations. The details here are unnecessary in the same way that an understanding of how a refrigerator works is unnecessary to be able to use it effectively. If you are not interested in these details, then go ahead and skip to the next section now.

If you want to continue reading here, then first, we will look at some domination concepts defining when one strategy is better than another. We denote the expected utility of strategy X as E(X). By "base", we mean all the information available in the decision model.

- Strategy A is at least as good as B in the current probability and value bases of $E(A) \geq E(B)$ for all feasible values of the included probabilities and utility values.
- Strategy A is better than B in the current probability and value bases if it is at least as good as B and $E(A) > E(B)$ for any allowable value of the included probabilities and utility values.

If there is only one strategy that is the best one, then that should be selected, but normally, we have overlaps between strategies that make it more difficult to directly determine which strategy is the best. In this case, it is appropriate to consider the number of values (the so-called support) a strategy has by examining for how many different assignments of variables in the bases (which contain all the possible numbers that represent the perceptions we have) the different strategies come out as the best. If, for example, strategy A is better than B for 2% of the feasible numbers, and B is better than A for 98%, it seems reasonable to choose B over A because it is much more likely that B is in fact the best strategy; that is, in a much larger proportion of all possible cases, B is a better choice. To facilitate these calculations, you need quite an elaborate computer program.

We will now illustrate a more difficult decision situation with a simple example (which also demonstrates that small problems are already difficult to solve without structured methods).

For instance, assume that we are about to implement a new IT system, and that we have two main strategies to choose from. One strategy consists of building up from scratch a somewhat limited system with internal resources, and the other consists of outsourcing a larger project for an extended system. After an analysis, we find that the risk of a total failure in internal development is less than 5%. We then have at least a 95% probability of obtaining a working system, albeit a somewhat limited one. If we outsource, the probability of subsequently being forced to carry out an internal development project and obtaining an even more limited system is 10–20%. This means that the risk of total failure is 20–30%.

As you can see, the problem is structurally relatively simple, but it is still difficult to give a reasonable and well-justified recommendation by just considering this *prima facie*. The processing problems we are facing are that: (i) we lack access to accurate probabilities, as the estimates in the data are necessarily uncertain, and (ii) a reasonable value scale is not easy to define.

If we instead ignore the requirement for unrealistic precision, we can rank the consequences: i) A full-scale system is better than an initially limited system, ii) An initially limited system is better than a system that has even more limited functionality and that must be built quickly, and iii) A system with even more limited functionality is better than a failed project.

This problem is short, but nevertheless it is not clear which strategy is the best simply from reading it. To be able to analyse it more structurally, we must start modelling the problem as a decision tree. In Figure 7.6 (which is the same as Figure 7.5), we can see the two strategies and their respective consequences in such a tree. The probabilities are stated at the edges of the tree as the intervals we specified above. Here we also have an underlying value scale for the consequences between 0 and 1. We give a value of 0 to the worst consequence (complete failure) and a value of 1 to the best (full functionality).

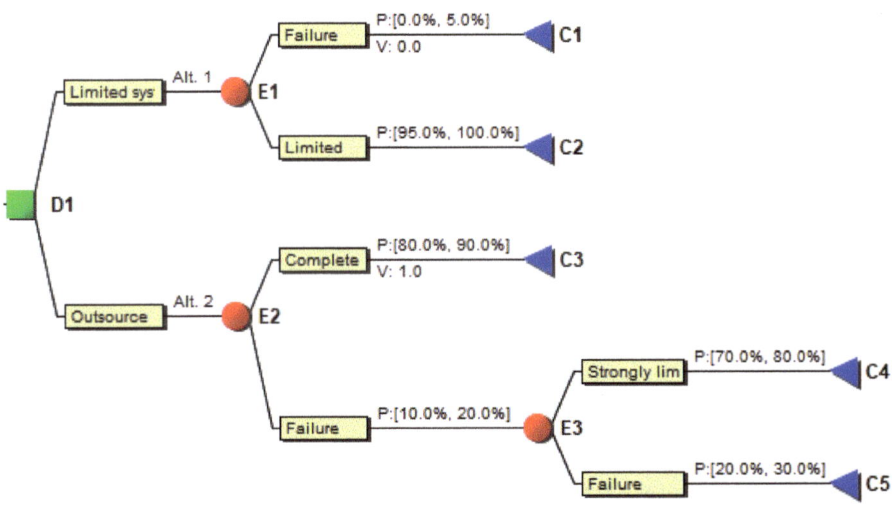

Figure 7.6. The decision tree modelling of the example.

After modelling the problem, an evaluation can be made. We use the expected value in the slightly modified version that we described above. Since the problem contains both intervals and comparisons, it is again slightly complicated to calculate manually, particularly as there are now dependencies between the two strategies. We therefore use the DecideIT tool for the analysis, which also gives us some additional information. The result of this analysis can be seen in Figure 7.7.

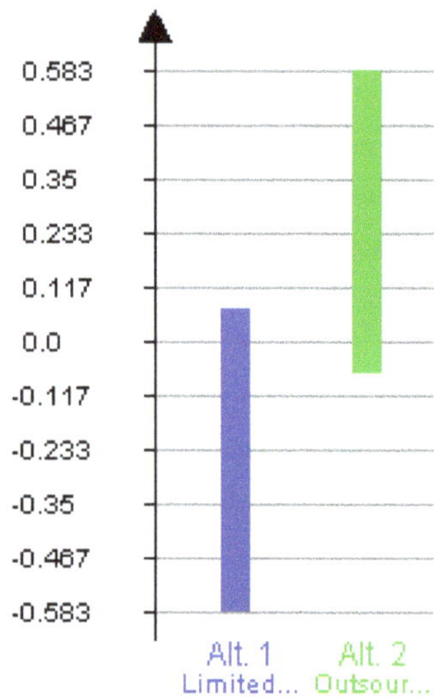

Figure 7.7. An initial evaluation of the decision situation.

What we see in the figure is how well the strategies perform relative to each other given the values in the bases that we have defined with our interval and relationship expressions. The higher the bar, the better the strategy it represents. The leftmost bar represents the strategy of building the system internally, and the rightmost one represents the strategy of outsourcing. It is now easy to see that the outsourcing strategy is clearly better than that of building the system internally. There is a small overlap, but it has no practical significance since it represents only a small part of the information bases and therefore can safely be ignored. It is thus evident that the best strategy is outsourcing, based on the information that has been provided. The situation is furthermore very stable in relation to changes in the input information. Decision problems like this, and many considerably more complicated ones, are easily manageable if we perform the analysis in this way. What was initially difficult to see becomes clear through this method, without the addition of any information that we do not actually have.

7.4. Sensitivity Analyses

A sensitivity analysis is indispensable in a robust decision-making process. The decision process involves continuously questioning the model. Have we really modelled and analysed the problem reasonably correctly? We should ask ourselves whether we have inferred the most relevant strategies, consequences, scenarios, and criteria. But the most common way to check the result is to vary the input probabilities and utilities as well as (if applicable) the criteria weights, to see how sensitive the decision is to changes. This is called sensitivity analysis and is normally used to find out so-called critical values, i.e., the limits within which weights, probabilities, and values must remain in order for the result not to change.

This is achieved by letting several variables alternate between the most and least likely, but still valid, numbers and studying how this affects the decision. Starting with the simplest model with fixed numbers for probabilities and values, we first look at the values of the consequences. The value of each consequence and the probability of each event must therefore be systematically varied upwards and downwards. If you have structural information, such as the knowledge that one consequence is worth more than another, there are dependencies that cause the variables to co-vary, which must also be considered.

Reconsider the platform change example. The sensitivity analysis could start with, for example, the probabilities being varied to see how this would change the decision. For instance, we might want to change the value of smaller losses to 0.2 and 0.4, respectively, (from 0.3) to see if this has any effect.

Table 7.3. A modified decision matrix with values and probabilities.

	Positive staff (p_2 = 65 %)	**Negative staff (p_1 = 35 %)**
Change platform	Big gains (v_2 = 1.0)	Big losses (v_1 = 0.0)
Keep platform	Very small losses (v_2 = 0.7)	Small losses (v_1 = 0.2 and 0.4 respectively)

If we insert our new numbers into the expression above, we will obtain new values for the second expected value.

$$E(\text{Change platform}) = 0.65 \cdot 1 + 0.35 \cdot 0 = 0.65, \text{ as before}$$

$$E(\text{Keep platform}) = 0.65 \cdot 0.7 + 0.35 \cdot 0.2 = 0.52 \text{ and } 0.65 \cdot 0.7 + 0.35 \cdot 0.4 = 0.60$$

It is still best to change the platform according to the calculation, so in this sense, the decision is quite stable if we consider this variable. One problem, however, is that it is only realistic to perform the sensitivity analysis in this way when we have few variables. As soon as we add more variables that we want to co-vary, it quickly becomes unmanageable. We can handle more complicated sensitivity analyses much more easily if, for example, we already have interval statements and comparisons for probabilities, values, and weights from the start. In that case, we just allow them to assume all possible values given the information we have, by means of a software tool.

Let us return to the example of outsourcing shown again in Figure 7.8 (which repeats Figure 7.5).

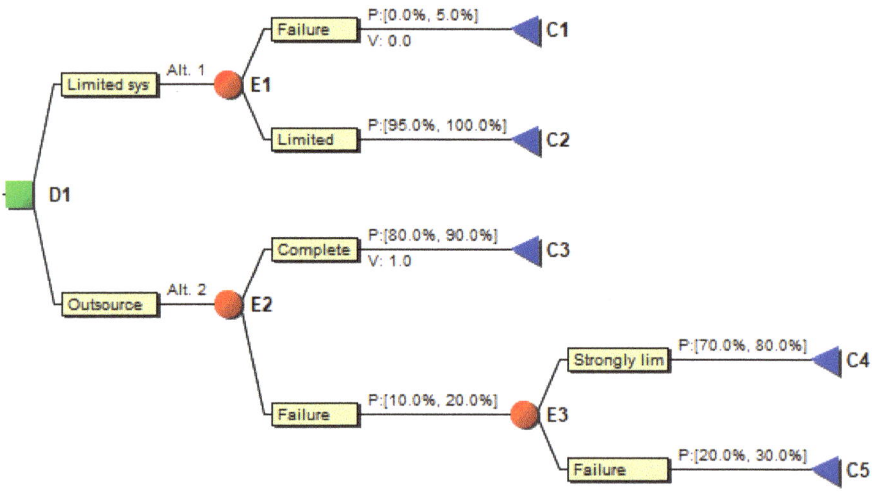

Figure 7.8. The decision tree shown again.

Earlier, we saw that the strategy of outsourcing was the best one. Now we will analyse the sensitivity of the information bases. We can do this in several ways. A tornado diagram is one method of showing how a strategy's expected value varies when the parameters involved are varied. The diagram shows, for example, how variations in the probabilities in a decision problem affect its end result. The diagram is sorted so that the probabilities with the greatest effect are at the top, with the remaining probabilities below them in decreasing order of influence. The width of each parameter indicates the influence on the expected value. The diagram thus resembles a tornado, as shown in Figure 7.9. Similarly, we can see how changes in the values and weights affect the result.

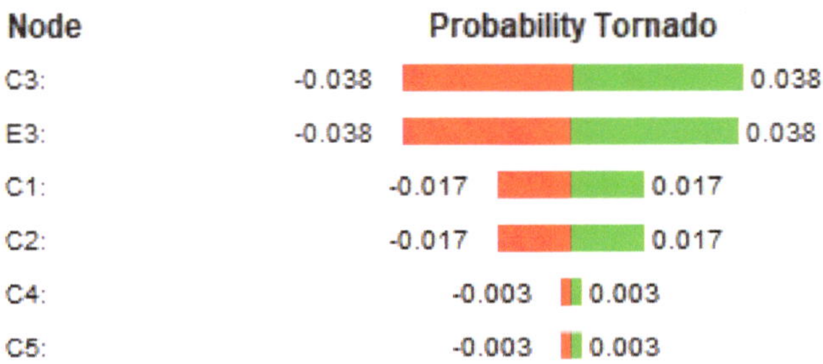

Figure 7.9. A tornado diagram.

An even better way to study the stability of decisions is to look at where the most important numbers reside. For example, when you specify an interval, it is likely that not all numbers in the interval are of equal importance, but rather that the numbers towards the middle of the interval add more "decision weight" to the problem. This could be seen as a kind of function representing the strengths that we assign to the different values. Figure 7.10 shows an example of how we might believe in the probability of success in building a limited system.

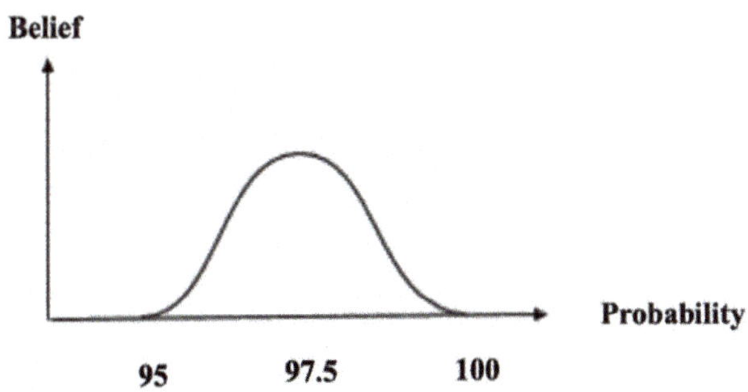

Figure 7.10. How important values can be distributed.

What we would like to know is how the decision situation looks when you remove the numbers closer to the interval borders and instead consider only the central ones. This is called contraction and can be done systematically with all variables, right up to the single number where you have the strongest beliefs in the values. In Figure 7.10, the strongest belief is at a probability of 97.5%. Figures 7.11 and 7.12 show what happens to the evaluation of the strategies when we systematically and continuously peel away the border numbers from left to right (increasing degree of contraction).

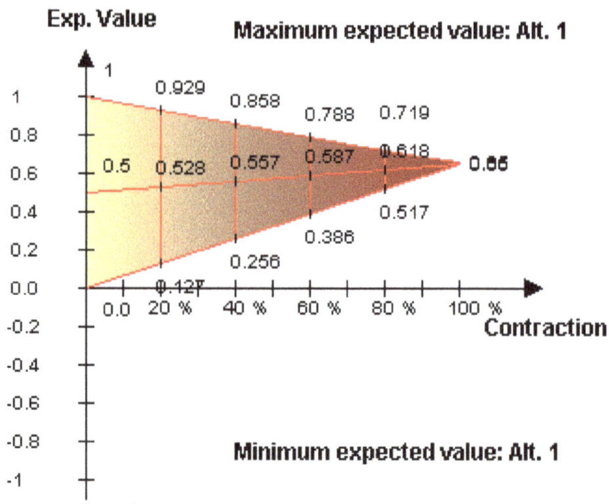

Figure 7.11. Focusing on central interval numbers.

For the first strategy (building a limited system), you can see how the result of the evaluation from the beginning (at 0% contraction) can be between 0 and 1. At 40% contraction, it is between 0.256 and 0.858, and at full contraction, it is 0.65. Correspondingly (but not shown), the values for the second strategy (outsourcing) are initially between 0.8 and 0.98, and finally reach 0.8875 at 100% contraction. In this way, we see that the decision is very stable, and that the second strategy is significantly better than the first. We can also directly study the differences between the strategies, as shown in Figure 7.12.

In Figure 7.12, we can see how the second strategy compares to the first. The greater the area of the triangle that lies above the x-axis, the better the second strategy is. We can see that that difference is quite dramatic. This means that the decision to choose the second strategy is very stable. In some cases, it may be more difficult to determine which strategy is the best (for instance, when the cone area in the figure is centred close to the x-axis). In that case, additional information must be gathered in order to determine the most suitable course of action. Through the tornado diagrams discussed above, we can then see which information has the greatest impact, so that we can obtain a better picture of how to allocate resources for continued analysis.

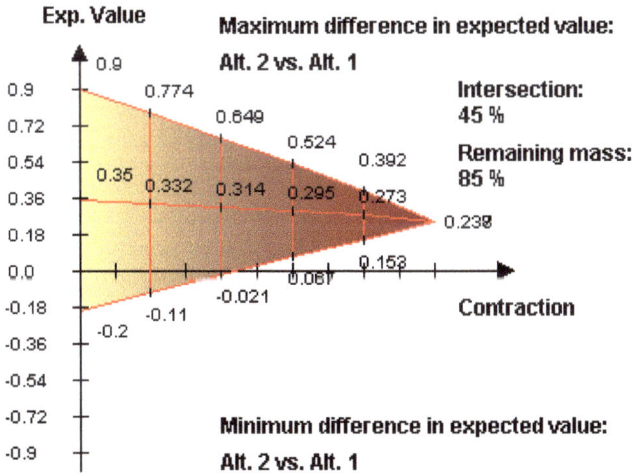

Figure 7.12. Comparison of the strategies.

An important observation can be made here from what is called the remaining mass in the figures. This expresses more exactly how strong the difference between the alternatives is. In this case, it is 85%, which means that 85% of the information points to the second strategy being the best and only 15% points to the first, i.e. the result is very stable. We will not go through all of the details here, but we will refer to more information that can be found in the tips for further reading and the appendix. We hope that this has shown the advantages of performing sensitivity analyses, and that with the right tools they are both manageable and informative. Finally, we will consider tools.

7.5. Tool Support

Advanced decision tools are easily able to handle all of the components we have discussed in this chapter, such as criteria and sub-criteria, weightings, strategies, events and probabilities, and values (utilities). In this way, we obtain a basis for the decision, where we can combine decision trees and criteria trees for one and the same decision problem. There are different types of tools that we can use to support this process, but we should use those that do not limit what we want to accomplish. Where information uncertainty is considered, we must be able to handle quantitative information in a reasonable manner. We must also be able to handle soft information such as rankings that can be difficult or even impossible to express in numbers. Furthermore, we need to be able to mix hard and soft information and to view the decision problem from different perspectives. The tools should be able to support all of this, point out the weak and strong strategies, and explain their characteristics.

The program we have used in this book is DecideIT, which is available at a discounted rate for universities and other public entities and at a standard rate for all other users. A one-year licence with full functionality is supplied for free with this book. Refer to the appendix for instructions and licence information. See also the paragraph below on further reading for more information.

7.6. Chapter Summary

We have reviewed various aspects of decision analysis and how it can be used to achieve rational, transparent, and stable decision situations. We have in this chapter mainly dealt with probabilities, and discussed how they influence decision outcomes. An important observation is that, as in multi-criteria analyses, it is practically untenable to use precise numbers for what is in reality uncertain information and where in practice we have neither full insight on the future, nor on our actual preferences.

Therefore, we must use models that are useful in practice, that allow us to provide imprecise information but still manage it, and that give us sensible directives. Otherwise, our decision-making will only be based on diffuse gut feelings and impulses. We have gone through various aspects of probabilities and risks, and how these can be systematically handled. We have also considered instances when even rather vague information can satisfactorily give an insight into which decision is the best.

In the following chapters, we will take a closer look at how to systematically incorporate decision-making into a project management process.

7.7. Reading Tips

These tips pertain to Chapters 5–7.

Transcending Business Intelligence addresses different aspects of decision and risk analysis in a simple manner, and also goes through some examples of how the analyses can be used in practice.

- Borking, Kjell; Danielson, Mats; Davies, Guy; Ekenberg, Love; Idefeldt, Jim and Larsson, Aron (2022). *Transcending Business Intelligence* (3rd edn). Stockholm: Sine Metu. Available free of charge from www.preference.nu.

A more comprehensive but more difficult book on the subject is *Deliberation, Representation, Equity,* which carefully examines uncertainty in decisions. It also discusses how this can work when people participate in political decision-making.

- Ekenberg, Love; Hansson, Karin; Danielson, Mats; Cars, Göran et al. (2017). *Deliberation, Representation, Equity: Research Approaches, Tools and Algorithms for Participatory Processes.* Cambridge: Open Book Publishers. https://doi.org/10.11647/OBP.0108.

Integrated Catastrophe Risk Modelling deals with various aspects of risks. The book focuses on flood risks but is applicable more generally. It introduces several useful methods for risk management.

- Amendola, Aniello; Ermolieva, Tatiana; Linnerooth-Bayer, Joanne and Mechler; Reinhard (eds) (2013). *Integrated Catastrophe Risk Modelling: Supporting Policy Processes.* Cham: Springer. https://doi.org/10.1007/978-94-007-2226-2.

A good overview of decision analysis can be found in the article "Decision Analysis: An Overview". It is a bit old but is written by one of the big names in the area and is still very relevant.

- Keeney, Ralph (1982). Decision Analysis: An Overview. *Operations Research* 30 (5), pp. 803–838, https://doi.org/10.1287/opre.30.5.803.

Kahneman's book is an excellent and systematic description of people's shortcomings regarding rational thinking and reasoning. In 2002, Kahneman received the Nobel Prize in Economics (to be precise, the Sveriges Riksbank Prize in Economic Sciences in Memory of Alfred Nobel).

- Kahneman, Daniel (2012). *Thinking, Fast and Slow*. London: Penguin Books. https://doi.org/10.1111/j.1539-6975.2012.01494.x.

If you want to learn more about the tool DecideIT, you can read the following two papers by Danielson et al. They go through the fundamentals of the tool without delving too deeply into mathematics.

- Danielson, Mats; Ekenberg, Love and Larsson, Aron (2019). DecideIT 3.0: Software for Second-Order Based Decision Evaluations. Proceedings of the Eleventh International Symposium on Imprecise Probabilities. *Proceedings of Machine Learning Research* 103, pp. 121–124.
- Danielson, Mats; Ekenberg, Love and Larsson, Aron (2020). A second-order-based decision tool for evaluating decisions under conditions of severe uncertainty. *Knowledge-Based Systems* 191, 105219. https://doi.org/10.1016/j.knosys.2019.105219.

If you really want to understand the details of the program and its mathematical background, you can refer to Danielson and Ekenberg's patent description.

- Danielson, Mats and Ekenberg, Love (2004). A Method for Decision and Risk Analysis in Probabilistic and Multiple Criteria Situations under Incomplete Information, U.S. patent 7257566.

Almeida et al.'s book is an overview of the multi-criteria area that goes through various processes and techniques.

- de Almeida, Adiel; Ekenberg, Love; Scarf, Philip; Zio, Enrico and Zuo, Ming J. (2022) *Multicriteria and Optimization Models for Risk, Reliability, and Maintenance Decision Analysis*. Cham: Springer. https://doi.org/10.1007/978-3-030-89647-8.

A somewhat older, but still very good, overview of the multi-criteria area has been written by Belton and Stewart.

- Belton, Valerie and Stewart, Theo (2002). *Multiple Criteria Decision Analysis: An Integrated Approach*. Cham: Springer. https://doi.org/10.1007/978-1-4615-1495-4.

Hubbard provides a good critical review of the area of risk management and discusses lots of interesting examples.

- Hubbard, Douglas (2009). *The Failure of Risk Management: Why It's Broken and How to Fix It*. Hoboken, NJ: John Wiley & Sons. https://doi.org/10.1002/9781119198536.

The Feeling of Risk is an entertaining overview of how we perceive risks by one of the most knowledgeable people in the field.

- Slovic, Paul (2010). *The Feeling of Risk: New Perspectives on Risk Perception*. London: Earthscan. https://doi.org/10.4324/9781849776677.

At the website www.sipta.org, there is lots of information on different ways to represent uncertainty in probabilities. Typically, the material is quite difficult to read but the website gives a good overview of the subject area.

The program we have used and reference in this book is DecideIT, which is complimentary with every copy of the book and can be downloaded from www.preference.nu/digitrans. The appendix describes how to install and use the program for structured decision-making. You can read more about the program at www.preference.nu. More about decision-making programs in general can be found at, for example, Wikipedia. Search for "decision-making software" or "decision-analytic software" for an up-to-date overview.

8. Project Portfolios

Projects entail a risk in all organisations, for the simple reason that resources must be invested in a project and the return or benefit is not expected until a later point in time. Risks were introduced as a concept in Chapter 7, but it is important not to forget that the work of a project manager and project owner is largely also about managing risks and their effects.

In organisations that work with projects, there are normally a number of parallel projects with different goals and in different parts of the organisation. For example, a company may have an IT project to develop the next version of its website, while the finance department is working to improve the budget process. How such projects are handled is an important issue: i.e., how are conflicts avoided and how can one ensure that the required benefits are delivered, that resources are used in a thoughtful way, and so on. All organisations should ask themselves these questions. And this is what project portfolio management is about: how we invest our money, select and evaluate projects, and so on. The important thing in portfolio management is to answer these questions from an organisational perspective and not from a project perspective. In other words, one must see what benefits the entire organisation, and not just specific projects.

This chapter and the next chapter will focus on a number of questions that an organisation should pose when working with projects and project portfolios.

 https://doi.org/10.11647/OBP.0350.08

8.1. The Project Portfolio and the Organisation

As we noted in Chapters 2 and 3, all organisations have a vision of what they want to be or achieve, some more pronounced than others. A retail chain's vision, for example, could be "We should make every day a little easier" (Adapted from Swedish grocery chain ICA), and a university's vision might be "We are a dynamic, innovative, and creative university driven by curiosity". Whatever an organisation stands for or wants to achieve, most of the change work is driven by projects, and thus it seems reasonable that project portfolios could be seen as a link between the desired achievement and the chosen investment.

A retail chain and its activities within the organisation can provide an example (the examples below are fictitious). The company has a vision to make every day a little easier for its consumers. It sets a tone and explains where employees need to strive. The next step is to break the vision down into concrete goals: what does it really mean to make it easier, and in what ways does this relate to the business model's value proposition, which we discussed in Chapter 3. Figure 8.1 shows an example of the types of goals that the vision can lead to, and projects linked to each. To "make it easy", for example, may mean that the retail chain wants to shorten the time it takes to shop for dinner for the family. To achieve this, they can choose to invest in a number of projects, in this case self-scanning and online shopping lists, both of which should, if implemented correctly, help the organisation to achieve their goals.

In this example, the project portfolio and the work it entails serve as a guarantor for activities that lead toward business goals and, ultimately, the vision. The starting point for a discussion in portfolio management is thus always the organisation's vision, strategies, and goals in the short and long term. This cycle should be seen as central to the organisation, and, put simply, it is an endless loop where the vision leads to goals that are realised through projects that in turn change and develop the vision.

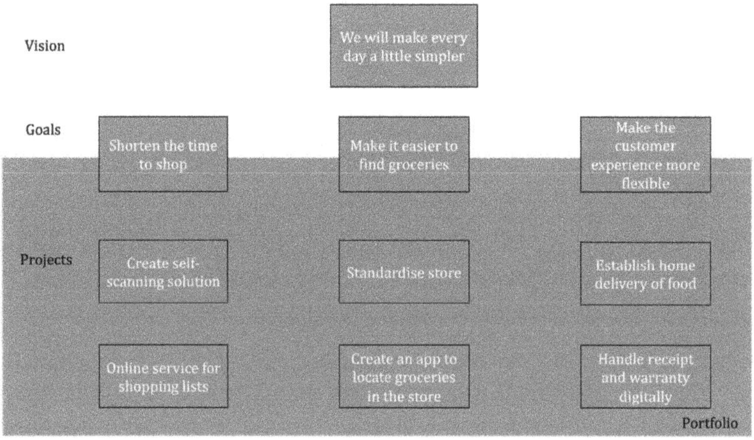

Figure 8.1. Connection between visions, goals and projects.

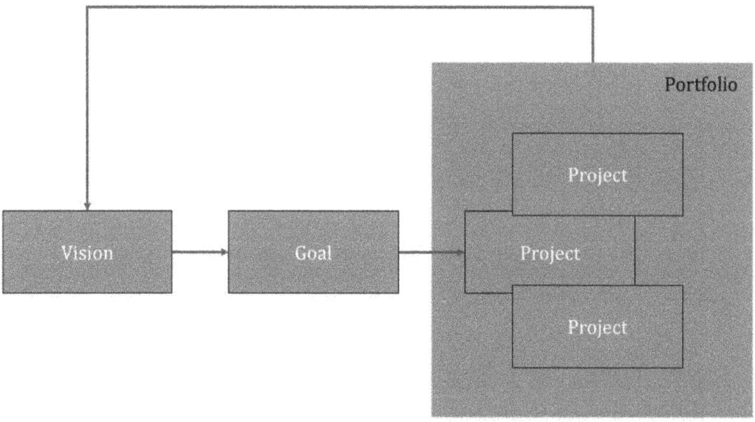

Figure 8.2. Vision/strategies, goals and projects.

8.2. Are We Investing in the Right Things?

The question of investing in the right things is relatively simple on the surface, but unfortunately while the answer may seem simple, it is not. Basically, this depends on how, and on what basis, we select projects, the methods that we use to ensure that our projects reflect our strategies and goals, and how we ensure that we have a good balance of different types of project, such as research, product development, and improvements to existing products.

No matter how someone chooses to work in an organisation, resources are limited and depend, for example, on what money is available for new investment, or which staff are available to work on projects. These limitations mean that not everything can be achieved, and organisations must choose where to put their resources. This choice is an important part of portfolio management. There are many methods and types of support that can be used to help an organisation make the choice, but each has both advantages and disadvantages.

Often, the decision situations with which we are faced are complex, and we need a decision process. A large proportion of the total working time is therefore spent on collecting, processing, and compiling information to create a reliable decision basis with all relevant information and all reasonable possibilities. As noted in the previous chapters however, decision-makers within an organisation are often required to make decisions based on a lack of clarity, and at worst on pure intuition. There is thus a great risk of making the wrong decision. The risk problem can be managed by introducing quality-assured decision-making processes that handle everything from idea generation to the identification and valuation of possible strategies to implement and follow up.

Most traditional decision models require relatively well-structured problems, however. By following a clearly defined process, the decision-maker can improve their overview of the decision material and the overall perspective of the problem. Such a work process cannot, of course, be simplified into a single formula, and must be well integrated into the organisation in order to effectively systematise and manage existing decision-making bases and uncertainties. We will present some examples that are common in project and portfolio management, and which gradually develop the decision model, pointing out the advantages and disadvantages of the respective methods. We will start with a simple method for project selection and end with an example of a multi-criteria-based model.

Common project models can be divided into two categories: quantitative and qualitative. Quantitative models create a basis for decision-making by quantifying and translating, for example, benefit or risk into money, while qualitative models are softer and focus on creating a discussion basis on which to work and ultimately from which to make decisions.

As you read about the below methods, consider how you think a more formal process should look. What is missing, and would prevent you from feeling comfortable making decisions based on the information each model contributes?

8.2.1. Quantitative Models

In order for quantitative models to work, information/data must be available, and preferably digital. Numerical methods have various problems that should be acknowledged when working with project portfolios. The fundamental problem is that benefits are difficult to quantify. How does one translate the effect of an IT investment that affects large parts of an organisation, or a redesign of a business process? Digitisation efforts are particularly affected by a redesign, as digitisation generally affects many parts of an organisation. For example, how can the benefit of investing in an intranet be calculated? This may seem like a simple problem, but the value of increased information dissemination that may lead to a more harmonious workplace where employees feel involved is very difficult, if not impossible, to quantify. Quantitative models are usually divided into scoring or points models and financial models.

8.2.1.1. Scoring Models

There are many designs for scoring models, but the basic elements are the same: points are given to different alternatives or portfolios. We considered these different types of models in our discussion of risk and decision analysis in Chapter 5. They are also used for these purposes, and to assign values to the various components that are included when choosing a project portfolio. These components may be the available alternatives, possible scenarios and their probabilities, the values of different consequences, and the relevant criteria and their relative weightings, as before. In portfolio management, there are multiple different variants in point models, which vary in their complexity and deliver vastly different results. The first model is based on estimates made by members of projects or experts within an organisation. They score different criteria on a scale (normally 1–5, where 5 is the best), and then rank projects on a scale where the highest average or total sum is equal to 1, and so on. For example, let us return to the retail chain scenario presented earlier in Section 8.1.

If we start with the six projects we used, and add a number of relevant criteria, an application could resemble the below calculation:

$$\text{Self-scanning} = 5 + 4 + 2 + 4 = 15$$

Table 8.1. Scoring model without weightings.

Criteria	How well does the project support our business?	Do we have the technical skill to carry it out?	How fast is the ROI?	Is the benefit of the project well-defined and believable	Average	Sum	Project ranking
Project							
Self scanning	5	4	2	4	3.75	15	2
Online shopping list	3	3	4	3	3.25	13	3
Standardised store	2	2	1	1	1.5	6	5
App to find groceries	3	3	3	3	3	12	4
Establish home delivery	4	4	4	4	4	16	1
Digital receipts	5	3	4	3	3.75	15	2

Here, because of past experiences of similar projects among other reasons, we have given the projects a number between 1 and 5 for each criterion, and then calculated the average and the total per project. The calculations provide the basis for a ranked list, where the best project is ranked highest (1). (It is best to have the highest average or the highest total sum. In this example, both metrics result in the same ranking.) From the list, we will primarily focus on the three top-ranking projects: establishing home delivery in the form of a shopping bag that can be ordered and paid for online and, if resources allow for it, implementing self-scanning in the stores. The advantage of this approach is that it is fast and relatively simple. However, it is also somewhat naive and illustrates several problems mentioned earlier in this chapter and in the discussion on decisions in Chapter 7.

For starters, we must rely entirely on people's ability to appreciate a situation and the significance of a given project within that context. If we ask an expert or participant in the project to choose a specific number on a scale (between 1 and 5), then we create a situation with large margins for error: how sure are we about the answers, really? For example, if you try to estimate for yourself how well you are doing in a course you are taking, it is not easy. Different people will perceive their own progress in different ways. Furthermore, we analyse the results by taking the average, or by adding the points together. What we miss or leave out in the process are the relationships between the criteria: can one criterion be more important than another? In the example, no distinction is made between the criteria, although in all likelihood there should be. In short, this process simplifies too much, which decreases the value of the results.

A better way, and in fact the most flexible way, is to use multi-criteria analyses. A multi-criteria analysis will, for example, rank or compare different criteria against each other in order to clarify how they relate to one another. If we develop our example by adding a weighting, the result looks as follows:

$$\text{Self-scanning} = 5 \cdot 0.3 + 4 \cdot 0.2 + 2 \cdot 0.4 + 4 \cdot 0.1 = 3.5$$

Table 8.2. Scoring model with weightings.

Criteria Weights	How well does the project support our business? 0.3 (30%)	Do we have the technical skill to carry it out? 0.2 (20%)	How fast is the ROI? 0.4 (40%)	Is the benefit of the project well-defined and believable 0.1 (10%)	Average	Sum	Project ranking
Project							
Self scanning	5	4	2	4	3.75	3.5	2
Online shopping list	3	3	4	3	3.25	3.4	3
Standardised store	2	2	1	1	1.5	1.5	5
App to find groceries	3	3	3	3	3	3	4
Establish home delivery	4	4	4	4	4	4	1
Digital receipts	5	3	4	3	3.75	4	1

When the two examples are compared, there is a difference in project prioritisation; digital receipts and home delivery are now equally important and should therefore be given equal priority. This is a trivial example that does not make full use of multi-criteria analysis, but it illustrates how a more structured decision model refines the result and delivers a more accurate decision basis. To show how a more thoroughly thought-out decision model could look, we will analyse the example with the help of a real multi-criteria analysis. As we have seen earlier, it is relatively useless to use precise numbers where we do not also have a clear picture of the differences between the values we are ascribing. A better method is to model the problem by using comparisons, both in terms of criteria and alternative values. We list the estimates in Table 8.3 under the respective criterion, numbering the project strategies as follows.

Project Strategies

1. Self-scanning
2. Online shopping list
3. Standardise store
4. App to find goods
5. Establish home delivery
6. Manage receipts digitally

Table 8.3. Criteria with strategy rankings.

Criteria	Ranking of strategies
How well does the project support our business?	1=6>5>2=4>3
Do we have the technical skill to carry it out?	1=5>2=4=6>3
How fast is the ROI?	2=5=6>4>1>3
Are the benefits of the project well defined and believeable?	1=5>2=4=6>3

Since this is a multi-criteria analysis, the strategies are, as before, first ranked under each criterion according to Table 8.3. In the table, the project strategies are represented by their numbers and are ranked, with the most preferred to the left. '>' means that a strategy is better than the next, while '=' signifies that they are equal within that criterion. Thereafter, the criteria are ranked too. The criteria rankings on a thermometer scale are shown in Figure 8.3. Here, a criterion that appears higher up is more important than one that appears lower down. The distances between the criteria indicate strengths, in the same way as in Table 6.11.

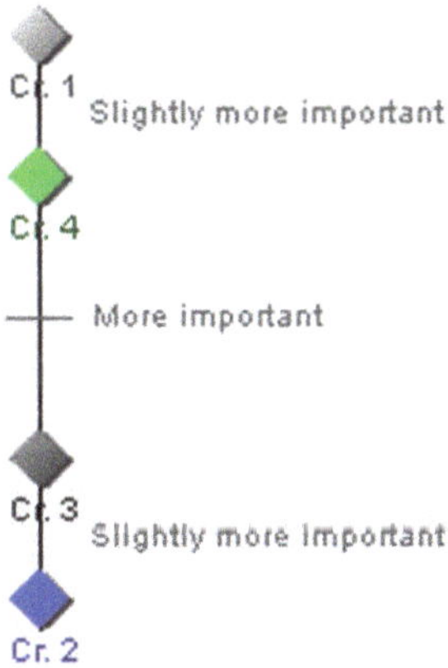

Figure 8.3. Criteria-ranking in the example.

In Figure 8.3, we can see that business support (criterion 1) is considered slightly more important than well-defined project benefits (criterion 4), which in turn are more important than the return on investment (criterion 3), which is perceived as slightly more important than technical knowledge (criterion 2).

The overall structure and results of the rankings can then be modelled in a single-level multi-criteria tree, as in Figure 8.4.

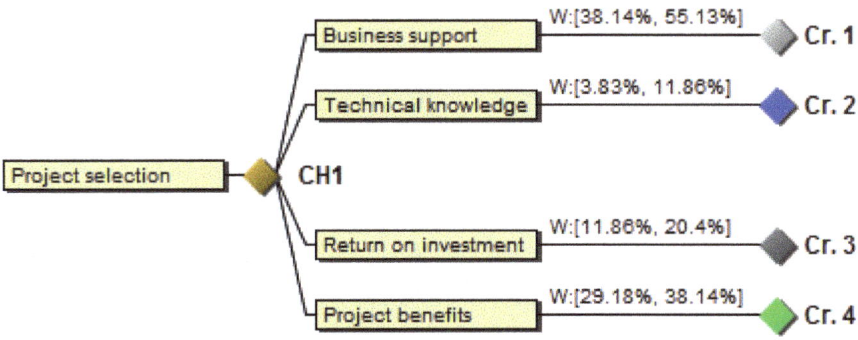

Figure 8.4. Multi-criteria tree.

How the strategies relate to each other can then be calculated and the result appears in a result window of DecideIT, as shown in Figure 8.5. An easy way to interpret the figure is to look at the vertical bars. The higher up a bar in the results window, the better the strategy it represents. We can thus see that self-scanning is the best (uppermost) option in this case, followed by establishment (which is the second highest), and so on. The strategy numbering is: 1. Self-scanning; 2. Online shopping list; 3. Standardise store; 4. App to find goods; 5. Establish home delivery; 6. Manage receipts digitally.

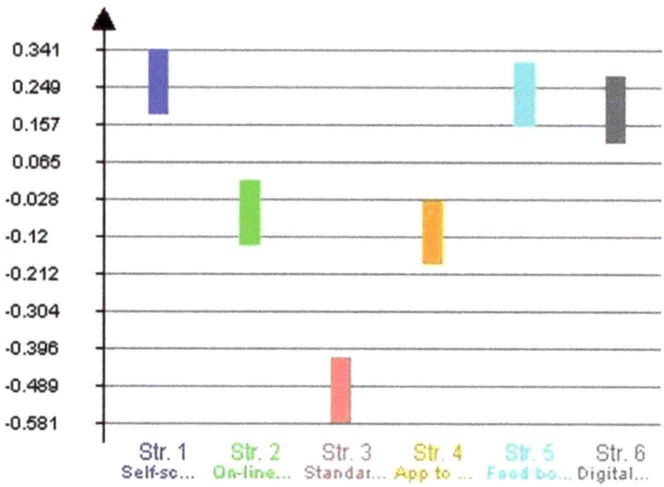

Figure 8.5. Analysis of alternatives and results.

Thus, in such an analysis, one must first rank the strategies under each criterion and then rank the importance of each criterion. Thereafter, the entire decision situation can be evaluated, while the complete set of rankings is also taken into account. Moreover, the effects of any uncertainty in the background information can also be studied to determine how reliable the solutions are, and whether more information would be required for a conclusive result. The details regarding this procedure were described in Chapter 7.

Table 8.4 shows the results of applying the different models. An interesting observation regarding the above three examples is that they generate different results.

Table 8.4. Comparison of project rankings.

Naïve method without weights	Weighted scoring model	Multicriteria analysis
Establish home delivery	Handle digital receipts	Self scanning
Self scanning	Establish home delivery	Establish home delivery
Handle digital receipts	Self scanning	Handle digital receipts
Online shopping list	Online shopping list	Online shopping list
App to find groceries	App to find groceries	App to find groceries
Standardise store	Standardise store	Standardise store

The variety of results in Table 8.4 indicates how important it is to think through the choice of decision model and to spend some time structuring the criteria and strategies as well as their relative importance. A general recommendation is to stay away from over-simplified decision models, since they often provide insufficient support for the actual situations that they claim to represent.

8.2.1.2. Financial Models

Financial models deliver analyses based on financial data, such as the speed of the return on investment, the anticipated monetary value of the investment at a future point in time, or various types of comparison between costs and revenues. This information is important and should not be disregarded, but its value from a project portfolio perspective is limited, as the models disregard the soft benefits to which IT projects in particular contribute, and also owing to the fact that IT projects tend to be complex and permeate large swathes of the business, which makes it difficult to pinpoint the effects of IT investments, as they are often dispersed across the organisation. The last, and perhaps most serious, drawback is that benefits must be expressed in monetary value, which we know is almost impossible for soft benefits. Despite these problems, the models are still used extensively in project portfolios, for the simple reasons that they are seemingly easy and inexpensive to use, and that financial arguments carry weight in organisational decision processes. Some examples of financial models used in portfolio management are presented below.

Present Value and Future Value

The analysis of present value and future value introduces the parameter of time and considers what the value of an investment will be if return requirements and fluctuations in the value of money are taken into account. The present value is derived by recalculating all of the project's payment consequences (expected payments and disbursements) since the project began, then adding them up, and discounting them according to relevant interest rates. Future value is instead derived by calculating the corresponding total at some point in the future. Normally, money now is preferable to the same amount of money at some point in the future (time preference). Future amounts may not be secure (What will sales actually be? How long will development take, and what will the hourly rates be?) and a compensation for the risk taken is desirable. The amounts are therefore calculated using an interest rate that includes both the time preference and the risk. The further into the future an amount falls, the less it is worth today (net present value).

The Payback Method

The payback method focuses on how fast an investment pays for itself, or how quickly money is returned (the repayment period). If EUR 1,000,000 is invested in starting to sell goods through a company's website and there is an increase in revenue due to the investment of EUR 200,000 per year, it will take five years to get the investment back (disregarding inflation and interest rates). In a situation where we are to evaluate prospective projects, we must define an acceptable payback period and compare the various projects to it. According to this approach, the method with the shortest payback or repayment time should be chosen. Unfortunately, it is rarely that simple, and there are other aspects that must be considered.

Benefit versus Cost

Another common method is to try to compare the utility of a project with the cost. Simply put, if the benefit of a project is greater than the cost, it is a good investment. There are certain challenges with this method, as it requires all parameters to be quantified (usually in monetary terms), which can be very difficult. Several researchers and organisations, such as the Gartner Group, have tried to create frameworks/models to calculate the benefits of an IT investment, so far without complete success, which makes the model valuable mostly in theory, but unfortunately not easily practically applicable to IT investments. It is simply too difficult to quantify the benefits, and it is often almost impossible to accurately pinpoint the precise benefits that an IT project will yield. Digitisation is a complex interweaving of IT use and organisational practices, and tangible organisational outcomes that someone claims stem from a digitisation project could be partly or wholly due to other factors, either internal or external to the organisation. Even if the benefits can be quantified, it is important to remember that this model only evaluates a specific investment from a cost/benefit perspective, and not whether it is right according to strategic reasoning, ethical, social, or other standards.

8.2.2. Qualitative Models

Unlike the quantitative models presented earlier, qualitative models focus on soft benefits and values and try to analyse them from a more holistic perspective. Examples of models used in projects and portfolio management are presented below.

8.2.2.1. Expert Groups

A common means of evaluating project portfolios is simply to use expert groups that, through discussion and possibly modelling, decide which projects it is relevant to start. This way of working is not as rigorous as, for example, multi-criteria analysis, but still works well in cultures and situations where consensus-building is important, such as Sweden. Of course, these discussions can be carried out with the help of more rigorous practices, such as workshops and modelling, but they lack the numerical basis that many quantitative models generate. The idea behind this approach is that since most consequences of IT use are difficult to quantify, we should instead focus on discussing and intuiting or "guessing" the value of the benefits.

8.2.2.2. Sacred Cow

Unfortunately, the sacred cow is an all-too-common way of selecting projects. In effect, this means that a project is proposed by someone in the organisation who has great power, such as the CEO, and because of this, the project is begun, since there is little or no opposition to a proposal from the CEO. These projects are seldom successful, and usually become empty shells without money or resources. Of course, there are exceptions. One is Steve Jobs' firm enforcement of the proprietary nature (patents or rights owned by the organisation) of Apple's products. This worked, because users in general were not interested in customising their computers, and were rather more focused on usability and function. Even though this decision took some time to be accepted by consumers, today it can be considered highly successful.

8.2.2.3. Necessity

All organisations have an outside world by which they are affected but cannot control. This sometimes forces them to run projects, such as new legal requirements that make it necessary to correct a product, increase security, and so on. Another example is a bank offering to handle customer banking issues via the Internet. This should be seen as necessary if the banks do not want to lose their market share. There are different types of requirements to which an organisation can be exposed. Their only similarity is that they force action and change. Operating systems such as MS Windows, OS X, iOS, and Android, which serve as a foundation for other products, are good examples of must-have projects. Microsoft no longer has a choice on whether to develop Windows further or not, since so much of their business depends on it. In these cases, project evaluation is unnecessary, and the focus should be on implementing the projects as smoothly and cost-efficiently as possible.

8.2.2.4. Product Improvement / Extension of Product

Today, organisations must work actively with their products and develop them continuously in order to compete within their field. There are examples in all industries and in almost all types of products. In the automotive industry, this process of renewing the design of an older model, or modernising its look and thus the user experience, is called a face-lift. In the IT industry, it is seen in updated versions of existing software, apps that can be expanded and that continuously get new features, and so on. Improving or expanding existing products is central, as it is not only cost-effective, but also extends a product's lifecycle, as these are becoming shorter and shorter.

8.2.3. Balancing the Portfolio

The challenge faced by the leader of a project portfolio is to find the right balance between different projects. They must decide which projects should be started so as to ensure that there are new platforms in progress, come up with new technology, develop new products, and improve existing ones. Each project idea is evaluated to ensure that it fits into the portfolio structure, so as to avoid a situation whereby, for example, as a product company, there are no new products in progress or too much time is spent on research. To support the work of balancing the portfolio, there are a number of tools that not only help us choose projects, but also visualise how the portfolio should look.

Instead of evaluating specific projects using quantitative and qualitative models, we can look at how our company portfolio is balanced, the types of projects we run, and match that with what kind of organisation we want to be. For example, a company should have a healthy mix of new development, improvement of established products, and in some cases research; if any of these is missing, the company risks being left without products in the future. By continuously analysing the balance of a project portfolio, one can invest in the right projects, i.e. those that will help the organisation to survive and be competitive in the future. Below are two examples of how this approach can be implemented. The first example is based on the model of the aggregated project plan and the second uses a Boston Consulting Group (BCG) matrix. Both models offer a graphic visualisation of the balance of the portfolio, which is important for explaining decisions to, and involving, stakeholders.

8.2.3.1. The Aggregated Project Plan

The aggregated project plan is a powerful tool for visualising, working with, and balancing project portfolios. The idea is to place projects in the model based on project type and show the major product and process changes they entail. Usually, projects are entered as shapes, where the area of the shape indicates the size of the budget. This not only provides a graphic depiction of the portfolio, but also enables us to see how the organisation's money is invested, and what proportion of investment is allocated to each project type. The following process is the starting point for coming up with a series of proposals for projects:

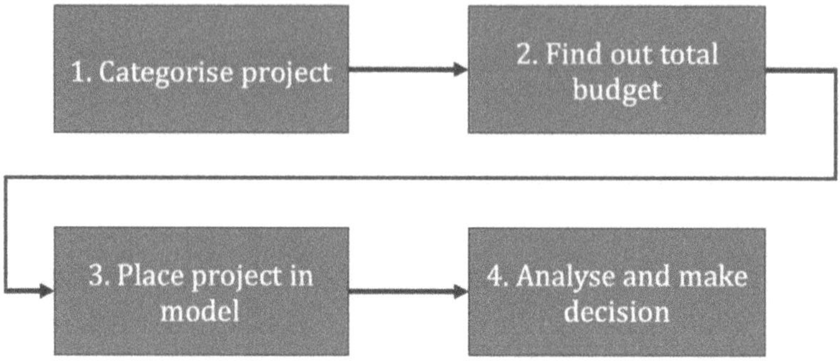

Figure 8.6. Process for handling project proposals.

We can use our retail-chain example. The following six projects are included in the example and the first step in the process is to arrange them into different categories. The categories can be determined by the organisation itself, but below we will use four common categories.

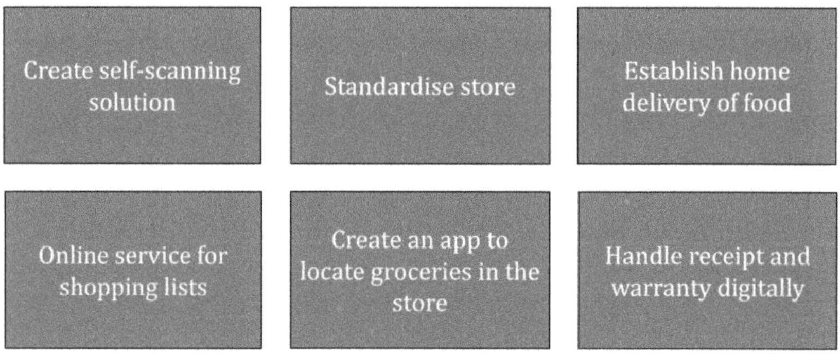

Figure 8.7. Sample projects.

The aggregated project plan uses four categories that combined cover all of the projects that are reasonable for an organisation to run. Categorisation is not an exact science, and a project can be assigned to more than one category. The four categories are research projects, product development, platform projects, and improvement projects.

Research Projects

Defining a research project is not easy, as it can relate to just about anything. However, unlike other projects, there is no requirement to deliver a particular product. A company can choose to start a research project to develop new technologies, such as 6G wireless technology, on which Ericsson and several other companies are working, or a faster algorithm for storing and retrieving data from Google's cloud. Such projects provide the technology necessary to develop the products of the future as opposed to a clear product that can be sold. Furthermore, research projects fail (i.e. simply do not deliver what was intended) relatively often. Research normally involves high risk, so failed projects are to be expected.

Product Development

A product such as a new car model or an IT system is usually developed through a project. Product development projects are arguably the most common category of projects, and organisations normally run a large number of them. This category is characterised by a product or service focus: i.e., it will deliver a product that will generate revenue for the organisation in the future. In other words, there is a great focus on delivery, costs, and schedule.

Platform Projects

In order to develop new products, it is sometimes necessary to create new technology, a new platform to build on, or a platform that enables, for example, specific software. Projects such as developing Windows or iOS are platform projects, as they form the basis for numerous innovations. A platform project is usually characterised by large budgets and relatively flexible time frames. Platform projects are usually very important within an organisation: think about what the next version of Windows means for Microsoft, or 6G for Ericsson. This type of project must succeed and can cost almost whatever is needed. Other business-related examples could be a new website as a platform for communication.

Improvement

Existing products, like everything else, have a lifecycle, a time span during which they are of interest in the market and create revenue. Depending on the product, this time span will vary, and it is the company's job to improve and expand existing products so that it can continue to make money from them. Improvements and changes to existing products can be anything from a face-lift of a car model, to new features in an app, or expanding a service portfolio. Projects of this kind are traditionally quite short and introduce a small number of changes/improvements incrementally.

In our retail-chain example, we can categorise the projects according to Table 8.5.

Table 8.5. Project categorisation, example.

Project	Category	Budget	Explanation
Create self-scanning solution	Platform	5000000	This creates a service that stores can offer their customers but also implements a new customer interaction that should be able to function as a platform for future services
Standardise store	Improvement	1000000	ICA works continuously with creating a better store and this is one more step in that process
Establish home delivery of food	Breakthrough	3000000	Establishes a new channel and a new market to reach customers with food
Online service for shopping lists	Improvement	500000	Refines and extends current services
Create an app to locate groceries in the store	Improvement	500000	Most stores offer maps if needed and this would be an improvement and extension of that
Handle receipt and warranty digitally	Improvement	3000000	Receipts are handled manually on paper and this would improve and extend the receipt process

The next step in the process is to place the projects in a diagram that helps us to visualise the portfolio. We analyse the projects and rank them based on the size of their impact on the processes, and the size of the product changes introduced. The size of the squares in our case indicates the size of the project budget. In Figure 8.8, it becomes clear that our main focus at present should be to improve what we have: we see self-scanning as a platform for the future, and home delivery as a way of establishing a new market, from which we expect future revenue.

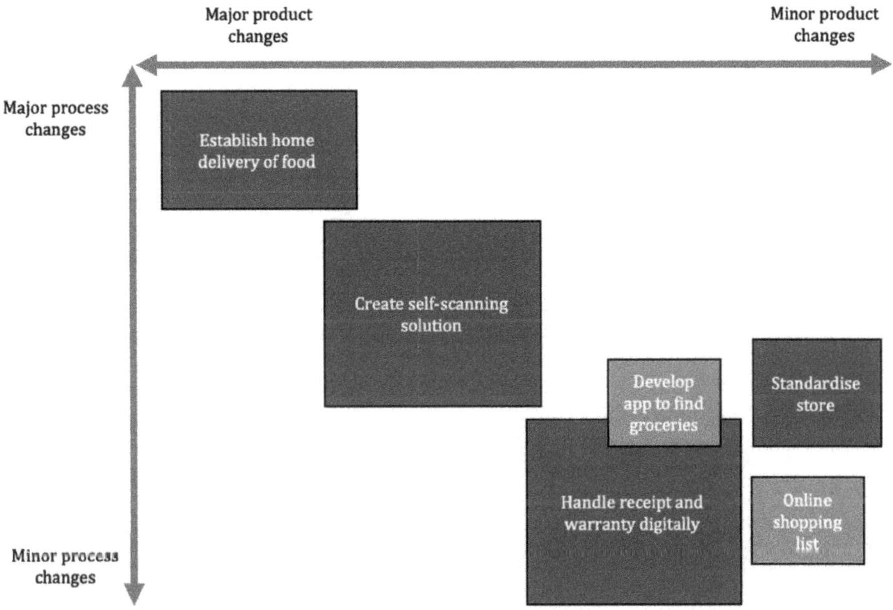

Figure 8.8. Application of the aggregate project plan.

When faced with the choice of whether to undertake new projects, we can place them in the model below to produce a scenario on which to base our decisions. This is not an exact science, and should instead be seen as a form of decision support that gives decision-makers a better overview and a powerful tool to support their individual decision-making processes. The important thing is that the process arouses reflection and discussion within the organisation. An organisation must decide where in Figure 8.8 it should be; should it focus on research or product development? This is primarily determined by the organisation's goals and strategies, but also by the industry in which it operates.

An organisation within the retail trade should reasonably focus most heavily on developing new products and improving existing ones, and far less on research projects.

8.2.3.2. Boston Consulting Group Matrix

The BCG matrix and other two-by-two matrices are common in management and leadership studies and practice, and also in project portfolios. They aim to place projects in one of four fields in order to achieve a balance suited to the organisation's industry. It is important to point out that the applications of such matrices can differ, because each organisation is unique, so it is not possible to provide a specific formula. However, BCG matrices relate to products, so it is important that we consider which product the project aims to improve or develop.

There are four fields in a traditional BCG matrix, and in our example, these are: (1) Problem Child, (2) Star, (3) Cash Cow, and (4) Dog. Most new products, such as an iPhone app or a specific car model, start out as 'problem children', in that it is always uncertain whether they will be successful. If the product creator is lucky, the problem child becomes a star thanks to its great development potential, and thus assumes a significant market share. One example of this is the Angry Birds game, which was a great success (and the fifty-second attempt by its creator company, Rovio, to produce a hugely successful game). After a while on the market, development potential decreases (but market share remains stable), and a product becomes a 'cash cow'. The company now makes big money from the product, but it has reached its peak, and from now on its market share will steadily decline and it will eventually become a 'dog', i.e., a product that is considered old and outdated.

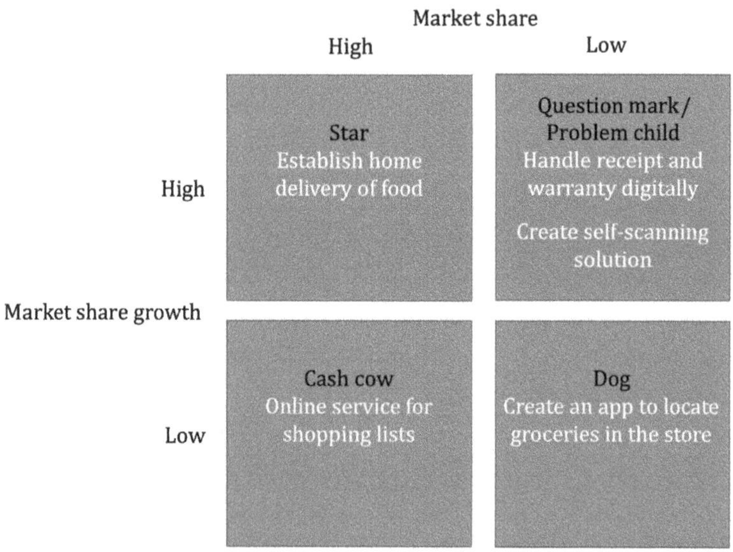

Figure 8.9. Application of Boston Consulting Group matrix.

There are many applications for the information we might glean from a BCG matrix, but from a portfolio perspective; its focus is creating projects that generate new products that will become stars of the future, updating and renewing existing products so that they can resume star status, and retiring products that have become too old and not profitable enough. The strength of any matrix lies in the graphic image that serves as a clear basis for making decisions from the outside, and that should provoke discussion in the organisation, thus leading to better decisions. If we apply the BCG matrix to the retail chain example, the process begins by first linking the organisation's projects to the products that they are striving either to develop or to improve. For example, a project for handling receipts is proposing a completely new product and would therefore be categorised as a problem child, as we do not know whether it will be positively received by customers.

8.2.4. Strategic Alignment and Agility

It is an established fact that IT initiatives are important for supporting an organisation's business, and are central to evaluating any project. The question is to what extent the proposed project aligns with IT strategies and, by extension, business strategies. Projects that do not support these strategies should never be given a green light, and projects that no longer support those strategies (i.e., because strategies have changed) should be discontinued. Over the years, a number of different models have been presented regarding the implementation of strategic alignment. The most elaborate and established is the strategic alignment model by Henderson and Venkatraman (1999), which model focuses on the link between business strategies and IT strategies from four perspectives:

1. *Strategy execution.* This perspective emphasises that business strategies not only drive design choices, but also IT infrastructure and the decisions around it. Business management sets the strategies and IT management implements them. In this way, there is a clear link between strategy decisions and IT decisions, as well as the design and infrastructure they use.
2. *Technical potential.* This perspective regards IT strategies as the basis of infrastructure and technical decisions at more junior

levels within the organisation. Senior managers should thus set an organisation's visions for technology and technology investment, and the IT staff are the architects who implement them. In this way, the vision is firmly linked to the business benefit, as it is developed at a higher level where individuals have a better overview of the business, and who leave implementation to the IT department.

3. *Competitive potential.* This perspective focuses on how IT affects strategies and goals. Not only does IT help achieve such goals, but it also creates opportunities for new strategies and the development of existing ones. This perspective is important for exploiting the opportunities that IT creates.
4. *Service level.* From this perspective, it is necessary that the IT department functions well and is structured satisfactorily. It is the role of management to prioritise and help with the allocation of limited resources. It is important, however, that this process is not conducted solely from a technical perspective but includes, for example, licences, investments, and project start-ups. The IT manager's role is to guide the group towards set business goals according to certain business priorities.

What is most striking about the above model is the close collaboration between the IT manager and senior managers. IT highlights the importance of active leadership at the highest level, and must support the business and its goals, which is only ensured through mutual cooperation. Another aspect that cannot be ignored is the fact that today there are many organisations that do not have their own IT department or internal IT skills. It is also reasonable to believe that the number of such organisations will increase, as more and more IT functions can now be purchased in cloud solutions. If so, it is important, as we highlight elsewhere in this book, that business managers shoulder their responsibility and drive IT issues as a central aspect of doing business. This requires insight on digitisation, either from within the business management team, or via external expertise consulted to support strategic dialogues.

8.3. Are We Using Our Capacity Correctly?

All organisations have the capacity and opportunity to invest in new ideas. Capacity is usually equated with resources, such as money, personnel, or machines. Resources are ultimately limited in all organisations, because no organisation has an infinite supply of money or staff, so these must be balanced, and require thoughtful decision-making. Deciding how best to use resources is not easy; it requires assumptions and, in some cases, even guesswork. Employees and their time often create bottlenecks in projects, so we will focus below on efficient use of time as a resource.

An important starting point is to define what time means to an employee, and how much time an employee has in an organisation. The simple answer is that most people work about forty hours per week; however, part of that time will be spent on internal meetings and administration, so this is not all at the project manager's disposal. Consultancy companies usually expect their consultants to work for around 85-90% of their time on billable activities. From a project portfolio perspective, it is unreasonable to expect that an employee will spend 100% of their time working productively. Of course, it is desirable to minimise the time that cannot be used for a project, but there will always be start-up and switchover time, or time spent on coordination that may not feel like "getting the project done", etc. There is also a tendency to underestimate this "non-productive" share of total working hours.

The most important way to manage an employee's time effectively is not to spread it thinly across too many different activities. An employee working on several projects or often engaged in other activities will be less efficient and more stressed. In essence, this is because they will spend time switching between activities, thereby reducing effective working time. One must also consider the relationship between the employee's competence and the task they are working on. The gaming industry uses the term "flow". If a game challenges us at just the right level, i.e., it is not so difficult that we do not progress in it, and not so easy that it becomes boring, then it has "flow". The concept of "flow" is relevant to this discussion because an employee's skills must be at the right level for, or at a level slightly below, what is required by a certain task. When competence is harnessed most effectively and an employee feels motivated, this will easily prompt efficiency of time and energy. The third and final variable is the working group, which, if it functions well, provides an employee with support and help, which increase motivation and improve team performance. It is important that team members complement each other, through similar levels of competence in different areas, and through a sense of collective responsibility.

To summarise, effective use of time is about ensuring that an employee can focus on several tasks at once, and that the challenge presented should be well-matched to a particular employee's competence.

8.4. How Well Are Projects Implemented?

Evaluating how well projects are carried out is not easy, but it nonetheless requires thought. This section will introduce and discuss a number of issues surrounding project implementation, before indicating a number of approaches to project portfolios.

There are two basic phases of project evaluation: during project implementation, and after completion. Both are important, although they have different goals.

Evaluation of a project after its completion places the emphasis on organisational learning, by giving the organisation an opportunity to decide what did and did not work, so that working methods and routines can be changed to improve future projects. Unfortunately, many organisations act regard such evaluation as wasted, unproductive time. This is a major mistake, as organisational learning and development are vital parts of successful project execution. Whilst there may be organisational guidelines to evaluate and draw lessons from completed projects, such activities tend to be poorly prioritised. In agile approaches, recurring retrospectives—reflection time allotted at intervals during a project—are one way of narrowing the gap between the idea and the practice of evaluating projects.

Evaluating a project during its implementation means finding and solving problems, and steering the project towards an end goal, or in our case deciding how a portfolio should be adapted in order to be "effective". Basically, both types of evaluation seek to create a basis for decisions, in order to change a way of working, or the way a project or project portfolio is run, and they should be seen in this light.

8.4.1. Follow-up during Project Execution

The most common way to follow up on a project is to use key performance indicators (KPI). They measure different aspects of the projects in a portfolio as well as the portfolio itself, and assign them a value or rating. The value, or grade, is then used by the project or portfolio manager as a basis for making decisions. Common KPIs include the proportion of time spent on project activities, the amount spent versus the forecasted budget, or the actual number of activities completed compared to the projected number. There are many other KPIs, but they all have one thing in common: they require accurate information to work. KPIs are clustered to answer questions about how a project, such as keeping to budget, is progressing. However, there are a number of problems with them that should be highlighted. They usually require quantification of what is to be measured, that is, aspects of a project must be translated into numbers that can then be analysed. This is not always so easy, because project progress often depends on nebulous factors such as customer relationships and employee motivation, which are difficult to quantify.

KPIs also define what is measured and how. This often leads to measuring what is visible (or identifiable) and easy to measure, and omitting aspects that are complicated or that have not arisen, which in turn can generate a misleading perspective on a project. Organisations also tend to focus on financial variables, as these are easily accessible and measurable, but they may not always be as rewarding or enlightening from a project perspective.

The follow-up process attempts to gain a fuller picture of a portfolio. Although KPIs provide many answers, they do not create a full image, because they focus too much on details. They raise the question of how one ever knows that one has a correct and complete picture of a portfolio. If, for instance, we use ten KPIs to evaluate a project (in reality there are usually more) in a portfolio, it will unfortunately be impossible to tell whether that number is sufficient for us to have a reliable decision-making basis. We must therefore simply guess that the number of KPIs we choose is sufficient, and this is not the most appropriate way of dealing with uncertainty.

8.4.2. Follow-up after Project Completion

Once a project is completed, it is important to follow up on and evaluate it. This results primarily in organisational learning and allows us to benefit from experiences, good and bad, gained during the project's implementation. There are certain questions that should be answered, such as: (1) How well did our assumptions and plans match up with reality? (2) How realistic were the time estimates? (3) How well did our methods work, and what can we do better in future? There are, of course, many more questions that could be posed, but time constraints and resources usually limit the selection along these lines. Exactly how a follow-up, or post-mortem as it is often called, works depends on how the organisation works, the kind of information that is required, and so on. What is important is not *how* it is done, but that it is implemented and its results provide useful lessons.

8.5. Chapter Summary

Project portfolios are basically a collection of guesses and bets about the future, but in practical terms they are a collection of projects that need to be managed in order to avoid conflicts, failures or mis-investments. How this is done depends largely on how an organisation views its projects and works with strategies.

This chapter has offered a range of ways of working, and has flagged the most important areas. We began by considering how certain projects are selected, and what such decisions are based on. We have highlighted the challenges in quantifying the benefits of IT projects, and have examined both the qualitative and quantitative models for doing so. The chapter then described two ways of visualising a project portfolio: the aggregated project plan and the BCG matrix. These models can easily produce a visual image of a portfolio. We then briefly presented a model for strategic alignment. The important thing to understand here is that an organisation's goals, strategies, and business models are constantly changing, and that it is therefore of utmost importance that ongoing project evaluation supports its current goals and strategies, and that action is taken if they do not. We ended the chapter with a discussion of resources and follow-up as vital parts of portfolio work.

The information we obtain from the models and the working methods can only provide help and support, not firm directives. It is almost impossible to create processes and systems in an organisation that give unequivocal answers about which projects we should start, which we should end, and which we should invest in. All of this depends on the wider context in which the organisation is situated and the current events affecting it.

This chapter has established the central concepts and issues that are important in project portfolio work. In the next chapter, we will focus on the implementation of projects, the challenges posed by such work, and the tools we can use to solve them.

8.6. Reading Tips

Below are a number of articles and books that provide more information about certain topics covered in this chapter.

- Pennypacker, James and Retna, San (2009). *Project Portfolio Management: A View from the Management Trenches*. Hoboken, NJ: Wiley, https://doi.org/10.1002/9780470549155.
- Ward, John and Daniel, Elisabeth (2012). *Benefits Management: How to Increase the Business Value of Your IT Projects* (2nd edn). Hoboken, NJ: Wiley, https://doi.org/10.1002/9781119208242.
- Enoch, Clive (2015). *Project Portfolio Management: A Model for Improved Decision-making*. New York: Business Expert Press.
- Moustafaev, Jamal (2017). *Project Portfolio Management in Theory and Practice: Thirty Case Studies from around the World*. Boca Raton, FL: Auerbach Publications, https://doi.org/10.1201/9781315367200.
- Frey, Thorsten (2014). *Governance Arrangements for IT Project Portfolio Management: Qualitative insights and a Quantitative Modelling Approach*. Wiesbaden: Springer Gabler, https://doi.org/10.1007/978-3-658-05661-2.
- Rajegopal, Shan; McGuin, Philip and Waller, James (2007). *Project Portfolio Management: Leading the Corporate Vision*. Basingstoke: Palgrave Macmillan, https://doi.org/10.1057/9780230206496.

9. Managing Projects

Management of digital transformation projects is basically about moving from Point A to Point B, delivering what is required within budget and schedule. The big questions are therefore: Is the road straight or curvy? Do we know the goal from the beginning, or do we learn from experience of a project, and continually negotiate the path we are taking? These questions can elicit different views on how projects should be run, but are still an important part of project management.

9.1. Goals and Definitions

In Chapter 2 we discussed the goals of organisations, and we use the same idea here in relation to projects. Goals are the objectives that an organisation wants to achieve, in either the short or long term, and how detailed they are depends on which level within the organisation sets them. A CEO sets broad goals that are then successively broken down into smaller, achievable goals via projects. There are different kinds of goals, such as personal goals, business goals and, most importantly in this discussion, project goals.

When talking about goals in a project context, it is important to emphasise that we are really talking about two types of goal: (1) Project objectives: the concrete goals of the project, such as building a house, delivering an IT system or designing a car, and (2) Impact goals: the expected benefit of the project, such as increased sales of a product, a new line of sporty cars or a stronger sense of competitiveness.

All goals are equally important, but project managers in organisations generally focus almost exclusively on project goals. Recently, however, organisations and project managers have increasingly begun to discuss the fact that project managers are also responsible for impact goals. We will examine this perspective later in this chapter. However, for

 https://doi.org/10.11647/OBP.0350.09

our immediate purposes, goals can be categorised into two distinct categories. The traditional school views goals as something that can be clearly defined and described in a requirement document or the like, whereas the non-traditional school sees goals as difficult to define and describe, and argues that they should therefore arise from learning and a direct understanding of the problems that a particular project is trying to solve. These different views on project goals are central to how we work and which processes we use. This in turn leads us to two basic types of project model: sequential and iterative.

9.2. Project Models

There are many project models (some of which are used more than others), such as the waterfall model, PROPS, Scrum, and Kanban. As noted above, they can be divided into two main categories: sequential and iterative. Below, we will review the models according to categorisation, and describe the different steps involved in each. It is important to highlight that hybrids and other types of mixed models may well exist, but our focus here will be on the simple, delineated models.

9.2.1. Sequential Project Models

Sequential models have a long tradition and have evolved from a need for structure and control. The best-known sequential model is the waterfall model, introduced in the 1970s by Winston W. Royce. The model is based on a sequence of activities, each of which produces information required for the next step. The process is intended to be carried out sequentially, thus ensuring a well-functioning, tried and tested system by the end. The waterfall model is characterised by rigorous control via documents and other deliveries, which was more necessary during the 1970s and 1980s when IT activities were largely run by technicians and were frequently disorderly, or at least not customer-focused.

In order for the waterfall model and models such as the V model to function optimally, a project must have a well-defined goal that does not change, because it is difficult to go back to the model and change the basic requirements that were set at the beginning of the project. The process starts by defining what should be accomplished, and how this might be done, which leads to a requirements document, and in many respects a contract then forms the basis for design and development.

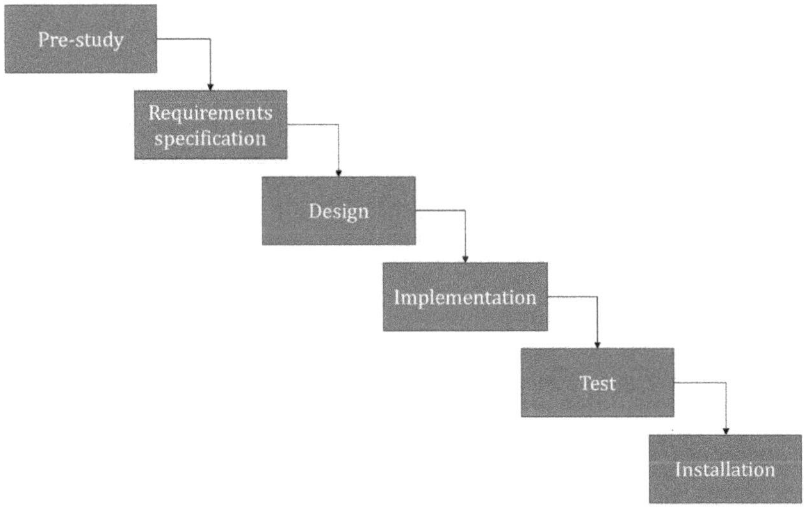

Figure 9.1. Example of the waterfall model.

Step 1: Pre-study
The first step (which is not really part of the project) is a feasibility study. This investigates whether there are enough resources, knowledge, time, and so on to carry out the project in a reasonable manner, within the budget and time frame that the customer has requested. If the answer is yes, the project continues, and if the answer is no, then it ends.

Step 2: Requirements Specification
Managing requirements or understanding the required functionality of an IT system is difficult and time-consuming, but a crucial part of the waterfall method. The requirements specification is the document that outlines the functionality that will be implemented in the system. When working to procure a new IT system, the requirements specification functions as a contract between the client and the supplier. As the requirements specification is important, requirements management will be discussed in more detail in Section 9.3.2.

It is common for this step of the process to be based on a customer's system description, for example, the main requirements (requirements that must be met) and set requirements (requirements that provide added value) that the system can deliver. The requirements specification process is about translating the customer's requirements into clear systems requirements that can be implemented and delivered.

Step 3: Design

Once the functions that should be included in the system are identified, it is time to create it. A systems design contains all the elements needed to build the system, including everything from visual identity, graphic design, and database structures to flow charts that describe flows in code or class charts. It should be possible to build the final system on the basis of this design. In order for a design to be implemented, it must be easy to understand, so that the developer, graphic artist, or other worker understands exactly what is meant. Common means of expressing design in IT projects include techniques such as the Unified Modelling Language (UML). This tool consists of different types of graphical representations of, for example, flows in the system, information, and how a user interacts with the system. UML is described in countless books and on the Internet, and some reading recommendations are listed at the end of this chapter.

Step 4: Construction

In this step, the system is built, according to the design document. Here, traditional system development processes take over and programmers, for example, create the system. Most of the work (in time) in the project takes place during this step.

Step 5: Integration

A company's IT systems must be integrated or interconnected. It is common to use an external system to manage logins, so that users do not need multiple passwords (single-sign-on). Data used by many sub-systems need to be shared, rather than duplicated, and so on. Integration is often one of the most difficult tasks in an IT project and it is usually the most competent technical staff who work on it.

Step 6: Test

When the system is fully integrated, testing starts. In this step, the functionality of the system is tested so as to iron out errors, both visible and hidden. Testing is a major aspect of IT and is often complex and difficult to implement properly.

Step 7: Installation
After the system has been implemented and tested, it is time to hand it over to the customer or to deploy it in the organisation, and put it into production. This is often a relatively complicated process that requires extensive collaboration with the customer and knowledge of many areas within IT.

9.2.2. Problems with the Waterfall Model

The waterfall model is still the central and most widely used model in many industries. However, we see major changes in, for example, how to produce goods and the length of projects, that have gradually caused the waterfall model to lose ground. The waterfall model was created when IT projects were large, required structure, had low-to-medium complexity, and it was still possible to set firm goals. Today, the world looks rather different and these conditions are not necessarily a given. IT is complex and a project's goal or functionality will typically be revised repeatedly during the project timeline. On the one hand, this is because it is difficult to define exact functions and there is a learning curve in any project; the customer simply becomes more skilled and more informed and, during the project, builds up their own and the organisation's knowledge of IT and IT systems. On the other hand, external and internal conditions can change, meaning that further IT support is required to keep the organisation operating effectively. The customer and the project now require greater interaction and visibility, and waterfall models suffer because the product development is invisible to the customer. It is only late in the process that the customer has the opportunity to test the system, and at that point they can have minimal influence on the end result. This lack of prolonged customer impact contrasts with the customer's need to be able to change and correct the target image and requirements during the project.

Another aspect of product visibility is that we are now also looking for more innovative ways to deliver IT systems or programs. This is especially evident with apps and games, which can be delivered to the customer in different forms. It is possible, for example, to buy a basic version of a game/app and then add features as you go. Agile methods allow innovative delivery, where a product can be accessed in increments. Unlike in the waterfall model, it is central and part of the working method to involve the customer during the project (as opposed to just at the start and the end), in order to deliver a flexible end product. The waterfall model also focuses on functionality, and the aim of the project is to ensure that all requested functions are available. This is a view that does not reflect current discussions about how in order to realise the benefits of a project, IT must deliver business value to motivate investments. Instead, flexibility and the gradual development of understanding of needs and possible solutions form the basis and primary focus of agile methods.

9.2.3. Iterative Methods: Focus on Utility

Iterative models (or agile models) are considered by many to be the next step in project management development, and in this sense represent 'the new'. Basically, iterative models are exactly what they sound like; work is done in stages and the plan, work, assess cycle is repeated over and over again. Some would trace the origins of iterative models or agile methods, as they are normally called, to the creation of Lean (coined in 1988 by John Krafcik), a cool for car production that has gradually evolved into a tool for realising value in all manner of projects. However, this change actually began even earlier because prototypes and iterative development have been concepts in the IT industry since at least the 1980s. The starting point for agile methods includes the business value, the benefit of activities and efforts to cut out "unnecessary work" or, in other words, work that does not create value, and to try to reprioritise those activities that at present seem most fruitful.

Agile methods were born out of a need to handle change in projects more smoothly. Recurring priority discussions between the "customer"—the client or project owner in whose business the project result is to be used—and the executors, who build the solutions, are central. Agile thinking is a popular solution to the challenge of managing difficult-to-understand initiatives, where the customer gradually learns more about their needs and how an IT solution can help to satisfy them, and where the developer gradually learns more about the customer's needs and operations, and about how technical solutions can be developed.

9.2.3.1. The Agile Manifesto

The agile manifesto was presented in 2001 and forms the basis of the agile method. It presents the philosophical ideas behind agile thinking, and how to look at work and projects. The manifesto presents four theses: individuals and interactions versus processes and tools; working software versus comprehensive documentation; customer collaboration versus contract negotiations; and responding to change versus following the plan. These theses, or approaches, form the basis of the agile movement and its methods.

Individuals and Interactions versus Processes and Tools
In agile methods, the focus is on the individual and their competence, and projects rely on a group being able to self-organise through communication between members to solve problems and undefined processes and tools. For this to work, a well-functioning team who trust each other and allow open communication, is necessary. The team members must also be competent in their respective areas and constantly strive to improve and develop themselves. It is important that they take responsibility for the group and for the work they have undertaken, and it is important that all members understand this and take it seriously. There has been some criticism of agile methods because self-organisation is regarded as difficult in practice. It requires all members to take on considerable responsibility and teams to be very tight-knit, which can be difficult as most companies have a resource pool that cannot change from project to project.

Functioning Software versus Comprehensive Documentation
It is important that the team builds, experiments, and works closely towards a solution, using prototypes instead of spending time on documenting. Evolutionary work with prototypes and modularised solutions is central to all agile models. Documentation is not productive, whereas designing and coding are. This does not mean, however, that there should be no documentation, but rather that one should document thoughtfully and effectively. Agile methods do not advocate long reports on functionality or changes.

Customer Collaboration versus Contract Negotiations
The customer is seen as a natural and important part of the project, and is expected to participate and make important decisions as it develops. Agile methods are based on a partnership rather than a strict customer-supplier relationship. This means that we should move away from the concept of "the customer", because in a sense there is no customer separate from the project in the agile world, since everyone works together on the project, preferably with the same target goal.

Responding to Change versus Following the Plan
The ability to respond to a customer's desire for change and the resulting learning curve are more important than following a predefined plan. Handling change smoothly is a basic principle in agile methods; we know that things will change and that the specifications may be proven wrong, and this should impact our approach. In the agile world, we start with what we know, which is documented and regarded as a living requirement specification. Everything that the project adds or changes along the way is a natural part of the work. This is described in more detail in the example of Scrum below.

9.2.3.2. Example of an Agile Method: Scrum

Scrum is the agile project method most widely used in the IT industry today. Methods always need to be adapted to the situation, and this applies no less to Scrum. Its name is a reference to rugby, and the cluster that starts the game. It is no coincidence that this word was chosen, as the success of Scrum, like that of many other agile models, depends on how well the project team works together, and requires them to work in tight-knit groups to inform each other and solve problems.

There are a number of concepts in Scrum that must be clear in order to understand and apply the method. For starters, there is a product backlog that contains all identified requirements. This does not mean that it contains all requirements; the backlog is usually an incomplete list that is continuously expanded or adjusted after discussions with the customer, and according to how the project is progressing. In addition to a product backlog, there is also a sprint backlog that contains all requirements or functions to be implemented in the next stage. The primary challenge for agile thinking is a situation where the goal is unclear and is continuously changing. To run the project, however, one requires the outside world to appear stable and unchanging. This is achieved in agile thinking through time-boxing, which involves setting a maximum time for a stage, to create a hypothetical scenario with a start date and an end date, and, above all, a clear goal that must not be changed. This time interval (which is usually called a sprint) is normally between two and four weeks long, depending on the project and what will accommodate the work, and once it is set, no goals can be changed, and no new work introduced for its duration.

The process represented by Scrum is led by a Scrum Master who is equivalent to a project manager. The concept of project manager does not exist in scrums; the teams are self-organising, and the Scrum Master is responsible for several administrative tasks, problem-solving, and managing external communication.

The overall workflow in Scrum is similar to that in many other project methods, including the waterfall model, in that it is about implementing functionality and creating a product. What should be implemented is documented in a backlog. This backlog is then changed as tasks are completed and shipped, or as new information renders older backlog entries irrelevant, inefficient or otherwise undesirable, i.e., if the old entries do not promise to deliver enough value in the updated backlog context.

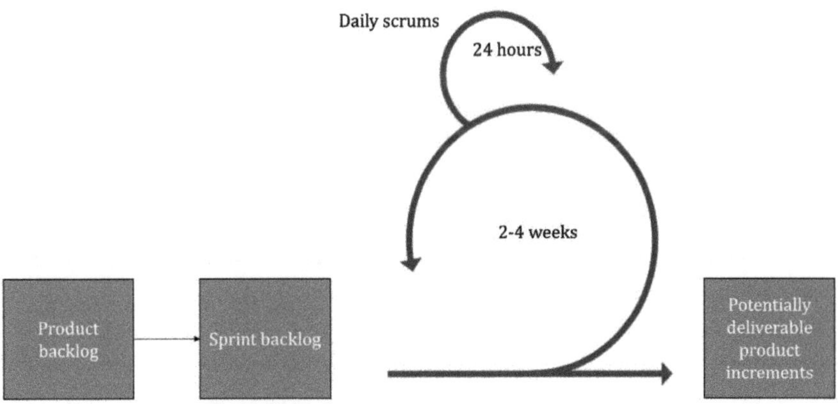

Figure 9.2. Scrum work process.

Step 1: Build the First Version of a Product Backlog

Since it is assumed that requirements cannot all be known from the beginning, this first step is about documenting requirements. This documentation can be achieved in different ways, such as through text, story or pictures. It is important that a product backlog is seen as a living list which, with the customer, is updated as changes arise, or new requirements are added. This can be done using the same approaches as for the waterfall method.

Table 9.1. Example of a backlog.

ID	Story	Estimate	Priority
1	Implement login using Facebook	3	1
7	Update graphical profile	4	2
12	Enable product name search	8	3
6	Update Tomcat server to new version	5	4
9	A customer should be able to see pictures of products	8	5
3	...		

Step 2. Decide What to Implement in the Next Sprint

The next step is to define what needs to be done during the next sprint, or which requirements to implement. According to Scrum, it is the customer who at this stage prioritises and decides what is done, on the advice of those who are technologically savvy, so as not to create problems with the sequencing of activities, and so that the task list is based on realistic time estimates. Once several functions have been selected, they must be refined, detailed, and explained, so that, for example, a developer can start programming the function once the sprint begins. Work time is estimated, and this determines how many functions can be accommodated during the two to four weeks of the sprint. The result of this sprint planning is what is usually called a sprint log, and the associated necessary technical descriptions. The sprint log contains a subset of what is to be implemented in the backlog.

Step 3. Development/Sprint

Work is now done on the function or other tasks that have been chosen for the sprint. The method is not set in stone, and even the waterfall model is possible. The most common approach is to split the work as a group and to then work individually with the support of other members. Each morning a fifteen-minute Scrum meeting is held, where the group members organise themselves by dividing the work and coordinating in a way that suits them. Each member of the team should ask: What did I do yesterday? What do I intend to do today? What can stop me from accomplishing what I set out to do today (so that I may request assistance)?

Step 4. Possible Delivery-ready Product

After every sprint, it is important that there is a sub-product that could theoretically be delivered to the customer; all the results of a sprint must be deliverable. This means that it must have been tested and integrated with previous deliveries. If it is possible that a function will not be completed within the specified sprint time, then the data will be returned to the reverse log and may be included in a later sprint.

Step 5. Show to the Customer

The penultimate step is to show the work to the customer. This allows for discussion of what has been done, and gives the customer the opportunity to test the prototype, provide feedback, suggest changes, and so on. Any additional changes made during this preview are added to the product backlog, to be sprinted at a later date.

Step 6. Sprint Overview

The final step is to evaluate the sprint: How did it work? What was good? What was bad? Is there anything about the working method that should be changed before the next sprint? This is an important step as it enables work changes, such as how time is spent. It is an essential part of Scrum to question and improve the model, to learn from previous sprints, and to improve the work process.

9.2.4. Problems with Agile Methods

We have previously discussed problems with the waterfall method, and agile methods equally have problems that should be noted. The first challenge is how well they really suit the way the market does business. In internal projects, this is not a problem, as the entire chain from financier to implementation can be controlled, but it is more problematic in a customer-supplier situation. Much of the business that is done within IT is about fixed price agreements, where a supplier takes on an assignment for delivery at a fixed price that is negotiated before the project starts. This way of working is the opposite of agile methods, where those involved have to be able to work more like partners with a current account. In reality, they do not know what the final price of the project will be, which makes the business relationship complex.

The second challenge is that agile methods require a team with the ability to self-organise without the involvement of an official project manager. This usually does not work completely smoothly. If the team is not experienced, coordination is required and the team will need support to self-organise. In larger projects, coordination between teams also becomes a challenge. The scrum masters must therefore meet in scrums (of scrums) in order to handle cross-team coordination. With six or seven people in a team, a third level of coordination will be needed. The larger the project, the more complicated cross-team coordination becomes.

The fact that the customer controls much of the work is the third challenge for the agile method. An ability to prioritise and drive the work forward requires relatively good knowledge of IT and systems development, which a customer normally does not have. In this case, one must guide the customer and converse with them in order to decide on sensible priorities. Also, sometimes customers may not be prepared to be as involved in the project as the method requires. In that case, someone on the developer side will have to act as the customer, thus introducing the risk that customer needs and priorities are not really understood or incorporated into the project.

9.2.4.1. Real-life Examples

In Chapter 2, we met an IT manager in a business area at a Swedish bank. To drive the development of systems there, IT managers work in projects. As mentioned in Chapter 3, they can run up to seventy parallel projects at a time. Here is what some of them say about working on projects:

> The projects I have been involved in have used the more traditional way of working, which is usually called cold waterfalls. I do not really like to call it a waterfall, because we have worked on iterations over time even though the project form itself has been a waterfall. You start with a needs analysis, then you go into a feasibility study. The needs analysis should show "what is the benefit, what is the value we get from this?", but you don't know what the price tag is. To find out, you need to do a feasibility study and in this, you go deeper into what solutions there are that you can develop to achieve the desired effect. With some luck, when the preliminary study is over, you will get an indication of what this will cost. Then you decide if you want to do it and then you go into a project.

The quotation above illustrates a common problem with agile methods. The cost of the project cannot be calculated with great certainty, and the project relies on a continual calculation of costs, which requires trust and cooperation, which do not always work. This means that many organisations work with hybrid models that combine sequential and iterative models to control the costs while utilising the positive aspects of agile methods.

> In the agile world that we are going into more and more, we ignore the formalities and the big plans, because they will still prove wrong. The feasibility study will be faulty, and you will not know what it costs. According to this approach, it is better to have agile cross-functional teams that are always in place and who can constantly follow up on what needs to be developed, because you can never know what you want. You know what outcome is needed, but how to achieve it? It is better to let the team take responsibility for that. The team makes small deliveries and makes sure the deliveries are executable early, so that we get something of value from the beginning, and then in theory we build on it. This is great, but it is not easy. You do not always know if it is best to run an agile approach or a more traditional one: "Now we collect all the resources we need and then we send out the people in the project." In the agile journey, it is the teams that build this to a greater extent; we start from the team. In some industries and areas, this works well and in others less well.

The quotation above certainly reflects reality. Seemingly good ideas can be difficult to realise. Agile methods are based on a sometimes too-perfect world, with a perfect team that can handle everything and has all the knowledge needed to organise everything itself, in close collaboration with the customer. Unfortunately, the reality is that project managers are not allowed to choose project members freely, and it is thus rare that self-organised teams work exactly as intended in a project. It is therefore important to work with different tools and at different levels. It is not wrong to make plans, even if they fail, because this makes us think about the future and teaches us about the situation, which in turn helps us to drive the project closer to success, regardless of method. And there can be situations where an agile approach is suitable.

> If you have an assignment to make continuous changes and improvements over a certain limited area in a company, such as a website, over a long period of time, then I strongly believe that there should be one or more teams working in the same area, where you should work agilely. There is a backlog (list of outstanding activities) of what it is you have to take and do. Over time, the teams will find out what is important. If you have flow in the work and a constant iterative dialogue with a product owner or area manager sitting in the middle of the team, then the agile method is perfect.

The connection between the IT department and the rest of the organisation has long been, and will continue to be, a key issue.

The quotations above show how important it is to think through the agile in an organisation: how should these thoughts be applied so that they deliver maximum business value and can at the same time be controlled? Using hybrid models is common and a division between overall architecture and how things are implemented is not only sensible but arguably necessary in today's complex, increasingly digitised world.

9.2.5. Which Method to Use and When

Which method to use and when will largely depend on the type of project and what kind of relationship the customer wants. Agile methods require the customer to actively participate in the project, and if the customer does not wish to do so, then it is safer to choose a more sequential model. In general, however, it can be said that the more uncertainty there is in a project, the more suitable an agile method will be. Conversely, the greater the stability, goal clarity, task familiarity, and size of a project, the more appropriate the waterfall method.

As noted, there are problems with both models, and nothing says that the waterfall model cannot be effective and deliver good results. Below are some examples of project types that fit each method.

9.2.5.1. Waterfall Model

- Fixed-price projects with a clear target.
- Short projects in which the limited time does not allow for changes.
- Projects whose goals are well-defined and relatively simple.
- Large projects whose tasks and solutions are familiar and possible to plan.

9.2.5.2. Agile Method

- Development of, for example, an app that you want to be able to deliver step by step.
- Unclear projects where the goal is not well-defined or clearly feasible.
- Complex projects in which changes are likely to occur.

This is a list of examples, as opposed to hard recommendations. In a given project, it is almost always possible to devise a way of using either method, or a combination of the two.

9.3. Common Skills, Tools, and Methods

Regardless of the method(s) used, there are a number of basic skills that a project manager should possess. Of course, needs vary between organisations and the tools and methods below should be seen as examples and suggestions of how to meet them.

9.3.1. Conducting a Feasibility Study

A feasibility study normally consists of five parts, each of which analyses a specific area of the project. It is important to point out here that these analyses cannot be made separately, because they will influence each other, so the feasibility study should be conducted as a whole. The five parts are: assessment of technology, economic aspects, legal aspects, operational considerations, and time schedule.

9.3.1.1. Technology

This part of the feasibility study is normally carried out by technically knowledgeable people who use an overall design to evaluate whether it is technically feasible to carry out the project. They also consider the technical solutions available and focus on ensuring that appropriate technology is used. It is important to ensure that there are technologies to solve the problem, and that it is possible to spend time changing an existing technology or developing new ones. Normally, there is no time to conduct research in a software or IT project.

9.3.1.2. Economy

Here we evaluate whether the proposed budget is adequate to implement the project. Another aspect evaluated is the question of whether or not the project will pay off, and usually a cost-benefit or business case analysis is carried out to ensure that the project will generate a profit, or other forms of benefits that might justify its resource consumption.

9.3.1.3. Legal Aspects

As more and more projects use open data or store information that may be considered sensitive, it is important to consider whether legal restrictions affect what data can be used, how it can be stored and handled, and how this affects the final product. Such analysis is normally conducted by lawyers with knowledge of IT-related issues.

9.3.1.4. Operational Considerations

This part focuses on the operationalisation of the proposed system or process. The focus is on how the intended change is to be introduced into the organisation. The underlying issue addressed is how to ensure that the IT system is accepted and utilised in the organisation and interacts well with organisational processes and practices. If we do not plan for implementation, the likelihood of resistance from future users is high, so there should be an analysis of what can be done to make the introduction as simple and painless as possible. This is about ensuring that you help the customer or recipient of the project to realise its benefits. One complicating factor is that project managers usually carry out one systems development project before moving on to the next one, and therefore in reality have very little opportunity to work to ensure that the desired benefits of a project are actually realised.

9.3.1.5. Timetable

Can the project be completed within the given time frame? This part is exclusively about ensuring that the time allocated to the project is sufficient to carry it out and that its individual stages are sensibly arranged.

9.3.2. Working with and Managing Requirements

Requirement management, or the process of understanding and defining a requirement, is relatively complex and consists of specification, analysis, and documentation. It often forms part of the pre-study work, but may well be a separate process that is carried out after a pre-study. There are many methods and processes for requirements management. Basically, requirements management consists of three aspects that are based on each other and when combined create a well-defined requirement. These are:

- Requirement definition. This is a requirement that is expressed in natural language, such as Swedish (rather than formal, artificial modelling language). This is primarily aimed at the customer as a way of creating an understanding of the project.
- Requirement specification. This is a structured description with all project requirements, which forms the basis for a contract between the customer and the supplier.
- Software specification. This is a technically detailed description of the requirements for the developers who will implement them. This can be created with the help of tools like UML (Unified Modeling Language).

If we put these together, we get the final requirements specification, which forms the basis for the continuation of the project. It should also include the relationships between the requirements and the external environment. There are many methods for obtaining requirements from the customer or the users, ranging from interviews to the analysis of systems specifications that customers have developed. More concrete examples of methods that can be used to obtain requirements are brainstorming, conceptual or process modelling, and working with prototypes. These different methods have their own strengths and weaknesses, and depending on the situation and type of system the customer is planning to build, different ones will be appropriate. Brainstorming is a convenient way to get started, or to find new ways to look at a problem. Modelling is most often used to analyse processes, and to determine how to improve them, or to chart what information the project should help in handling, and which conceptual data structures are needed to capture that information. Prototypes involve visualising something that can be complex, to test the usefulness of a certain functionality or to provide experience of potential user interfaces.

There are thus many methods with which to create a clear overview of requirements. It is important that the project manager understands the difference between each and chooses carefully, as it can be costly to choose the wrong one. The point is to find a mix of requirement management methods that works, and to deliver a result at the lowest possible cost. It is also important to understand that requirement management is a generic kind of knowledge used in both agile and sequential methods. The difference depends on when it is done and how many of the requirements are handled; agile methods focus on what is to be implemented in the immediate next step, while sequential methods identify all requirements of all steps before the project can start.

9.3.3. Time Estimates

> *It is difficult to make predictions, especially about the future.*
> Karl Kristian Steincke, Danish politician

Estimating time frames is undoubtedly one of the most difficult activities in a project, but it is of utmost importance that these are as correct as possible when planning a project as, for example, cost (and often price) directly corresponds to hours spent on a given activity. There are a number of methods for estimating time, but in essence, it is about using past experience and/or statistics to estimate how long an activity takes.

Estimates can, however, be more or less elaborate. What has never been done or experienced cannot be estimated, and then it is better to accept the help of experts who may have additional insights.

Before considering methods for estimating time, it is important to note that the planning horizon has a major impact on the quality of any estimate. The more distant the future of an activity, the greater the margin of error, and vice versa. This will have a greater impact on sequential methods, which require us to estimate the entire project and all of its stages before it has started, unlike iterative projects, where only the activities closest to us in time are considered.

Take a moment to imagine that you are expected to estimate how long it will take to do something that will happen in eight months' time. Now do the same for something you will do tomorrow or next week. Which is easiest? It is nonetheless important to understand that we must actively work on estimations throughout a project, and adjust them according to what we learn from tasks we have already completed. For example, if our estimates are constantly 10% too high, then we can probably correct our estimates for all upcoming tasks by reducing them by 10%.

Below we will discuss some methods for estimating time frames: work breakdown, historical data, and experts.

Work breakdown structure (WBS) is a common tool used in a variety of applications, and, in addition to time estimation, helps us to understand the activities that are part of a project and its scope. There are numerous variants of WBS, such as product breakdown structure (PBS), which is often used in agile projects, because it focuses on products and regards functions in IT systems as products, in line with the agile view of business value.

WBS is about breaking down a project into smaller parts known as work packages that one can estimate with relatively great certainty. This process creates a tree that describes the project's steps or tasks. The process is then completed by adding together the times for completion of the various levels in order to work out how long it will take to complete the project. We use the ICA example from Chapter 8 to illustrate what a WBS looks like (Figure 9.3). This is not a complete example, but illustrates the hierarchies that are used, and the gradual division of the work into smaller parts. There are main groups, such as design, which in turn consist of a number of sub-activities. The breakdown should continue until clear work packages are defined.

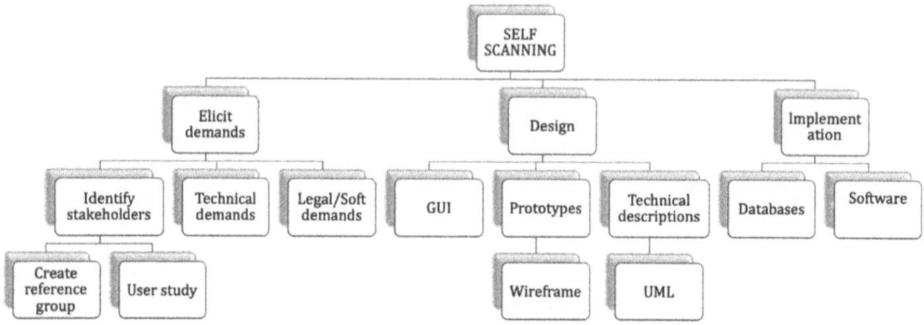

Figure 9.3. Example of high-level WBS.

9.3.3.1. Historical Data

Using historical data for estimation is a reliable method, when possible, since it offers facts: the end result, or how long a past project actually took. The most common way to work with historical data is to look at similar projects that the organisation or others have undertaken, see how long they took and use this as an estimate or as the basis of an estimate. For this to work, it is important that the organisation works actively to finish projects to a good standard, that employees learn from what they have done in the past and, above all, document the projects in a way that allows them to reuse the information. It is important to point out, however, that the tasks must actually be the same, that the project context is similar, and so on, otherwise there is a risk that the estimates will be incorrect because the projects are too different.

9.3.3.2. Experts

Seeking help from people inside and outside the organisation is a common and well-tried approach to estimation. All organisations have experts in different areas, and the underlying assumption is that if someone is good at something, like programming, they are more likely to be able to estimate how long an activity within their field of competence will take. The Delphi method asks a number of experts to individually estimate how long activities will take. The results are collected and a group discussion with the experts then follows, giving an opportunity to review, compare, and discuss the individual estimates before reaching a final estimate. This approach can provide well-founded estimates, but takes a long time and is costly, so care is needed in applying it.

9.3.4. Risk Analyses

There are many opinions and theories about risk analysis. The topic was discussed in Chapter 8. Here, we will focus on balanced and realistic risk analyses, which can be used in an organisation when working on certain projects.

The purpose of risk management is often to minimise losses in a rational manner. Ideally, it would be nice to minimise all imaginable risks, but it is usually too expensive to obtain protection against everything. An important part of a rational approach to this is risk analysis. When conducting a risk analysis, we examine the consequences of the different strategies and how they should be valued. We must then also try to anticipate what can happen and estimate the probabilities of the relevant events (which are often termed 'incidents' in IT-related risk analysis). As in decision-making in general, it is often difficult to obtain the necessary information for the analysis (or here, to make sure that all relevant risks and countermeasures have been considered, and to be sure to prioritise them adequately relative to the importance of the actual problem). In this work, we use the decision-analytical components and methods that we discussed earlier in this book.

A risk analysis is usually part of a decision-making process and is intended to systematically identify the risks involved. It usually contains assessments of risks and vulnerabilities which analyse all threats, at least to some extent. The potential benefits of risk analysis are significant; for example, they include adequate cost recovery, increased productivity, a better focus on safety, and increased general awareness. A major function of risk analysis is to create efficient processes for handling incidents before they occur, when they occur, and when they have occurred. A lack of such measures can be very costly.

There are different methods and tools for risk analysis, including everything from simple checklists that only require a few hours of effort, to analyses that may require several people's work over multiple months. Qualitative risk methods are sometimes useful when reliable data for quantitative methods are not available, and can be used as screening methods for preliminary assessments. One problem, however, is that they are very rough, and it is difficult to really distinguish between the various mid-level risks. Quantitative methods seem more accurate and are sometimes included as branches of the decision trees used for overall risk and mitigation analyses, making it possible to obtain a complete picture of the situation.

Quantitative methods are usually divided into deterministic and probability-based analyses. A deterministic analysis is based on the seriousness of an incident's consequences. In probability-based analyses, we also consider the frequency of the events. We will continue to use values (or sometimes utilities) to quantify the perceived effect of the outcome. (Some risk analysis literature uses a different and more confusing terminology that mixes the concepts of consequence and value.)

To deal with a risk, we must essentially answer three questions:

- How high is the probability that an incident will occur?
- If an incident occurs, how big is its impact on what interests us; that is, what is the value of the consequences?
- How should countermeasures be managed so that the risk is reduced, and any adverse effects become acceptable?

Answering these questions will allow a better understanding of the risks and create a situation in which they can be prioritised and addressed.

In practice, it is almost impossible to obtain precise information on risks. People have tried to come up with solutions to the problem, and many models—in some cases, remarkably strange ones—have been proposed. The more developed methods use event trees, which attribute probabilities and costs to tree nodes in the same way as decision trees, and then a more or less reasonable aggregation of the values used is performed. A common method of aggregation is the use of any variation in the expected cost of an incident, where the probabilities of the consecutive events are multiplied by the cost of the consequences of the event, as we have seen before.

As we might expect, decision trees, and decision-making methods generally, are very useful here, especially in more complex situations, and can be used constructively to model the relationships between possible risks and countermeasures. When we have an idea of the probabilities and effects, we can go further and evaluate the risks to understand which ones must be handled instantly, which should be managed over time, and which can be ignored. Normally it is not feasible to mitigate everything according to time and cost constraints.

9.3.4.1. Evaluation

First, we show that the simplest evaluation methods work because they are relatively common. The simplest methods assume that we have attempted to quantify probabilities and values on a scale of, for example, 1–5 or 1–10, while others handle more qualitative measures such as small–medium–large. Such scale models allow analysts to express the different values in a relatively coarse format.

We want to emphasise that it is not, as we have seen in the section on procurement, a particularly good idea to use this type of scale. Methods of this type can, however, sometimes be useful for gaining an overview of a situation. But they rarely suffice for more qualified analyses. Now, suppose we have a list of risks:

Table 9.2. Example of a risk matrix.

#	Risk	Probability	Effect on project
1	Illness of consultants and employees participating in the project	Mid	Mid
2	Customer changing and expanding functionality	High	Mid
3	Incorrect technology choices or innovations that make the selected technology outdated	Low	High
4	Resistance from the organisation complicates the introduction of the IT solution	Mid	High

The next step in the process is to create a picture of the risks and to determine which should or should not be managed. The risks must therefore be ranked. We show here a simple matrix model, a heat map, for handling qualitative scales (low–medium–high), which provides an easy way to visualise the risks graphically.

Table 9.3. Graphic visualisation of risks with analysis.

		Effect		
		Low	Mid	High
Probability	Low			3
	Mid		1	4
	High		2	

The risk analyst can now use the matrix to sort the various risks based on how they perceive their probabilities and effects, where, not surprisingly, an event with a high probability and high effect is more serious than an event with a low probability and negligible effect. After entering the risks into the matrix above, in Table 9.3, we get at best a coarse ranking of the risks. Green can mean that the risks are negligible, yellow that they should be remedied, orange that they should definitely be remedied, and red that they must be remedied. What remains is to decide on which risks to address. It is usually reasonable to focus primarily on the risks in the Orange and red fields, and secondly on those in the yellow fields.

This can work as a first analysis, even though it is greatly oversimplified. The problem, however, is that most risks are classed as medium without any indication of how they should be ranked. A less experienced risk analyst is already able to distinguish between catastrophic, unacceptable, and acceptable risks without the help of analysis tools, so the problem that remains is determining the order of the risks so that they can be systematically managed. When the risk hierarchy is obvious, there is no need for a model, and for the interesting risks, models such as the heat map are little or no help.

Another fairly popular method is to use a scale such as the one below, where the expected loss (value) of an event can be calculated based on the value (v) of various losses and the probability of occurrence (f).

$ 10: v = 1
$ 100: v = 2
$ 1000: v = 3
$ 10,000: v = 4
$ 100,000: v = 5
$ 1,000,000: v = 6
$ 10,000,000: v = 7
$ 100,000,000: v = 8

Once in 300 years: f = 1
Once in 30 years: f = 2
Once in 3 years: f = 3
Once in 100 days: f = 4
Once in 10 days: f = 5
Once a day: f = 6
10 times a day: f = 7
100 times a day: f = 8

The expected losses can then be estimated using a formula, for example, based on a weighted average where these f-numbers are weighted together with the values.

One problem with this method is that the possible values are spaced too far apart. This issue can be partially solved by using decimal numbers for v and f, but then we should instead use the much more versatile tree models, as described below.

Trees can provide a much better overview. As we have seen earlier, a decision tree consists of three types of nodes: events, outcomes, and choices. Tree models are also extremely useful for managing risks.

Suppose we are assessing the effects of a project delay that has given worrying signals. We have a value scale between 0 and 1, where 0 indicates that the situation is catastrophic and 1 that everything is unfolding as it should.

Table 9.4. A risk matrix with values and probabilities.

Delay	> 6 months (p_1 = 5 %)	3–6 months (p_2 = 10 %)	1–3 months (p_3 = 25 %)	No delay (p_4 = 60 %)
Effect	Complete losses (v_1 = 0)	Large losses (v_2 = 0.1)	Negligible losses (v_3 = 0.3)	No losses (v_4 = 1)

In the same way as for decisions, expected values are commonly used for risk analyses. The information is thus also synthesised here into an expression that weighs the values against the probabilities. We usually speak of expected loss, giving rise to a risk measure such as $E(H) = p_1 \cdot v_1 + ... + p_n \cdot v_n$, where H is the incident.

If we insert our numbers into the expression above, we get the expected loss as a result of the incidents:

$$E(\text{Delay}) = 0.05 \cdot 0 + 0.1 \cdot 0.1 + 0.25 \cdot 0.3 + 0.6 \cdot 1 = 0.685$$

The expected value has the great advantage of being clear and easily calculable, as long as the probabilities and values are known.

If tree models are being used, then it is also possible to directly model the subsequent consequences of the parent consequences to obtain a more detailed analysis. For example, we can model the consequences of a serious delay, such as customers disappearing, liquidity problems, redundancies, and so on. All of this works completely analogously to the decision tree models.

As we will see below, another advantage is that risk trees can easily be linked with decision trees, thus providing an overall impression of both risks and countermeasures and how we should best manage and prioritise them.

Again, with the exception of simple situations, there is little realistic hope of getting a useful guide from numerically accurate methods. As discussed earlier, this can be solved by using decision trees with imprecise input data, where a probability lies within a confidence interval, instead of being ascribed an exact number. We can also use comparisons if we lack quantitative data. In this way, we get considerably better data when we carry out risk analyses.

9.3.4.2. Mitigating Risk

To mitigate a risk is to prepare for unfortunate outcomes or to ensure that they do not occur, or at least that their probability of occurring is very small. There are basically four ways to counteract risks: avoid, share, reduce, and transfer.

- Avoiding risks is usually about evaluating and selecting other solutions or making other choices to find less risky alternatives. One common way of doing this is to choose proven working methods and technical solutions instead of untested ones.
- Sharing a risk means, for example, choosing to work with another organisation meaning that each organisation is only exposed to a portion of the risk.
- Reducing a risk means acting so that the risk becomes smaller, for example, by hiring an external expert to go through the project or by placing staff members with the greatest experience in time-critical activities on a project.
- Finally, the risk can be transferred to someone else. An obvious example is if one insures against a risk through an insurance company.

We can look more closely at the simple example of project delay above. Suppose that the anticipated delay depends on a lack of internal competence, which can result in a delayed delivery to the customer. The analysis can now be expanded and clarified through trees, which makes it possible to specify sequential events. We therefore continue to assume that the delay can have different effects in terms of market share.

After a more detailed analysis, we find that if the project is delayed for more than six months, the supplier has more than a 50% probability of losing the entire market as a result. This is a catastrophic scenario, which we estimate as having a value of 0. However, even less catastrophic scenarios involve substantial losses (value: 0.2–0.3).

If the delay is instead between three and six months, the supplier has a probability of over 75% of losing a very important customer (value: 0.2–0.3), but with a little luck (less than 25% probability), everything will go well (value: 1.0).

If the project is delayed by between one and three months, the supplier has a less than 30% probability of losing the customer (value: 0.2–0.3). Of course, if there is no delay, nothing will happen (value: 1.0). The event tree in Figure 9.4 shows the aggregate risks.

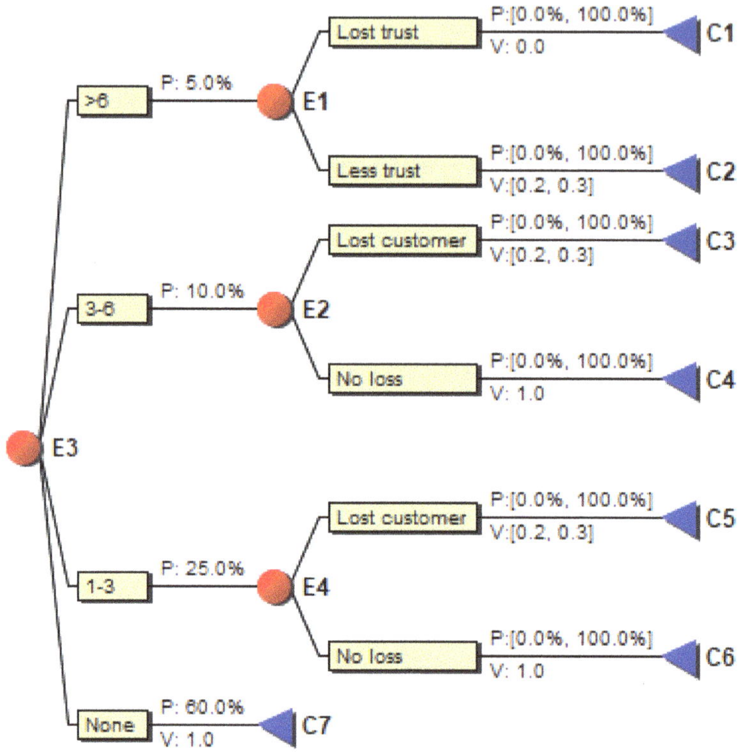

Figure 9.4. Project risks in a tree format.

The company can now decide, in order to mitigate the risk of delay, to recruit a smaller or larger group of technicians, for example. The effect of recruiting a larger group means that there is more than a 90% probability that there will be enough qualified personnel to implement the project on time, and a maximum 10% probability that the delay will be between one and three months. The risk of even later delivery is non-existent. At the same time, the costs increase so substantially that the company risks a 20–30% probability of bankruptcy. The supplier perceives this outcome as negatively as losing the entire market. In any event, the costs will be so significant that the value of a successful project will be significantly lower. The value of delivery in both cases thus decreases (by 0.2), as the costs of saving the project in this way are so large.

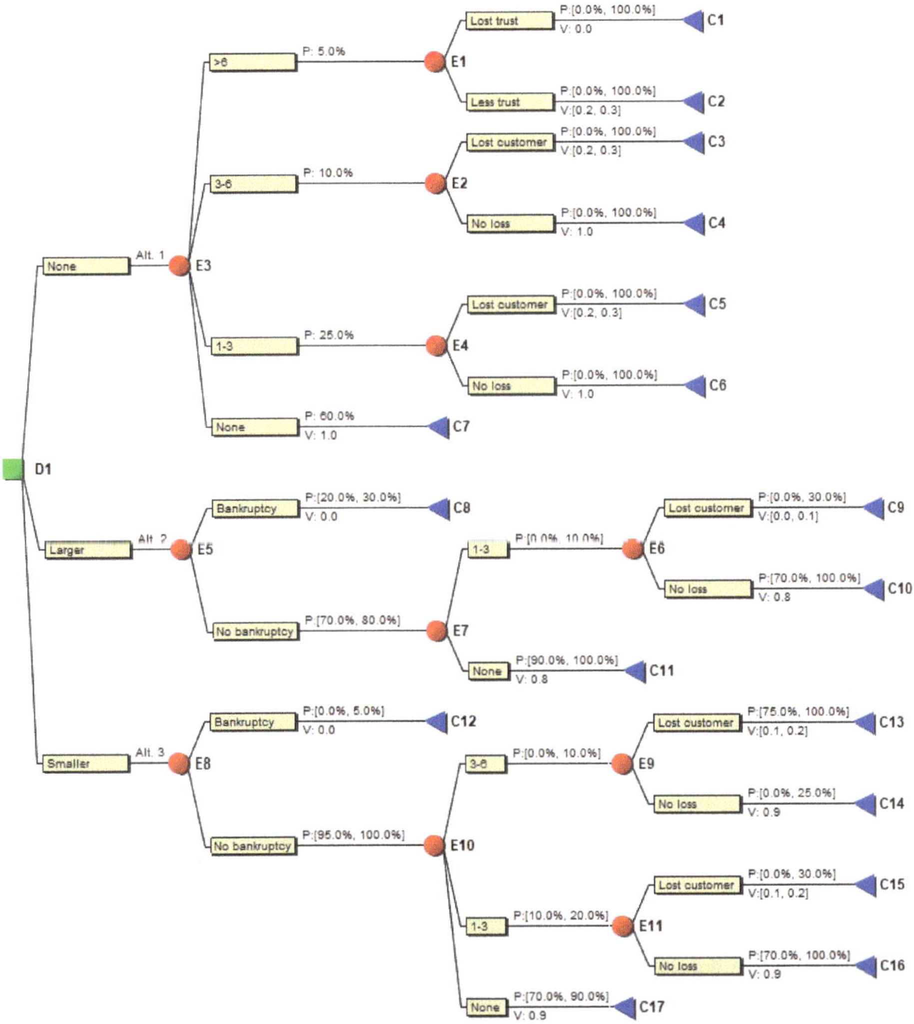

Figure 9.5. A decision tree for the above example.

Recruiting a smaller group is cheaper and means that the bankruptcy risk is below 5%, but the probability that the project can be implemented in time then drops to 70–80%. The risk of a one-to-three-month delay is 10–20% and that for a three-to-six-month delay is less than 10%. The value of a successful project also decreases here, however (by 0.1), thanks to associated costs.

The risks, as expected, have different effects depending on what is done. We therefore have a classic decision problem that naturally combines the risk analysis with the decision regarding the company's course of action. Figure 9.5 shows this reasoning in its entirety.

After modelling the problem, the evaluation can be made, and the results can be seen in Figure 9.6.

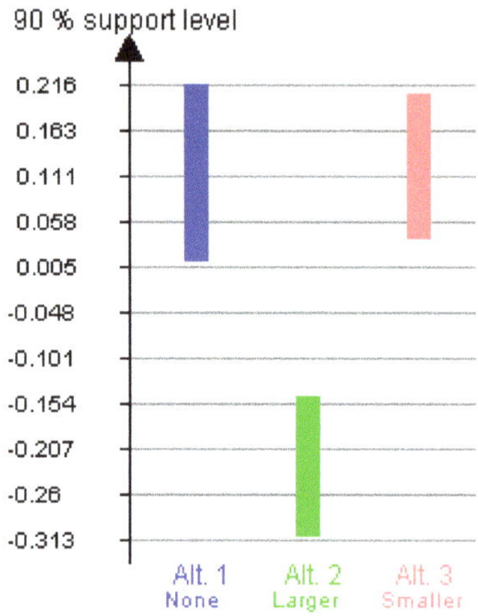

Figure 9.6. Result of the decision and risk analyses.

In Figure 9.6 we see how the alternatives perform in relation to each other, given the background information. The further up the bars they are, the better the options they represent. It can now be seen that the alternatives of either not recruiting at all, or recruiting a smaller group, are clearly much better than recruiting a larger one, based on the information available. The two better alternatives are rather similar, with no risk mitigation (Alternative 1) and a somewhat larger range of potential outcomes. Recruiting a smaller group (Alternative 3) appears to be slightly better, with a smaller range and a somewhat higher mean expected value.

9.3.4.3. Create and Establish a Follow-up Process

The last task in the risk analysis process is to establish a system for continuous monitoring during the project. We will discuss this in more detail in the next section. Monitoring the project is part of the project manager's responsibility. The work process runs throughout the project and helps the project manager to correct plans and current approaches. In its most basic form, the work process looks like this:

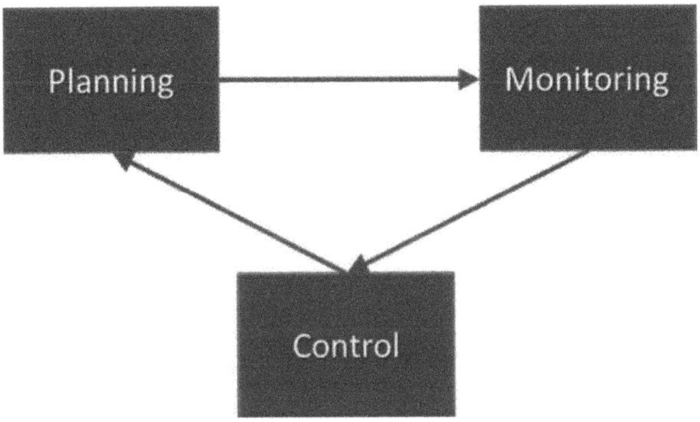

Figure 9.7. Planning, monitoring and control process.

Figure 9.7 shows a traditional work process for monitoring and controlling projects. It is a loop with a plan for what is to be done, monitored via, for example, KPIs and correct plans and behaviours. The most interesting areas to monitor/follow up on depend on the context and the type of project. In general, however, four areas of interest can be noted: (1) risks, (2) budget, (3) resources, and (4) goal fulfilment. Information is required to be able to monitor them and make decisions about which changes should be implemented. How information is collected is not important in itself. The important thing is to understand the composition, which will be a mix of quantitative and qualitative data and more free-format sources, such as reports, from project members and the project manager. The monitoring process is about setting up an information flow, getting members to report on how their work is progressing, the rate at which money is spent in relation to goal fulfilment, and so on. The major challenge in monitoring a project is to find a balance between information needs and the opportunity and willingness of members and other participants in the project to deliver. It is all too easy to create a process requiring a large amount of data, with members spending hours reporting the status of various activities, which is not cost-effective, and will eventually become tiring. The basic rule is to automate as much information collection as possible. For example, financial data can be retrieved from the financial system; a consultant's billable hours can probably be found in the time-reporting system used by almost all consulting companies; and so on. It is important that the project manager explains, and points out to participants right from the start, the importance of reporting what they do, the status of activities, and so on, so that this becomes a natural part of the workday.

Exactly how the follow-up and control process in a particular organisation looks is not our main topic, and instead we focus on which questions require answers in the different areas of risk, budget, resources and goal fulfilment.

Risks

- Have probabilities and effects changed compared to the plan?
- Have new risks arisen and old ones disappeared?
- Are risks handled correctly?
- Have new risks arisen that need to be dealt with?

Budget

- How much money has been spent compared with the plan?
- How does the requested change affect the plan?
- Are the cost estimates correct?
- What corrections need to be made?

Resources

- To what extent are the resources used?
- Are the resources used for the right things?
- Have the right staff been allocated to the right tasks?

Goal Completion

- Do activities end on time?
- Are the time estimates correct?
- Do planning and working methods work?
- Do forecasts need to be updated?

There are, of course, more questions to answer. Questions must be tailored to the specific situation and the above questions should therefore be seen merely as examples of basic questions. The questions and answers mean that plans must constantly be updated to reflect the changes and decisions being made.

9.4. Chapter Summary

In this chapter, we have discussed how projects can be managed and implemented. Projects are a key route for an organisation to realise benefits and value offerings, since they involve activities that bring the organisation closer to its goals and ultimately realise its vision.

We have looked more deeply into two areas: project portfolios and individual projects. Project portfolios are simply about making sure that money is invested, and that other resources are spent on the activities and projects that bring an organisation closer to its goals. If project portfolios focus on the holistic, then projects are more specific, and focus on a specific investment.

We posed and answered questions such as how projects are selected and resources used, in order to ensure that the right course of action according to the goals set is taken.

Project management is difficult and requires a number of skills and the ability to change roles frequently, for instance between leading and marketing a project without much preparation time. It is important to remember that all projects involve risk and the project manager has a great responsibility to manage them properly. We have discussed a number of risk management approaches, from fairly simple to more complex multi-criteria analyses.

The purpose of this chapter was not to give a comprehensive overview of projects and portfolios (there are entire books on these topics), but to situate the project in the context of its benefit, and how this benefit is realised.

What a project manager chooses to do, or how they choose to manage a portfolio, is ultimately up to them and their organisation. Here we have indicated a number of areas that are important to consider, and suggested a number of ways of working. How you proceed with and apply them is your choice!

We are now starting to approach the end of the book, but before wrapping up, we will look at digital transformation in higher education, and in doing so, move towards a global perspective.

9.5. Reading Tips

- Brewer, Jeffrey L. and Dittman, Kevin C. (2023). *Methods of IT Project Management*. West Lafayette, Purdue University Press, https://doi.org/10.2307/j.ctv2ckjpzf.
- Hopkin, Paul (2017). *Fundamentals of Risk Management: Understanding, Evaluating and Implementing Effective Risk Management*. New York: Kogan Page.
- Haimes, Yacov Y. (2016). *Risk Modelling, Assessment, and Management*. Hoboken, New Jersey: Wiley.
- Koelsch, George (2016). *Requirements Writing for System Engineering*. Berkeley, CA: A Press, https://doi.org/10.1007/978-1-4842-2099-3.
- Bjarnason, Elisabeth; Unterkalmsteiner, Michael; Borg, Markus and Engström, Emilie (2016). A Multi-Case Study of Agile Requirements Engineering and the Use of Test Cases as Requirements. *Information and Software Technology* 61, https://doi.org/10.1016/j.infsof.2016.03.008.
- Sutherland, Jeff (2014). *Scrum: The Art of Doing Twice the Work in Half the Time*. New York: Crown Business.

10. Globally Sustainable Digital Transformation

In this book, we have mostly covered digital transformation from a business perspective. But there is also a broader global sustainability perspective on transformation, as exemplified in this chapter by higher education. The Covid-19 pandemic accelerated the transformation and opened the world's eyes to understanding the possible impacts (both positive and not-so-positive) of transformation. For example, in the realm of higher education, one could compare the many universities in Sub-Saharan Africa that were forced to shut down overnight to the quick and successful shift to online teaching made by European universities.

In the UN policy brief "Leveraging Digital Technologies for Social Inclusion", a key message is: "Covid-19 is accelerating the pace of digital transformation. In so doing, it is opening the opportunities for advancing social progress and fostering social inclusion, while simultaneously exacerbating the risk of increased inequalities and exclusion of those who are not digitally connected."

Furthermore, the brief argues that the accelerated pace of digital transformation risks increasing the social exclusion of already vulnerable groups who are not digitally literate or connected.

UNESCO published a guide in 2021, "AI and Education: Guidance for Policy-makers". The authors state:

> However, while AI might have the potential to support the achievement of the Sustainable Development Goals (SDGs) of the United Nations, the rapid technological developments inevitably bring multiple risks and challenges, which have so far outpaced policy debates and regulatory frameworks. And, while the main worries might involve AI overpowering human agency, more imminent concerns involve AI's social and ethical

 https://doi.org/10.11647/OBP.0350.10

> implications – such as the misuse of personal data and the possibility that AI might actually exacerbate rather than reduce existing inequalities.

AI is agnostic, in the sense that it can be implemented and used for both bad and good. AI is about technology, or a group of technologies that are normally implemented along with other technologies that increase their impact, for instance in learning analytics. AI and deep technologies can thus be seen as potential components of transformation, which ought to be carefully considered when preparing for change.

There is little consensus on how to define AI. UNESCO has used a pragmatic definition:

> AI might be defined as computer systems that have been designed to interact with the world through capabilities that we usually think of as human.

This definition implies that what we think of as AI will change over time. As our digital tools become more powerful and help us to solve more complex tasks, we get used to them, and start viewing them as normal automation rather than "intelligence". According to this perspective, AI is always at the frontline of automation; handling "intellectual" tasks that we previously had to rely on people to perform. This relativistic character of AI also tends to lead to blurred lines between AI and other technologies. For example, is learning analytics about AI, at least partly? The issue of intelligence also relates to philosophy. There is some dispute over how far the I in AI relates to the I in human intelligence, HI. Can AI be used without HI? The human decision component might be easy to underestimate in the context of AI. As with all other digitisation, this book argues that it would be unwise to believe that AI will provide value without mindful human consideration of when and how to apply it.

Observing transformations through AI in higher education and research, three serious gaps become visible:

- The first is the gap between expectations and reality. This is discussed in a 2022 EDUCAUSE report on AI. As is typical for IT-related products and concepts, AI might also eventually meet a winter of discontent when the hype surrounding it leads to disappointment and criticism in the face of little or no tangible benefits.

- The second gap is between developed countries and less developed countries, in particular in Sub-Saharan Africa. This is evidenced by the many shutdowns endured by many sectors in Sub-Saharan Africa during the Covid-19 pandemic, and the resulting setbacks they have caused. African countries are hardly visible in the statistics for research on AI (except for South Africa, which has 2000 AI publications). In the chart below, Sub-Saharan countries (black bubbles) show almost no research activities and very low GDP per capita. Figure 10.1 plots countries by the number of AI publications, GDP per capita, number of all scientific publications (bubble size), and region (colour).

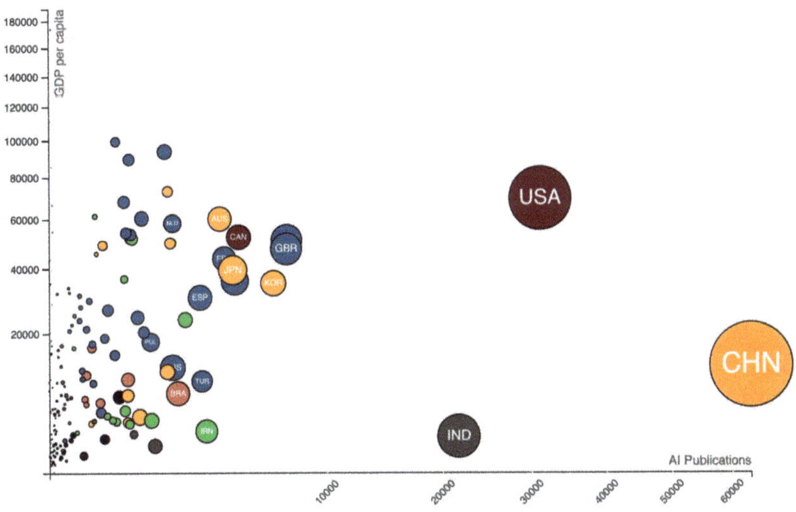

Figure 10.1. AI publications in Scopus vs GDP per capita by country and region.

- The third gap is between the business sector and higher education; the latter is lagging behind. This is detailed a bit more in the next section. If higher education, or certain parts thereof, is indeed lagging behind the business sector, it will fail to adequately prepare students for work life, and will increasingly find it difficult to interact with a more digitised business environment.

10.1. Digitisation in the Higher Education Sector

Higher education institutions and doctoral education can play a very important role in addressing the most burning issue of our time: sustainable development. Digitisation, if governed and implemented in an inclusive way, can play an important role in accelerating the positive impact by universities in meeting sustainable development goals. However, experience over the years shows that this is not a quick fix. It has taken time for universities to start to engage heavily with SDGs. The higher education sector has been slow to adapt to digitisation.

As mentioned in Chapter 1, for other parts of society, the Covid-19 pandemic accelerated the digital transformation of higher education, although most universities still have not started to prioritise digitisation projects. This means that whilst huge transformative processes have begun both for SDGs and digitisation, globally speaking we are still at the beginning. Research conducted by Boston Consulting Group shows that only about 30% of companies are successfully navigating digital transformation. There is no reason to believe that universities are doing any better.

For AI, the situation is in an even earlier phase. In 2022, EDUCAUSE found that very few higher-education institutions had implemented AI. Typically, only 1–4% were using AI for the twenty-four tasks examined, with three exceptions: proctoring (6%), plagiarism detection (20%) and chatbots/digital assistants (11%). For about twenty tasks, more than 40% of the institutions had no plan to use AI at all. However, quite a large share of planned projects is in the "tracking potential—planning/piloting" mode, which is typical (and perhaps sensible) for new areas of investment.

10.2. Need for a Higher Education Process Framework

Transformation in general is difficult, and digitisation is even more so. As a result, sound frameworks are needed to support higher education institutions and the sector in their digitisation processes.

In the study "Digital Transformation in Higher Education: A Framework for Maturity Assessment" (see Reading Tips), researchers explored and recommended a framework for maturity assessment, based on experiences from the United Arab Emirates, an advanced country driving digital transformation. The framework is based on the consulting company Deloitte's 2019 digital transformation assessment framework. This measures four processes: learning and teaching; enabling, e.g. library services; research and planning; and governance. Compared with the missions of the knowledge square (see Figure 10.3 below), one could ask if the innovations and services to society are underestimated in this model.

Researchers also mapped certain challenges for digitisation in higher education: (1) holistic vision, (2) staff competencies and IT skills, (3) data structure, data processing, and data reporting, (4) redundant systems, (5) third-party reporting systems, (6) manual entries, e.g. middle man, and (7) potential use by customers. This list shows the most important challenges (identified by 28-78% of the respondents). The EDUCAUSE special report on digital transformation in 2021 emphasises four barriers: (1) antiquated and siloed technology ecosystem, (2) lack of technology governance, (3) lack of necessary skills, and (4) change management difficulties.

These two findings from UAE and EDUCAUSE are similar but not the same and illustrate the necessity to carefully map maturity and challenges before starting or re-starting a digitisation process. A transformation must start with a thorough understanding of where the organisation is at, what the transformation is intended to achieve, and realistic planning for how to move towards the intended goals.

To successfully reap the benefits and manage risks and challenges, a framework for digitisation is helpful. This applies both when considering a certain university function that is being digitally transformed "end-to-end", for example online education, and when the university takes on a comprehensive transformation, considering all four of its missions: education, research, innovation, and services to the society.

A framework can be roughly divided into four phases (see Figure 10.2), however since digitisation is not a finite process, it is shown as a circle. Digitisation is not a destination; it is rather a permanent state of evolution.

Figure 10.2. Framework phases (inspired by Slidebooks consulting).

While many top-rated consulting companies offer frameworks for digitisation, including maturity assessments, few details are publicly available, probably because this is a revenue-generating part of the companies´ business. Little research exists on frameworks for higher education. In the article "Deep Dive into Digital Transformation in Higher Education Institutions", Mamdouh Alenezi discusses seven existing consulting companies' models for digital transformation in higher education institutions. In addition, it discusses the KPMG, Microsoft, and Google frameworks in more detail. To facilitate digital transformation in higher education, the paper suggests focusing on poor prioritisation, decentralised decision-making, internal resistance, digital literacy of the faculty, and a narrow view on return on investments. The author thus subscribes to a belief in centralised, forceful transformation efforts imposed on the institution, and the fact that the benefits of such transformation may be difficult to determine monetarily. This mindset is beneficial to consulting companies aiming to sell digital transformation projects to higher-education institutions.

A comprehensive digitisation process framework for higher education requires a holistic approach that takes all aspects of the university mission (here illustrated as education, research, innovation, and service to society, the so-called knowledge square) into consideration.

Extra challenges arise for institutions that completely or partly commit to open operations, here understood as open education resources (OER), open science and open innovation. "Open" implies a broad interaction with all members of society and might, but need not be, free of charge. It could also denote access that is restricted to a (large) collaborating network. For resource-poor countries, inclusion in "open" networks could be highly valuable, but it is increasingly likely that openness presupposes digital access. Some degree of digital transformation is thus a prerequisite for interacting with and benefiting from other institutions' open initiatives.

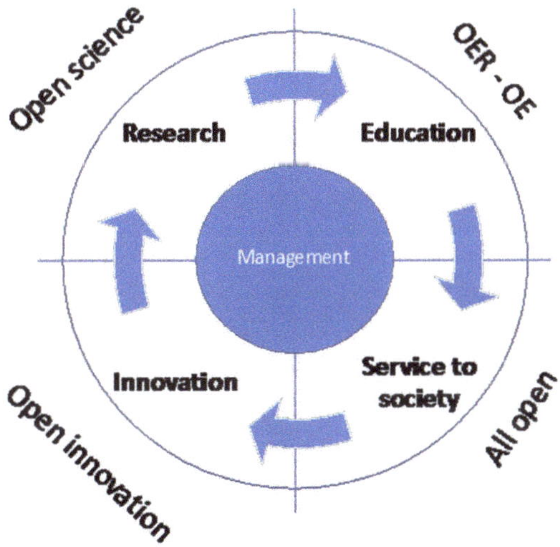

Figure 10.3. The knowledge square and open processes.

10.3. Aligning Higher Education Frameworks with SDGs

As discussed earlier in this chapter, digitisation efforts and policies have accelerated, and it is now one of the top twelve issues on the UN 2030 agenda. The importance of digitising higher education to meet the SDGs is widely acknowledged.

With the knowledge square in mind, universities have several tasks in relation to digitisation and SDGs. These include conducting research, building knowledge, and contributing to the global agenda for SDGs; educating students at all levels; empowering citizens to utilise digitisation and to engage with SDGs in their daily and professional lives; contributing to lifelong learning for all segments of society; and innovating on digitisation and how to better cope with the 2030 agenda.

The European Union gives high priority to digital transformation and sustainable development, both in its policies and programmes. The EU has launched the Digital Education Action Plan for 2021–2027, and the European Commission launched the Digital Decade Policy Programme in July 2022, stating in its press release:

> The Digital Decade policy programme is the way towards a more innovative, inclusive and sustainable future for Europe. Unlocking the potentials of the digital transformation, specifically by setting up and implementing multi-country projects, will pave the way for a competitive and sovereign Europe.

The Higher Education Sustainability Initiative (HESI), put both digitisation and the SDGs on their agenda at their 2022 Global Forum:

- Transformation of higher education post-Covid-19, including challenges and inequalities for those that lack capacities for rapid digital transformations and online learning.
- Integrating Sustainable Development Goals into higher education.

From a global perspective, digitisation requires missions to serve for the good, e.g., inclusion and sustainable development. Without such global missions, it is likely that individual higher education institutions will take a smaller, more inward-looking view of what their digitisation efforts should achieve. An important mission for higher education is expressed in SDG 4: to ensure inclusive and equitable quality education and promote lifelong learning opportunities for all. The "for all" implies a need for global cooperation. The UN organised the Transforming Education Summit in September 2022. In its discussion paper on digital learning and transformation, three recommendations and three principles are suggested as a guide for digitisation. These recommendations and principles can be of use to all higher education institutions, whether they are embarking or re-embarking on digitisation processes.

	PRINCIPLES		
	PUT THE MOST MARGINALIZED AT THE CENTER	FREE, HIGH-QUALITY DIGITAL CONTENT	PEDAGOGICAL INNOVATION AND CHANGE
1. Ensure connectivity and digital learning opportunities for all	✓	✓	✓
2. Build and maintain robust, free, public digital learning content and platforms	✓	✓	✓
3. Focus on how technology can accelerate learning by enabling evidence-based instructional practice at scale	✓	✓	✓

Figure 10.4. Recommendations and principles to guide digitisation in education.[1]

10.4. Chapter Summary

In this chapter, we have zoomed in, from a helicopter view on megatrend impact on the globe, identifying digitisation and AI as two of seven such trends – to some key issues for higher education institutions in meeting the challenges from an increasingly digitised world and at the same time observing the transformation of higher education to accelerate the impact of the SDGs while entering digital transformation. This is a tall order, but steps are increasingly being taken in this direction. The impact of digitisation has been accelerated by the Covid-19 pandemic, which also has made more visible three important gaps that need to be closed: between north and south, between expectations and reality and between the business sector and higher education.

Digitisation has in the last few years assumed a much more prominent place in work towards the sustainable development 2030 agenda. This is thanks to studies, influence and advocacy from many actors—and has not been without resistance. The Covid-19 pandemic was an eye-opener, which also accelerated policy surrounding digitisation. Now the leadership of global institutions such as the UN, UNESCO, and regional organisations such as the EU promote digitisation in all sectors through sector-specific and societal goals, including the SDGs.

1 Thematic Action Track 4 on 'Digital Learning and Transformation', Discussion paper (Final draft – 15 July 2022), https://transformingeducationsummit.sdg4education2030.org/AT4DiscussionPaper.

We have discussed how digitisation, AI, and deep technologies can be important for sustainability. And we have discussed how digitisation can be critical to the successful achievement of global higher education missions, and increase the impact of the SDGs. However, digital transformation is neither painless nor easy, and is not a destination; it is a permanent state of evolution. To better reap its benefits, meet its challenges and handle its risks, we have discussed the importance of using a framework for digitisation in higher education.

Several studies of such frameworks have been discussed, and we note that there is an obvious need for further research and development of holistic frameworks for higher education institutions to increase the success rates of digitisation processes.

We have also introduced some recommendations and principles for digitisation in education as a starting point for combining frameworks for the digitisation of higher education and sustainable development, and particularly SDG 4 for Education.

In Chapter 11, we will try to connect this chapter to earlier parts of the book, and will summarise its contents as a whole.

10.5. Reading Tips

Reports that provide a bird's eye view of what is happening globally, i.e., what trends to expect, the impact they might have, and where the "we" fits into this global picture, are always interesting. We recommend a report from Australia's National Science Agency:

- Naughtin C.; Hajkowicz S.; Schleiger E.; Bratanova A.; Cameron A.; Zamin T. and Dutta A. (2022). *Our Future World: Global Megatrends Impacting the Way We Live over Coming Decades.* Brisbane, Australia: CSIRO, https://www.csiro.au/en/research/technology-space/data/our-future-world.

The below report, with a forward-looking 2050 perspective, is helpful in shedding light on the (previous) lack of attention to digital transformation in the UN system and in work towards the SDGs.

- Nakicenovic, N. et al. (2019). *The Digital Revolution and Sustainable Development: Opportunities and Challenges.* Report prepared by The World in 2050 initiative. International

Institute for Applied Systems Analysis (IIASA), Laxenburg, Austria, https://doi.org/10.22022/TNT/05-2019.15913.

EDUCAUSE is an important open source of information, research and studies for those interested in higher education and technology, and particularly digital transformation. Here we recommend a few papers and publications that have been helpful in framing transformation and higher education.

- *EDUCAUSE Review: Special Report | Digital Transformation*, https://er.educause.edu/toc/educause-review-special-report-digital-transformation.
- *EDUCAUSE Review: Special Report Artificial Intelligence: Where Are We Now?* (2022), https://er.educause.edu/toc/educause-review-special-report-artificial-intelligence-where-are-we-now.
- McCormack, M. (2021, August 6). EDUCAUSE QuickPoll Results: Institutional Engagement in Digital Transformation. *EDUCAUSE Review*, https://er.educause.edu/articles/2021/8/educause-quickpoll-results-institutional-engagement-in-digital-transformation.

Harvard Business Review is also a good source for papers and articles on "practical digital transformation and AI", particularly for those with a business approach. Recommended reading includes:

- Davenport, T. H. and Redman, T. C. (2020, May 21). Digital Transformation Comes Down to Talent in 4 Key Areas. *Harvard Business Review*, https://hbr.org/2020/05/digital-transformation-comes-down-to-talent-in-4-key-areas.

Four academic papers are frequently used to focus on what global digital transformation is about, particularly in higher education. Gong and Ribiere clarify the definition of digital transformation.

- Gong, C. and Ribiere, V. (2021). Developing a unified definition of digital transformation. *Technovation* 102, 102217, https://doi.org/10.1016/j.technovation.2020.102217.

Alenezi, Holmström, and Marks et al. delve into frameworks, and their research can be helpful for those preparing to start (or restart) a transformation process.

- Alenezi, M. (2021). Deep Dive into Digital Transformation in Higher Education Institutions. *Education Sciences* 11 (12), p. 770, https://doi.org/10.3390/educsci11120770.
- Holmström, J. (2022). From AI to digital transformation: The AI readiness framework. *Business Horizons*, 65 (3), pp. 329–339, https://doi.org/10.1016/j.bushor.2021.03.006.
- Marks, A.; Al-Ali, M.; Atassi, R.; Abualkishik, A.Z. and Rezgu, Y. (2020). Digital Transformation in Higher Education: A Framework for Maturity Assessment. *International Journal of Advanced Computer Science and Applications* (*IJACSA*), 11 (12), https://doi.org/10.14569/IJACSA.2020.0111261.

Boston Consulting Group is one of the leading consulting companies offering valuable insights into digital transformation, AI, and deep technologies. Two of its reports on these topics are:

- Forth, P.; Reichert, T.; de Laubier, R. and Chakraborty, S. (2020). *Flipping the Odds of Digital Transformation Success*. Boston Consulting Group, BCG, https://www.bcg.com/en-nor/publications/2020/increasing-odds-of-success-in-digital-transformation.
- *What CEOs Need to Know About Deep Tech*. (2022, May 16). BCG Global, https://www.bcg.com/publications/2022/ceos-need-to-know-about-deep-technologies.

Studies of policy systems, policy development, and decisions are crucial for those wishing to understand what is happening and will probably happen in the world, and how they or their organisations can influence or take part in important development processes or fight against unwanted development. From a strategic perspective, it is always important to monitor and understand policy development relevant to one's organisation. Some see this as conducting intelligence to understand, interpret, and be prepared for what may come.

Here we suggest two reports that influence decision-makers. The Independent Group of Scientists report, issued every third or fourth year, is very important. We have also selected the DESA/UN policy brief as an example of precise policy work, which is read by politicians and civil servants.

- Independent Group of Scientists appointed by the Secretary-General. (2019). *Global Sustainable Development Report 2019 The Future is Now: Science for Achieving Sustainable Development*. United Nations, New York, https://sustainabledevelopment.un.org/gsdr2019.
- DISD/DPIDG. (2021). *Leveraging Digital Technologies for Social Inclusion* (Policy Brief UN/DESA Policy Brief #92:). United Nations Department of Economic and Social Affairs, https://www.un.org/development/desa/dpad/publication/un-desa-policy-brief-92-leveraging-digital-technologies-for-social-inclusion/.

The main messages from UN systems are normally issued by the Secretary General. Here, we have selected two documents relevant to digitisation and the SDGs. In addition, we also recommend the outcome document from the 2022 UN High-Level Political Forum on sustainable development.

- *Secretary-General's Report on "Our Common Agenda"* (2022), https://www.un.org/en/content/common-agenda-report/.
- *Secretary-General's Roadmap for Digital Cooperation* (2020), United Nations, https://www.un.org/en/content/digital-cooperation-roadmap/.
- *Outcome | High-Level Political Forum 2022* (2022), United Nations, https://hlpf.un.org/2022/outcome.

Some high-level forums can set goals for global cooperation, as in 2015, when certain heads of state and prime ministers first formulated the seventeen SDGs. More operational policies, such as the policy paper for the Transforming Education Summit Track 4 in September 2022, are developed at a lower level. It is good to understand how international cooperation paves the way for setting goals for digital transformation in education. UNESCO is the key UN agency for education (and science), and it decided to promote AI (both its opportunities and risks) and to offer policy advice early on. As a third reading suggestion, we have selected the UNESCO Institute for IT in Education. The IITE is a small but important operational entity under the UNESCO umbrella. Inclusive transformation for sustainable development is at the core of its strategy.

- *Thematic Action Track 4 on Digital Learning and Transformation Discussion Paper,* https://transformingeducationsummit.sdg4education2030.org/AT4DiscussionPaper.
- Miao, F.; Holmes, W.; Huang, R.; Zhang, H., and UNESCO. (2021). *AI and Education: Guidance for Policymakers,* https://unesdoc.unesco.org/ark:/48223/pf0000376709.
- UNESCO IITE. (2022). *UNESCO IITE Medium-Term Strategy for 2022-2025.* UNESCO IITE, https://iite.unesco.org/about-unesco-iite/.

In Europe, the European Union is setting the tone for policy development. If you are to operate in an EU environment, you definitely need to be aware of the relevant policies and developments in your area. For our purposes here, digital transformation, sustainable development, and higher education, two policy documents are selected for further reading, one providing a close perspective on education, and the other a broader EU scope.

- *Digital Education Action Plan* (*2021-2027*) | *European Education Area,* https://education.ec.europa.eu/node/1518.
- *The Digital Europe Programme | Shaping Europe's digital future,* https://digital-strategy.ec.europa.eu/en/activities/digital-programme.

11. What Is This All About?

This book's fundamental message is that valuable digital transformation does not start with the technical details. A strategic view of digitisation starts with the question of what is to be achieved, what one already has (a resource-based view), and how this relates to what others have, offer, and demand (a positioning view).

What "one" wishes to achieve is not obvious. It is not even obvious who "one" is. Given that our starting point is from within an organisation, the organisational management is of course relevant, but it is not enough in itself. Management or owners only lead or own to the extent that others allow them to do so. Other important parties in the strategic dialogue are, therefore, the co-workers and collaboration partners, but also the intended customers or users. And in an increasingly connected (through digitisation) world, there are also other actors and aspects to note and include in the organisational direction process: e.g., other affected parties, regardless of whether or not they have a strong voice at present, and the ethical considerations of oneself and others. We have talked of the surroundings as an ecology, without discussing techniques for environmental scanning and scenario work, because you can read about these elsewhere. But again, we want to emphasise that a strategic approach to digitisation need not turn into myopic navel-gazing. Every organisation operates in an environment, and organising (both internally and externally) is about developing functional ways of relating to others.

11.1. The Ecology Perspective and a Strategic Grip on Digitisation

A starting point for relating to one's environment is to adopt a business-ecology perspective, not least when one seeks to orient oneself in

 https://doi.org/10.11647/OBP.0350.11

digitisation issues. There are many large and strong actors, but none of them controls everything. A rich picture, looking beyond your immediate surroundings, can help you perceive developments that can become important to your future. In Figure 11.1, we provide examples of a host of actors.

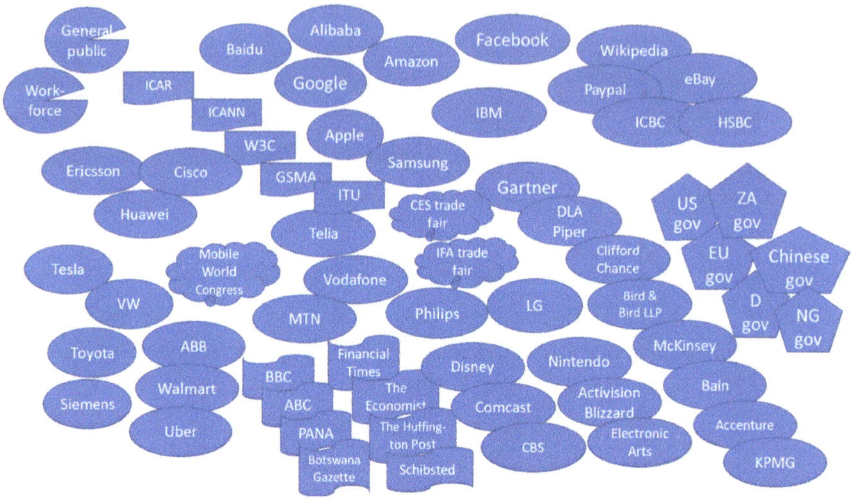

Figure 11.1. Actors in a digital business ecology.

Even trade fairs, like the Mobile World Congress, play important roles in shaping shared views, increasing the similarity of product offerings, and spreading news. The operators acting as middlemen between users and ICT networks, like MTN and Vodafone, hold a key position that makes them important. And if you are a sufficiently large actor, you wield a certain influence over standards through your own successful goods and service offerings.

Since digitisation is important for both physical production and the products themselves, the actions of industrial companies like ABB, Siemens, Volkswagen, and Toyota are significant, and not only because of their products. For example, Toyota has achieved considerable influence through its manufacturing philosophy. Other manufacturers generate impact through the launches of new and digitally innovative products. In Figure 11.1, Tesla is illustrative of this category: their innovation is not confined to the car's construction and steering, but extends to the sales model, by breaking away from the traditional car-dealer setup. As for Apple and their showrooms and stores, this choice is partly based on

Tesla's need to change potential customers' conceptions of the product category. That change is such an important task that Tesla does not wish to delegate it to partner organisations. Such a choice can also be motivated by cost considerations, as when the Chinese brand Lynk & Co followed suit.

In the distribution step, there are large actors, like Walmart, with a strong emphasis on efficient purchasing systems, logistics, and shelf-space profitability in shops, i.e., profiling that presupposes wide-ranging computer support. Newer actors, like Uber, have chosen to make their connecting services app-based: the physical meeting takes place directly between the trip operator (the driver) and the trip buyer (the traveller). There are also giants, like Amazon and Alibaba, that have done away with the bricks-and-mortar store for efficiency, but for whom logistics is an integral part of the offer, since the majority of goods traded are still physical.

Our views, both as individuals and as individuals working within wider organisations, are to a large extent shaped by media companies like BBC, ABC, PANA, and *Botswana Gazette*. Innovators, like *Huffington Post*, contribute to new ways of using digitisation in news production and the spreading of news. More traditional actors, like the Norwegian media group Schibsted, can also prove successful in understanding, using, and further developing digitisation's potential, not least by seeking to detect and influence readers' views and actions. Directed ads are, after all, a great source of income. But of course, search engine companies like Google and Baidu, social network services, like Facebook, and easy-access encyclopaedias like Wikipedia, have all come to occupy prominent positions in the shaping of our views, both directly (even on the question of digitisation itself) as well as in everyday habits and patterns.

Exchanges between individuals (e.g., of views and ideas, via network builders like Google and Facebook, of goods, via sites such as eBay, and of money, via actors like PayPal) have also been dramatically impacted. Companies that are close to the market for such services, and the image of how business can be conducted via the affordances of digitisation have also been affected. Banks, such as ICBC and HSBC affect the development of digitisation, both through what they do and do not help to finance, and through the services they do *not* offer, thus leaving space for new entrants to find business opportunities and develop niches.

For example, crowdfunding and crypto-currencies do not (yet) pose a threat to banks, but they exemplify developments in finance that have largely been driven by new actors because traditional banks have not chosen to try to cater to certain needs.

Counsellors like Gartner, which focus on digitisation issues, or more general management consultants, like McKinsey and Bain, wield large influence over views among companies and the launching of new concepts. For example, Gartner's hype cycles, published annually since 1995, contribute to shaping the image of what types of IT-related goods and services are emerging, and which are promising or overrated, well-established or outmoded. If they announce that light-cargo delivery drones, artificial-intelligence platforms-as-a-service, or blockchain are becoming really hot topics, this is not simply a statement of a state of affairs. It will also cause other actors to try to develop and launch products of the same kind, and lecturers and writers will read up on and market the trendy concepts. Management consultants will contribute by marketing catchy business concepts, like McKinsey's *The next-generation operating model for the digital world*, and Bain's *Digital strategy for a B2B world*.

In addition, governmental regulations, and the opportunities and obstacles they create, also influence the development of digital initiatives. Some government regulations and actions have a direct impact on how digitisation can be conducted, like the General Data Protection Regulation in the EU, or China's firewall against Internet. Others may impact digitisation more indirectly, for instance international admission and visa rules, which necessitate rich digital contact if the obstacles raised by physical travel restrictions are to be overcome (replacing physical presence with virtual contact). Trade restrictions impact how geographical placement of physical production can viably be designed to serve specific markets. Governmental regulation is, in turn, fertile ground for law firms, whose interpretations and treatment of intellectual property issues become increasingly important to digitisation ventures.

In classical electronics, established actors like Siemens, Philips, and LG have been eclipsed by companies that have successfully entered the smartphone and tablets sector, like Apple and Samsung. But the traditional actors still provide much of our digitisation environment, and trade fairs, like CES and IFA, play a role, both for the traditional actors' calibration against each other and for their launches—via wholesalers and retailers—to customers and users. Entertainment actors, like Disney, Comcast, and CBS, and perhaps even more so digital game companies, like Nintendo, Activision Blizzard, and Electronic Arts, are increasing in importance. Their products are popular and economically important, but perhaps more significantly, they shape our views of what is presentationally and visually modern. Animation in films and computer games, storytelling, visual design, and actors' looks and performances all affect our perception of what is modern and competent (or outmoded and amateurish), even when it comes to administrative support systems, information meetings and customer contact. Appearance and fashion in design and presentation have become very important for our willingness to adopt, or even to access, content and functionality.

These actors, and many more, take part in shaping the environment where our digitisation initiatives are seeking to get a foothold. A realistic view of how this shifting environment looks—and how it has shaped and continues to shape both our private and work-life habits and views regarding digitisation—is essential for the ability to think strategically regarding digitisation.

Some of the development depends on chance. Unforeseen opportunities and obstacles crop up, and are to some extent dealt with intuitively and in an improvised manner. It is of course possible to be lucky, and many of the companies mentioned above have been just that. But they form a minute section of the myriads of promising initiatives and ideas that continuously arise—the majority of which fail and founder.

Today, it is more common to think that to succeed, we need to take control over the development. Such control consists of understanding one's surroundings and being able to act in them. For this reason, we have dedicated a large portion of this book to the importance of knowing where one wants to head and what to do in order to get there.

This is why we spent Chapters 5, 6, and 7 on structured decisions and decision bases, procurement competence, and probability and risk management. In some cases, it is about choosing how to formulate strategies and act in accordance with them. In other cases, it is about exploring and preparing for possible futures. Organising and digitisation are continuously ongoing processes that need to be maintained. Then comes the actual enactment of the strategies. Since business development—and not least digitisation of businesses—is largely carried out via projects, we spent Chapters 8 and 9 on the managing of projects and project portfolios.

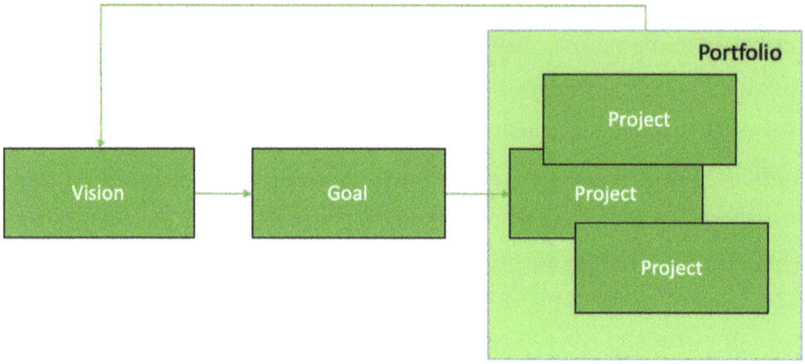

Figure 11.2. The project portfolio in relation to the organisation's visions and goals.

Projects are not carried out for their own sake. They do not fill their role in organising a business until that which they have helped develop has become a part of everyday life. To get there, it is important that the project does not disconnect from those who are to use the project results. Those involved in the project will, over time, be both bound by the solutions they have taken part in developing, and will develop an understanding of these solutions (see Figure 11.3). But if the intended users and other affected parties do not adopt the solutions and develop an adequate understanding of them, it will be difficult to realise the intended value from the ventures.

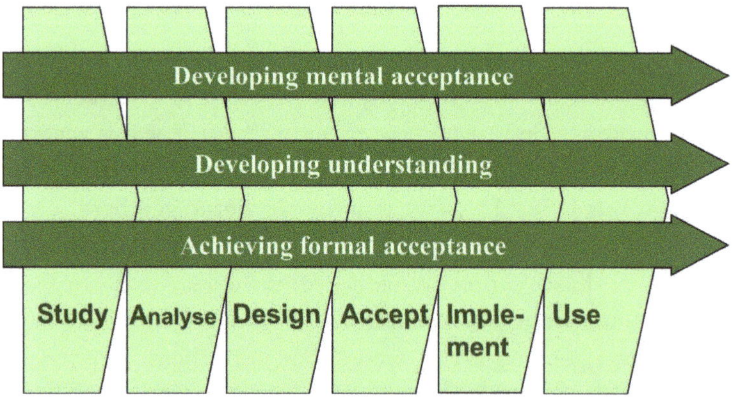

Figure 11.3. The importance of anchoring project results in the organisation.

11.2. The Business Focus

In all, what we have presented illustrates that for organisations, there are both external and internal perspectives of digitisation to handle. One way to summarise what your business focuses on in a digitised environment is to use Hambrick's and Fredrickson's (2001) strategy diamond (see Figure 11.4).

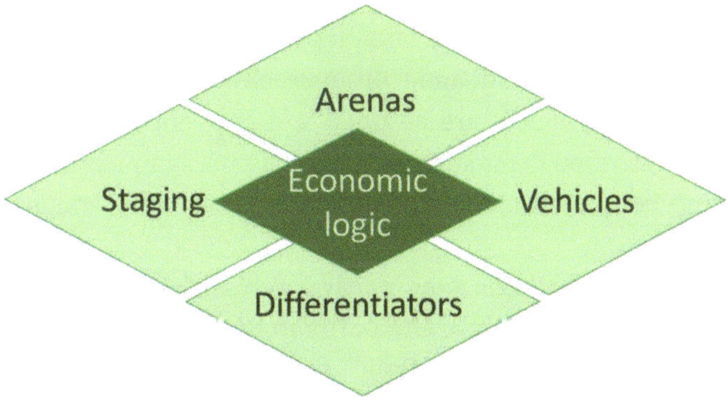

Figure 11.4. The direction of an organisation illustrated as a strategy diamond.

Arenas are about the type of product, market segment, core technology, market channels, etc.

Differentiators are how one intends to stand out from one's competitors, via customer adaptation, image, price, etc. Since arenas and differentiators vary depending on the product, we have not delved into these here, but we have provided examples of different sectors and product types (Chapter 3).

As we have emphasised, much of an organisation's operation is about *not* being different. Most of what an organisation does will be similar to what others also do, and the goal is rather to not be markedly less efficient or effective than others. **Vehicles** concern choosing suitable combinations of in-house activities, collaborations in different forms, competently buying units or services, etc. These are important decisions for all kinds of ventures, whether unique or not. We have primarily concentrated on collaborations in the form of outsourcing (Chapter 4) and in-house development (Chapters 8 and 9).

Staging is about the order and pace at which we take our development steps. Our message has been to place importance on preparation, not least on decision bases and evaluation of alternatives. There is rarely as great a need for rushing ahead as one is led to believe. Being well-prepared and deliberate in these steps can generate value and help avoid unnecessary mistakes.

To succeed in generating value and avoiding mistakes, structure and method are indispensable. We have gone through the phases of both the decision process and project management. We have made an important distinction between the waterfall process (where one sequentially progresses from investigation, analysis and decision, to development and implementation) and agile or interactive processes (where the goal and how to reach it are so uncertain that one must continually reconsider and refine the goal, action alternatives and priorities, and the relationship between them, along the way, as one learns and achieves a clearer picture).

Finally, **economic logic** was partly discussed in connection with business models in Chapter 3, and partly in the decision and evaluation sections and the project portfolio discussion. The basic idea is, naturally, to achieve value from the digitisation venture that matches, and preferably exceeds, the expended resources. A business needs to make ends meet economically, but as we have noted, this does not necessarily mean that it must always do so monetarily. There may be other important considerations, and an enterprise can be viewed as a portfolio of initiatives.

Digitisation connects our world and can make the distinctions between industries increasingly hazy. This impacts the arenas to a large extent. The informing and contact-enhancing aspects of digitisation also make it increasingly more reasonable to work in coalitions and to outsource tasks to partners and service providers. This influences the directional choices on the righthand side of the model (Vehicles). The more our venture builds on digitisation, the more imitable it becomes. This means that differentiation can only be expected to last temporarily. If we do something innovative (and successful), others will soon copy it. Similarly, we can choose to be fast followers rather than forerunners, provided that we pay attention to others' development.

Regarding steps and speed, it is important to remember that digitisation is only swift when it comes to automation. As soon as people are involved, the situation changes; we neither think faster nor function fundamentally differently than in ancient times. Thus, it is important not to let the idea of Internet time or the speed of technical development lead us to believe that people do not need time to think and to reconsider, or that change of habits will take place instantaneously. As for the economic logic (the last and central part of the model) properly performed digitisation can provide value. But, as we noted already in the Preface, digitisation does not in itself guarantee value realisation. Insufficiently analysed, digitisation can be the catalyst that speeds up poorly designed operations and make them quicker and more misguided. The goal focus, the organising, and the control of the ventures, are important to make them beneficial rather than harmful. In order to get a strategic grip on digitisation we must organise with value realisation in mind, something we have kept returning to and provided examples of in this book. Now, let us sum up what each of the previous chapters has highlighted before the book's conclusion in Section 11.8.

11.3. Strategy, Goal, and Business Model

When discussing how digitisation can contribute value to an organisation, the organisational goals should be the starting point. We have emphasised that IT, the technical aspects that enable digitisation, do not have value in themselves. It is only when IT contributes to valuable digitisation and goal achievement, that it becomes beneficial. This presupposes that the goal is clear.

In Chapters 2 and 3, we pointed out that there are some real challenges to handle. It is important to consider the different time perspectives at play in an enterprise; what is important in the short run, and what is important in the long run? This, in turn, is affected by the smallest elements of the organisation, the people who constitute it, all having their own goals with their work, and in life in general. It is also important which financial and non-financial goals are formulated. Depending on stakeholders, different goals differ in importance, which in turn poses demands on how the organisation chooses to balance its goal fulfilment. Discussions, reviews, and negotiations about goals and goal fulfilment are therefore important. A step towards succeeding with goal fulfilment is to develop and formulate strategies. To work strategically means to have a long-term plan for achieving goals, and here, too, people in the organisation have several challenges to handle. Seldom, if ever, is there complete data of suitable form and sufficient quality. Or there is too much data to sort and make sense of. It is also important that the organisation reflects on strategy views and how to coordinate strategies across levels of the organisation. And a part of this is to formulate the ways in which digitisation forms part of the strategies, rather than just being the task for a specialist function in the organisation. As with goal formulation, it is important, here too, to make room for a dialogue between the organisation's members in order to move from words to action.

To accomplish this move from word to action, people in the organisation also need to develop an idea about which paths the strategy offers – and how digitisation contributes to making each path as accessible as possible. One way of describing the way forward is to formulate a business model and to identify how digitisation affects its constituent parts. This includes an analysis of the content of the value offering and of the relation to collaboration partners. And which activities and resources that are critical to creating the value offering. But it is also important to define who the intended customers are and how development of customer relations and customer channels can be achieved. And, of course, to identify how all of this generates both revenues and costs. This analysis is not only to be performed regarding new business models; it is as relevant for existing ones stemming from an era of more analogue information flows.

Today, it is possible to find several examples of digital business models, ones that have arisen thanks to digitisation. They have some traits in common, for example contributing to bridging or alleviating the gaps and fissures in our daily lives through increased access to products and decreased time consumption. They also often build on brokerage of products and/or building of networks.

However, a business model only provides certain analytical perspectives. Having identified the different parts of a business model, and the importance of digitisation in each, it is time to consider organising digital competencies and resources.

11.4. Organising Competences and Resources

In order to create or refine a value offering through digitisation, efforts at different levels in the organisation are needed. One such effort is to create a conducive organisational setting, as discussed in Chapter 4. This involves, among other things, to create roles and responsibility structures that clarify who is to be part of setting the agenda for how digitisation can contribute to the business. Should the marketer, the controller, the IT manager, the customer support staff, the managing director, and/or someone else be involved? And how should this involvement be designed; should it be to contribute with ideas about new ways of digitising, to actually decide about the conducting of projects, or to be the one who finances the venture? We have not suggested any unequivocal answers to these questions, simply because the answers vary. In line with our recurring message that IT has no intrinsic value, we have however underlined that co-workers from the core business have an important role in the organisational digitisation. A more technical perspective, for example from the IT department, if there is such a department, can of course be relevant, but needs to be coupled with perspectives from the core business. Depending on the size and management philosophy (for example regarding the degree of centralisation/decentralisation), it is possible to consider both central and local involvement.

As a result of the different roles and shifting responsibilities of the co-workers, and therefore, different perspectives on how digitisation can contribute to the development of the value offering, co-workers' ideas and contributions need to be coordinated and balanced in different ways. Connected with this, we have argued for continuous communication with little specialised jargon, with job rotation and joint planning between the parts of the organisation. This increases the possibilities for a broader range of experience and the ability to adopt others' perspectives, allowing IT to be the catalyst for the business that it has the potential to be.

Yet an organisational effort that we have highlighted is the choice to let one or more external actors become involved in the organisation's digitisation. Are there others (than ourselves) who can deliver ideas and support for IT use in a better way and/or at a lower cost? Can we learn something from entering a partnership with a supplier, either by adopting the industry's "best practice", or by adopting a more tailored solution made possible through close collaboration with a supplier? Or are certain parts of our business too strategic and sensitive to allow external parties to support and develop digitisation there? We have not provided any unequivocal answers here either; both cost-cutting and strategic reasons play their part in decisions regarding outsourcing IT.

Regardless of the reasons, the relation between the organisation and its suppliers will need to be managed, and we have pointed at both more formal, contractual control mechanisms, and less formal, trust-based approaches. Even though there are indications that more complex collaboration can require less formal control mechanisms to really build mutual understanding and will to develop the collaboration, we hold that a number of different management control mechanisms are at play in a buyer-seller relation. When one is organising one's digital competencies and resources, there will be a need to make decisions of differing magnitude. Some decisions, like investments in certain types of IT infrastructure, can seem minor but can have far-reaching consequences for the organisation's ability to create value. To act strategically, when taking such decisions, needs to involve deliberations regarding risks in relation to the organisation's adopted strategy and organisational goals.

11.5. Decision-making and Risk

Since well-founded decisions and, not least, the balancing of risks, are important to strategic acting, we have devoted Chapters 5, 6, and 7 to decision-making and risk management. This is something that any organisation will come up against on a daily basis, and it is of fundamental importance if the organisation is to be able to develop and meet the goals set for it. As shown, decision-making can take many forms, some requiring less deliberation than others. How to address the decision situation depends on the type of problem faced. It is worth repeating that it is still too common in organisations that decision-makers rely on gut feeling and on their own, often less-than-solid experience when making decisions. This has led many organisations to sustain the belief that effectiveness and efficiency can be achieved by letting bureaucrats create static rule structures. That path leads to considerable, and often unnecessary, waste of resources and sub-par performance.

Decision situations are often complex; then, there is a need for a decision process. A considerable portion of the time spent in organisations is devoted to collecting, processing, and assembling sets of information meant to serve as bases for decisions, and including all relevant information and all reasonable courses of action. Still, people in an organisation make decisions on unclear grounds and pure intuition. The risk of making the wrong decision, decisions that do not contribute to goal achievement and value creation, is then considerable. This can be dealt with by introducing deliberate and quality-assured decision processes that handle the cycle from idea generation, via identification and evaluation of possible paths of action, to implementation and follow-up. Following a clearly defined work process will make the fundamental elements clearer. Decision-makers will also get a good overview of the available material, and it will be easier to understand the decision problem in its context. A well-structured decision basis will support the identification and specification of additional information needs. Such a process can of course not be summarised in a simple formula; it needs to consist of a process that is well-integrated into the organisation, a process that systematises and manages the bases for decisions and the existing uncertainties.

This has led us to argue for such deliberate processes. They are fundamental for achieving good quality in decision and strategy work. The processes should encompass both risk analysis and decision making and the sets of information underlying the decisions should have their different components clearly specified. This is not always easy to accomplish, too often leading to not even trying. In this book, we have attempted to demonstrate how it can be done and that there are different types of support available for doing it. To achieve good decision quality in strategies requires good decision bases, with clear reporting of different priorities. This is especially important when there are goal conflicts, and no alternative is the best on all accounts. When several decision-makers are involved, or when there are influential stakeholder groups, it can be wise to collect explicit prioritisations from each party to understand how they differ, but also to be able to demonstrate the degree of compromise needed. Another important aspect is to not hide the uncertainties in the decision bases behind mean values or other singular estimates; otherwise, the awareness of the uncertainties in the information is likely to suffer. The same goes for priorities. If one is uncertain about priorities, it is best not to try to guess based on the available information. The guessing is easily forgotten when a solid-looking result is obtained from calculations based on the guesses.

The basic guidelines are thus fairly simple. First, establish what one wants to accomplish, the goal(s). (Remember that "one wants to" in an organisation is likely to be the negotiated view of a number of stakeholders.) Then, identify strategies that could possibly lead to achieving the goals. Based on the goals, derive a clear criterion structure to assess the strategies. This also includes obtaining a good sense of the environment and developments there, to assess how the strategies could be affected by, or perhaps could even affect, the environment. Of course, there are almost always considerable uncertainties, which need to enter the analysis in the form of different scenarios and some type of assessment of the likelihood that they will occur. The effects of one's own actions and of what happens in the environment, will need to be grasped and formulated in consequence analyses.

To sum up, the following phases should be handled in the decision and risk evaluation processes:

- Identification of the problem(s)
- Structuring of it/them so that the components and their relationships become clearly visible
- Information collection leading up to a detailed basis for decision
- Modelling of the problem based on this basis (preferably with a graphic tool)
- Evaluation of the model, including aggregation and analysis of the information
- Feedback and repetition of earlier steps, if needed
- Preparation of a report with instructions and recommendations

The starting point is thus to make clear what the decision or risk analysis is about, and what should be included and excluded, A problem can typically be scrutinised under different criteria, and the values of the action strategies will then depend on which criteria it is judged by.

- When structuring the problem, the components of the decision situation are defined.
- The criteria and their priorities, and the action strategies, are formulated.
- The priority of the different criteria is noted by assigning weights to the criteria. Consequence analyses are also performed and shape an image of the values of the consequences. This includes performing scenario analyses

and estimating probabilities for different events. Especially when performing risk analyses, the consequences of different strategies and how they can be valued need to be determined.

- Then, the strategies are evaluated based on the components, and the result is consolidated in an assessment, where the strategies are evaluated along the criteria and an overall assessment of the decision situation is made. If the more obviously infeasible action strategies are discarded, the remaining ones can rather easily be evaluated by the well-established method of applying expected-value calculations, summing them up across criteria by using the assigned weights.

In addition, it is necessary to assess the risk exposure and understand how to handle it. This is done by analysing the effects of uncertainty in the background information to see how robust the solutions are. This is called sensitivity analysis. Note that it can be very difficult (sometimes almost impossible) to derive relevant weightings, values, and probabilities with precise numbers. Instead of assigning precise numbers, we have shown how to work with comparisons and intervals. This can help the organisation to understand the scenarios that could arise, and how to reduce the negative effects if something that cannot be entirely prevented should occur. The goal is of course to select the action strategies that have the greatest potential (at acceptable risks). But ultimately, it is about decisions and decision quality. If the decisions are to be well-anchored and lead to action, it is, as discussed in Chapter 5, important to include those affected, as far as possible, in the process.

A normal outcome of a decision process, particularly with regard to digitisation of business models and organising of digital resources, is that projects are started in the organisation. They can vary in resources and time, but regardless of size, they contain a host of situations requiring decisions.

11.6. Project Portfolio and Implementation

Working with projects and portfolios is a central part of realising strategies and achieving the desired value. In Chapters 8 and 9, we described project work. The question of which models to use (waterfall, agile, or hybrids) is not the most important concern; rather, the most important issue is to keep the desired benefits in focus. Project portfolios are, to a large extent, the bridge between what one wants to accomplish and how one actually goes about doing so. This requires choosing projects in a deliberate manner. The specific way of doing so will depend on the particular organisation. However, it is important not to disregard formal methods because they are too time-consuming and costly. Instead, one should ask what it will cost if things are not done right, i.e., if the projects that are best for the organisation (including the organisation's societal responsibilities) are not chosen.

Another important aspect is how to make sure that there is a clear connection between the projects conducted in an organisation and the organisation's strategic goals. This is not only about starting and evaluating projects, it is also about closing or ending projects that no longer support the strategic goals of the organisation. Traditionally, organisations are good at starting projects, but rather poor at ending or closing them down. The reasons tend to stem from organisational politics.

That we place digitisation and value as central in this book, affects how we have chosen to view projects and project portfolios. From a project perspective, it is important to focus on projects that deliver value, and important to be clear on how business management and IT management collaborate. Furthermore, it is important that decisions are taken from a business value perspective, and not for strictly technical reasons, and that the way in which one evaluates projects focuses on value creation and not only on project goals and implementation. From a project perspective, this may point to an agile approach where business value is central, but it is not that simple. Organisations do not exist in a vacuum – rather in a business ecology. Therefore, they have to relate to many more stakeholders than just customers, which affects the situation in different ways. Because of this, we have provided examples demonstrating that many organisations choose to use hybrids of traditional and agile methods, which, if done properly, can be successful. There is no single perfect way of working which is the best in all situations; every organisation must find its own ways. Theory and models can serve as help, support, and inspiration, but they need to be adapted to the organisation's needs and model users need to make them their own, not slavishly follow a rule book.

Projects are the dominant mode of working with change and organisational business development. There is no reason to believe that this will change soon. Therefore, the ability to work effectively via projects is of utmost importance to an organisation's future success, especially when it comes to digitisation and how it can help to create value.

11.7. Sustainable Development

Digital transformation was accelerated in all sectors by the pandemic. In higher education, many more institutions entered comprehensive change and innovation processes, driven by the needs of students and teachers. Some stopped at the "online teaching" step, and many more are still not in a position to enter a full transformation process. It is also difficult; only about 30% of companies are reporting success. Assembling the right team of people in four domains – technology, data, process-people, and organisational change capacity – is an important key to success. Today, we observe the need for sound frameworks for the transformation of higher education, frameworks that are publicly available and that facilitate higher education, as well as supporting the value proposition and direction of sustainable development. True sustainability ought to take a global perspective. There is a risk that digital transformation from a strictly local perspective will create or reinforce digital divides. Focusing on the "for all" in SDG 4

> To ensure inclusive and equitable quality education and promote lifelong learning opportunities for all.

can serve as a lodestar for keeping a global perspective.

11.8. Digital Transformation and Value

From time to time, there is reason to ask how far the digital transformation can or will go. Is there an end to it, or even a slowing down? Will the following three transformation conjectures hold?

1. Everything that can be digitised will eventually become digital;
2. All physical goods (of sufficiently high value) will eventually become digitally augmented;
3. Everything that can be fully digitally transmitted will—after an initial period—become essentially free of charge.

Will these conjectures come true? The future remains unwritten, and only time will tell the true transformative effects of digitisation. This book has pointed out the components of digital transformation, as well as likely trajectories.

Digitisation affects everything around us and brings with it both great problems and great opportunities. It poses significant challenges, and we need to make clear to ourselves what we want to accomplish. We also need to understand how to do so in an effective manner and at a reasonable cost. To achieve success in an enterprise, it is not sufficient to simply introduce automation and different kinds of information system because without proper control and insight, these risk being ineffectual or harmful. We have therefore examined digital transformation, taking as our starting point what an organisation is and how it should be controlled. We have focused on the organisation, the goals and value creation, the processes, decisions and enactment. We have dealt with understanding goals, organising, and decision-making (obtaining and using adequate information to understand risks and opportunities and how they should be handled and pursued). We have also dealt with how to manage processes and organisational functions. Remember, digitisation works as a catalyst; it reinforces, it is not unequivocally good. It can make poor operations worse and exacerbate poor decisions. But properly used, in a well-designed enterprise that is heedful to what is going on in the surrounding business ecology, digitisation opens up new possibilities and strengthens our ability to take advantage of them.

Appendix

A licence for the decision-supporting and decision-analytical software DecideIT is included with this book and the software can be downloaded from https://www.preference.nu/digitrans while stock lasts. This program is a user-friendly decision support tool developed for MS Windows by Preference AB and has been used in Chapters 5–9 of this book. It can handle various aspects of decisions with multiple criteria, as well as event trees (probabilities). There is no need to enter precise information in order to receive adequate decision support. Instead, rather vague information can still suffice to find out which decision alternative is the preferred one according to the available data. DecideIT has several positive properties and features, such as:

- A good overview gives a better overall picture.
- It is easy to document, review, and adjust the underlying data.
- Hard problems are solvable within a reasonable time frame.
- The program supports imprecise probabilities, consequence values, and criteria weightings.
- It supports rankings of values, weightings, and probabilities instead of, or combined with, numerical data.
- It supports the evaluation of combined multi-criteria and event-probability decision problems.
- It provides simple ways to detect a lack of information.

In real-life problems, it is usually impossible to assign precise numerical values to the different components of a decision, and there is thus a need for representation and evaluation mechanisms that can handle (sometimes severe) incompleteness of information.

DecideIT allows the construction of models that are actually useful in real-life practice, in that they allow decision-makers to only provide

https://doi.org/10.11647/OBP.0350.12

imprecise information but still gain important insights into the decision problems at hand. This contrasts with decision-making that relies on unrealistically precise information, or decision-making based on diffuse gut feelings and impulses.

For this short introduction to the tool, the decision example consists of whether a company should acquire and implement a new information system or not. This simplified situation contains only three alternatives: investing in one of two vendors' systems, or making no investment.

To start a session, first launch DecideIT. Double-click the D icon in the program menu or on your desktop.

To begin modelling, click the New symbol in the toolbar. In the File menu, you can also create a New model, Open an existing one, Close or Save a current model, and Exit the program. But most menu commands also have easy-access symbols in the toolbar, and where applicable we will refer to those in the first place.

A pop-up dialogue will appear, in which you can select the model type and the number of alternatives (which the program calls strategies). In this example, we will use a multi-criteria model of the kind we saw in Chapters 5 and 6.

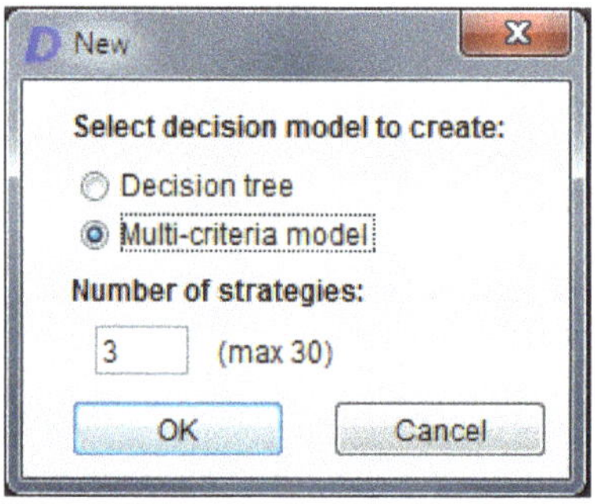

The default number of alternatives is two, but we will have three in the example. Enter the number of alternatives and click OK. In the next pop-up window, the number of criteria for this multi-criteria decision situation is entered. To keep this example simple, we will keep the default of two criteria, although the program can handle up to 300. Both the number of criteria and the number of alternatives (which we will call strategies henceforth to comply with the program terminology) can be changed later. The numbers entered now are only for the initial model.

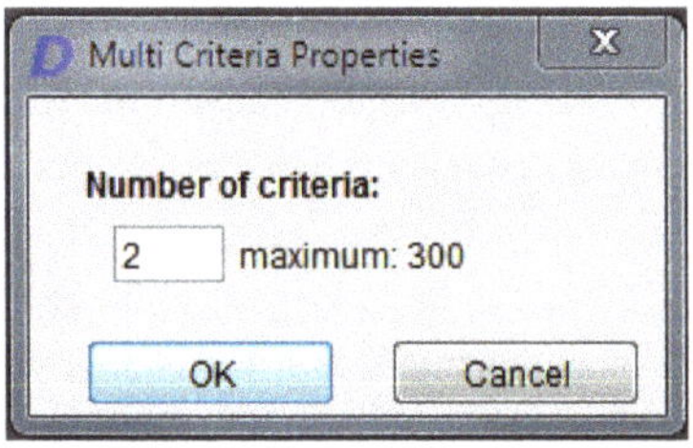

Click OK to create an initial model. The program now enters its basic mode, with access to all open models. There can be as many as fifty open models, but we will only have one open.

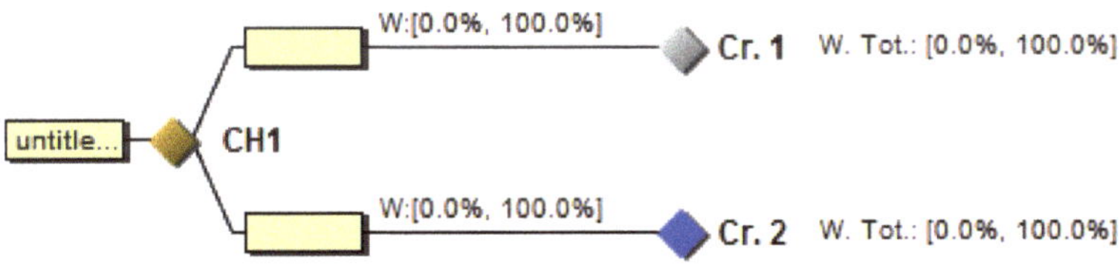

Each open model resides in a separate window. On top of all windows are the menu bar and the toolbar.

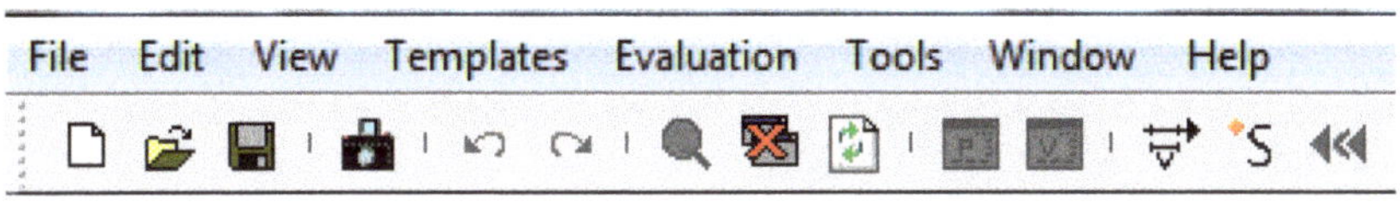

Several of the items in the toolbar are grey at any given moment when running the program. This only shows that not all functions are applicable at all times and with all models.

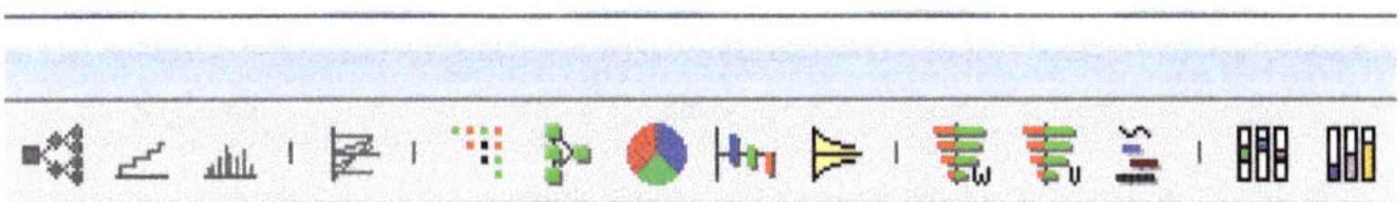

In our example, we must decide whether to invest in a new information system for customer service. The old one is increasingly inappropriate given the new market demands and expansion plans of our business, but it could work for a couple of years yet. The choice is between system vendors A and B, with a third strategy of deferring the investment for a few more years, to the end of the current system's projected possible lifetime. Reasons for deferring the investment include the strategy and market outlook of the business, as well as the expected development plans of the system vendors. On the other hand, important market shares might be lost if and when the market takes off in a near future.

The decision model is initially constructed in three steps. It is important to follow these steps in order. They are:

1. 1. Identify and name the criteria and the alternatives
2. 2. Enter value estimates for each alternative under each criterion
3. 3. Enter importance estimates for each criterion

Step 1. Identify and Name the Criteria and the Alternatives

In this simplified example, we will use only two criteria: cost and performance. Let us enter these label names into DecideIT by right-clicking on the respective criteria.

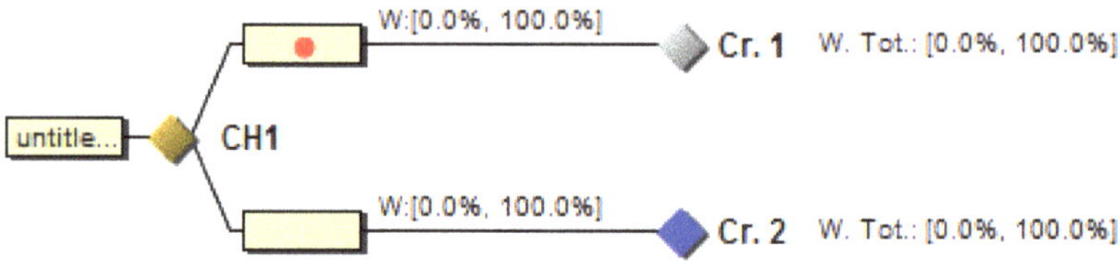

A dialogue box will then appear, in which you can enter the criterion name.

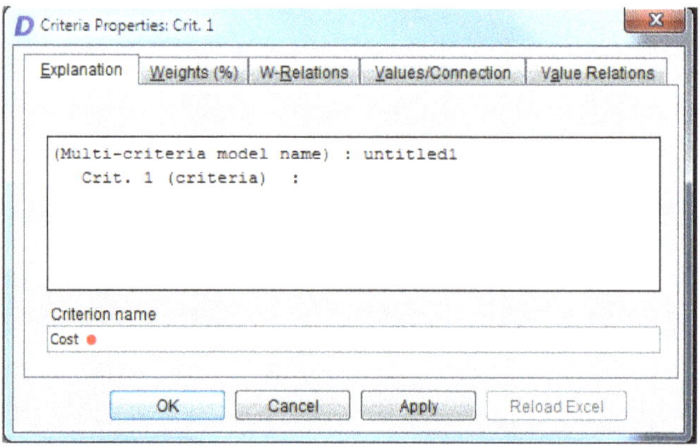

Click OK and enter the other criterion name in the same manner. You can also name the decision problem in a similar way, by right-clicking on the leftmost rectangle. Your model will then look like this.

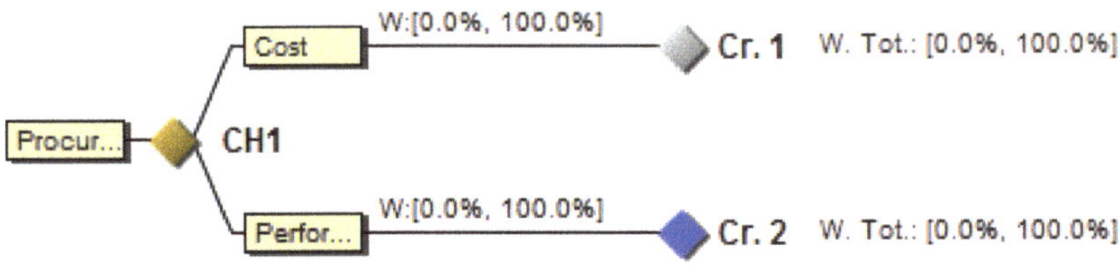

If you like to have the labels fully visible, you can enlarge the rectangles by clicking on Tools > Settings, and entering a larger pixel width for the rectangles either in the form of a number, or simply by pulling the handle.

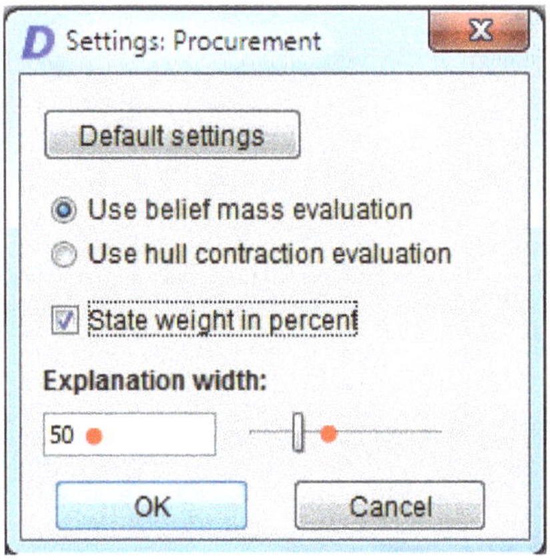

The first step is now almost finished.

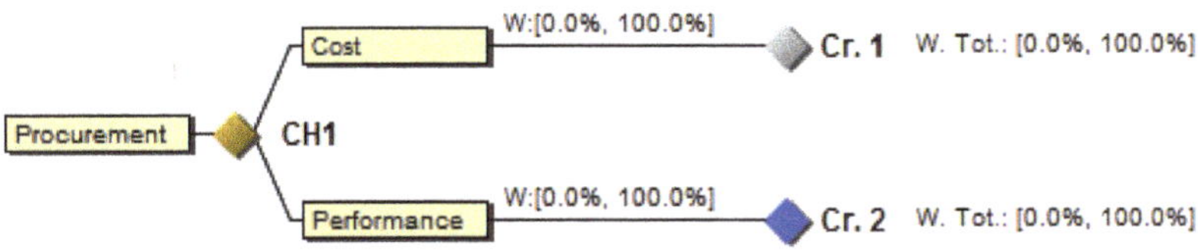

The only sub-step that remains is ascribing names to the strategies. Select S from the toolbar. In the dialogue box, enter the names by clicking Rename. As you can see, here it is possible to edit the number of strategies (alternatives) if necessary in a later phase of the analysis.

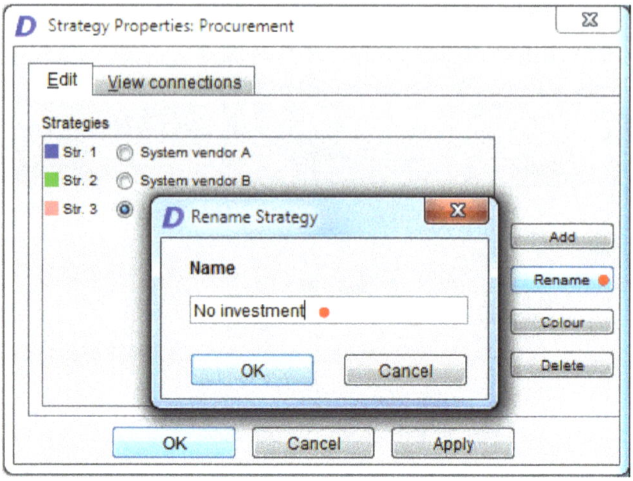

This concludes the first step.

Step 2. Enter Information about the Strategies (Alternatives).

The values of each alternative under each criterion can be entered in two ways: either as (imprecise) numbers or as rankings, the latter in case there is a criterion for which it is hard to give numbers. This could be a criterion such as business image, however both our criteria here are reasonably quantifiable. Assume that the costs for each alternative have been estimated as follows for the next three years of operation:

System vendor A: Between 2.9 and 4.2 MEUR
System vendor B: Between 3.7 and 5.5 MEUR
No investment: Between 0.6 and 1.1 MEUR

The strategy not to invest still incurs licence and maintenance costs.

To enter the costs in DecideIT, right-click on the Cost criterion. In the dialogue box, select the Values/Connection tab. In this tab, the cost of each strategy can be entered as a fixed number (seldom used), an interval, or an interval with a most likely number. In our case, we have intervals and thus select the second option for the radio buttons on the left. Note that higher costs are less desirable, thus the costs are entered as negative numbers. The ranges of the intervals express the degree of uncertainty of each statement.

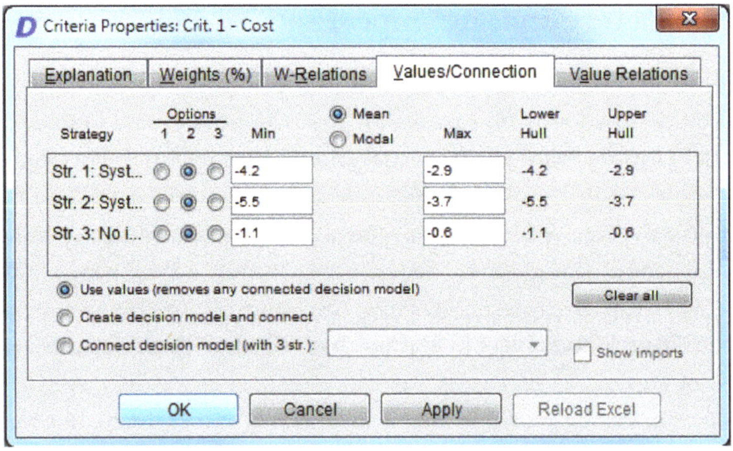

Let us now assume that the performance is a combined measure of number of customers, revenue per customer, and customer satisfaction. In a real-life case, these would be separate criteria, but to make this example more manageable, we have concatenated them. Assume that this combined measure generates the following estimates:

System vendor A: Between 45 and 75
System vendor B: Between 55 and 90
No investment: Between 10 and 35

These are entered in the same manner, by right-clicking on the Performance rectangle and selecting the Values/Connection tab.

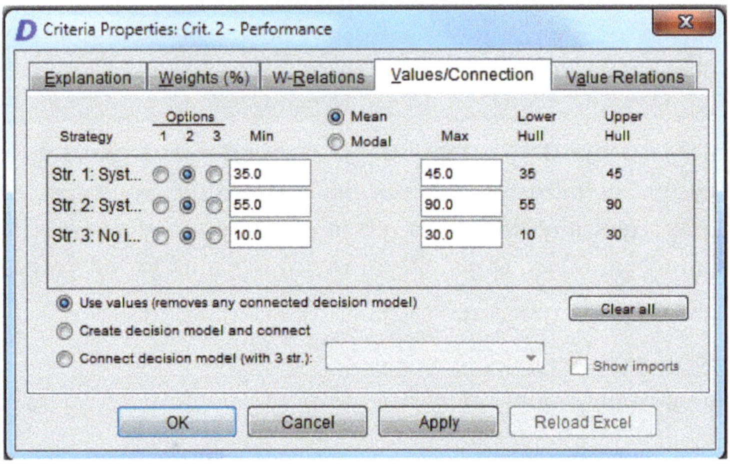

Click OK. This concludes Step 2 of the data entry.

Step 3. Determine the Importance of the Criteria

We have two criteria, and next we must input their relative degrees of importance. It should be noted that it is the importance between the criteria in this decision problem that should be compared. For example, if the difference in cost between the alternatives is small, then the criterion cost is ranked low for this particular case. This does not indicate anything about the general view on cost within a business, which is often at the top of any agenda. Thus, the range of possible numbers for each criterion is the object of comparison. To view these so-called scale spans, open the scale pop-up window. In this window, we can see that cost ranges between 0.6 and 5.5 MEUR while performance ranges between 10 and 90 points. Thus, the cost range [–5.5, –0.6] should be compared to the performance range [10, 90].

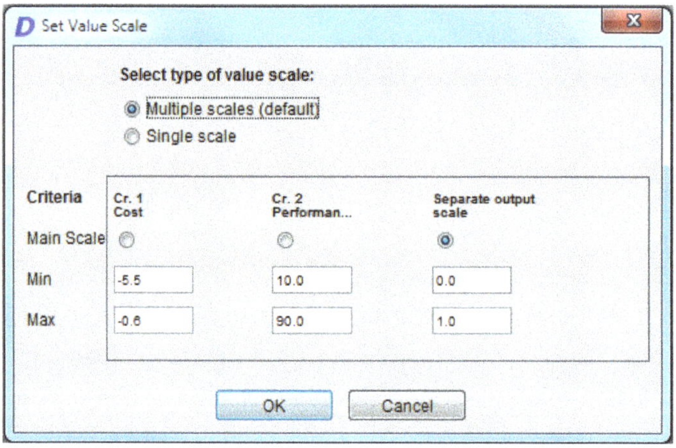

Given these value scales, the team of decision-makers finds that the difference in performance between the best and the worst outcome is more important than the difference in cost between the best and the worst outcome. They apply the following weights to the respective criteria:

Cost: 35%–45%
Performance: 55%–65%

Note that, as for values, the weights can be entered as fixed numbers (although one rarely knows precise numbered weights), as intervals, or as intervals with a most likely percentage. The widths of the intervals express the degree of uncertainty in each statement.

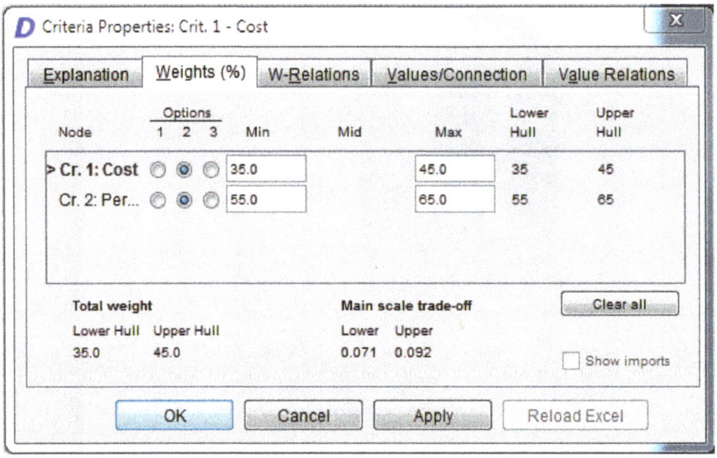

These statements of the criteria's importance are all we need to be able to evaluate the decision situation. After the three data entry steps, the next step is to evaluate the decision situation.

Step 4. Evaluation

To start evaluating, begin with the main evaluation window. It is reached by clicking the toolbar item . The following evaluation result window will then appear.

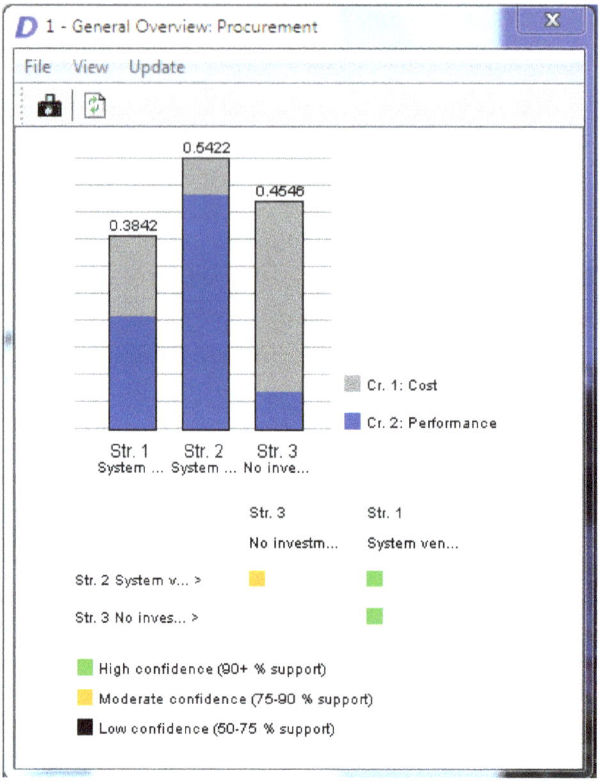

In this window, you can see in the upper half that Strategy 2, investing in a system from vendor B, is the preferred strategy (alternative of action). The heights of the bars reflect the level of preference for each option, with the numbers on top of the bars indicating the percentage of fulfilment compared to a fictitious optimal alternative. Such choices as 'the best performance for the lowest cost' seldom exist in reality (and if they do, they are often easily identifiable without a decision analysis tool). In the lower half of the window, there are comparisons of how much confidence can be put into one strategy being ranked above another. We can see that Strategy 1 (vendor A) receives high confidence, while vendor B wins over no investment with moderate confidence. In this example, the result is due to there only being two criteria. A larger set of criteria is usually more discriminative when it comes to confidence levels.

Next, you can gain an overview of where the confidence in the belief in the different strategies is allocated. To find that out, consult the pie chart by clicking  in the toolbar. The following pie chart will appear.

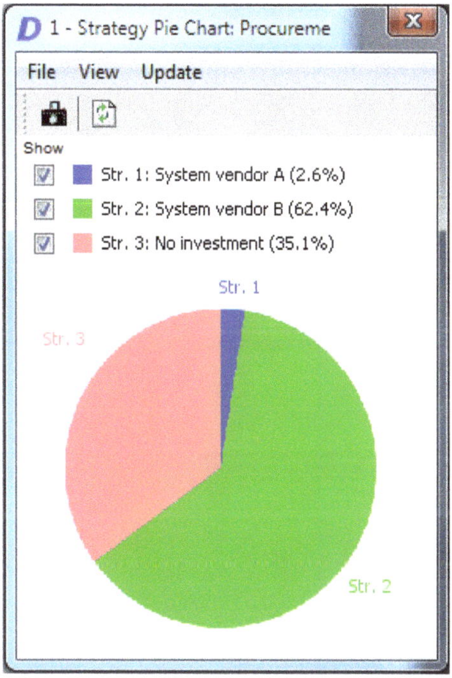

From it, you can tell that Strategy 1 is lagging very far behind and can reasonably be excluded from any further analysis unless we receive more favourable information. Around two thirds of the belief rests on Strategy 2, and the rest on the non-investment strategy.

Next, you can investigate the overlap in results for the three strategies. By clicking in the toolbar, a dialogue pop-up appears in which you choose at which confidence (support) level you want to investigate the possible resulting ranges for the strategies. Since 90% is a reasonable level of support, you can keep that and click OK.

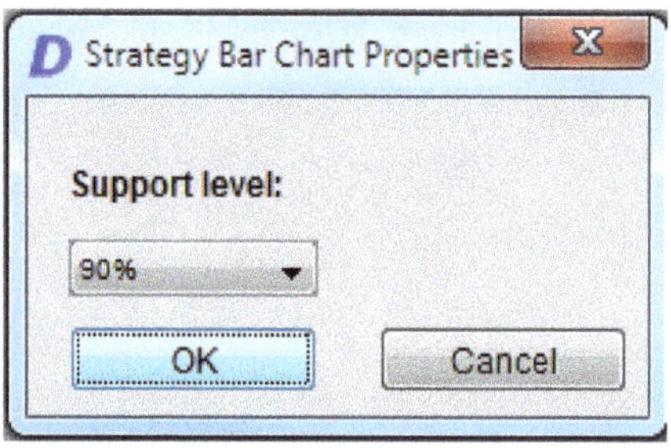

Now you can see what you have already been shown, presented in a complementary way, this time as resulting values relative to each other, i.e. the number 0 indicates equally as good as the average of all strategies. As opposed to the two previous ways of displaying the results, this one will be affected if an inferior strategy is removed. This is why this function is presented as the third means of illustrating the evaluation results.

Again, Strategy 1 is clearly inferior. If a decision is imminent, Strategy 2 is the preferred option. But in a real-life scenario with more time, it would be important to go back and revalidate the input information.

Note that this example does not in any sense purport to be realistic in its input values, number of criteria, or alternatives. It was conceived only to demonstrate DecideIT in the easiest possible way. On the contrary, a more realistic case has more alternatives valued under maybe 5–10 criteria or more. It is when the situation becomes more complex that the DecideIT tool shows its strengths by showing results that the human mind is not possible to compute.

Installation

How to install DecideIT on a Microsoft Windows PC (valid for Windows 7 and higher):

1. Download the program from the Preference website www.preference.nu/digitrans.
2. Follow the installation instructions.
3. Once installed, click on the DecideIT icon on your desktop or program menu to start the program for the first time.
4. The program will ask for your licence key (see below).

Licence Key Entry

This book comes with a one-year single-user licence for DecideIT. This licence is valid for one year from its entry into the program. After its expiry, you can continue to use the program in demo mode or purchase a renewal from Preference AB.

The first time you start the program, you are prompted for a licence key. You should enter the key into the relevant subfields.

Once the licence key is entered, the expiry date is determined by the program and you are good to go for one year.

DecideIT licence key
971F-B82-06B-1B8-FCF

The appendix and licence key are courtesy of Preference AB, the company that manufactures and sells this product. If you buy a renewal licence once the year is up, you should enter the new key through by clicking Help > Enter License Key.

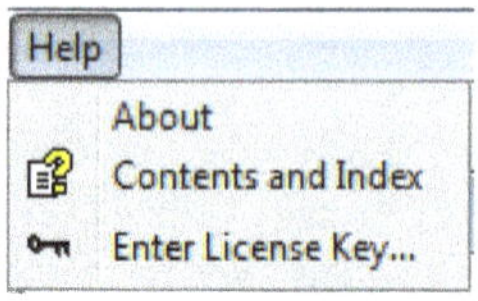

After this step, the new key will be validated and the old one, whether valid or not, will be removed from the program.

List of Illustrations

The figures in the appendix are unnumbered and intended to support the running text with illustrations on how and where to click.

Notes on Figures

All figures in Chapters 1 and 11 were created by Alf Westelius.

All figures in Chapters 2–3 were created by Mathias Cöster.

All figures in Chapter 4 were created by Cecilia Gullberg.

All figures in Chapters 5–7, all figures in the appendix, plus Figures 8.4, 8.5, 9.4, 9.5, and 9.6 were created by Mats Danielson using the software DecideIT from Preference AB, Stockholm, Sweden, with permission.

All figures in Chapters 8 and 9, except those mentioned above, were created by Gunnar Wettergren.

Figure 10.1: Creator OECD. Copyright: https://www.oecd.org/termsandconditions/. 30% or less of a complete work or a maximum of 5 tables and/or graphs taken from a work is granted free of charge and without formal written permission provided. OECD.AI (2023), visualisations powered by JSI using data from OpenAlex, accessed on 1/4/2023, www.oecd.ai.

Figures 10.2 and 10.3: Creator Gard Titlestad, The knowledge square and open processes.

Figure 10.4. Creator Gard Titlestad. Inspired by 'Digital Learning and Transformation', Discussion paper (Final draft – 15 July 2022), https://transformingeducationsummit.sdg4education2030.org/AT4DiscussionPaper.

All figures were created in 2022 and 2023 in Stockholm and Uppsala, Sweden, except for Chapter 10 whose figures were created in Bergen, Norway in a manner described above.

Index

About the Authors

Mathias Cöster is PhD and Associate Professor at Uppsala University, Department of Civil and Industrial Engineering. He researches the impact of digitisation on industries, organisational business models and price models. He also researches how organisations develop control systems for realising sustainability strategies. He has co-authored several books and frequently lectures in various educational contexts.

Mats Danielson is Full Professor in Computer and Systems Sciences at Stockholm University, Senior Advisor to the President, and UNESCO Chair Professor. He is former Dean of the Faculty of Social Sciences as well as former Vice President for External Relations, Innovation, and ICT. He has a PhD in Computer and Systems Sciences as well as university degrees in Computer Science and Engineering and in Economics and Business Administration. He worked in the software industry for almost twenty years before joining academia to work with research as well as algorithm and software design and development within decision analysis and support.

Love Ekenberg was Full Professor in Computer and Systems Sciences at Stockholm University and a UNESCO Professor. He had a PhD in Computer and Systems Sciences, as well as a PhD in Mathematics. He worked with risk and decision analysis, i.e. development of products and methodologies within these areas, for around twenty years.

Cecilia Gullberg is PhD and Assistant Professor in Business Administration at Södertörn University. She has ten years' experience of studying the intersection between accounting, organisation, and digitisation with regards to how roles, competences and processes of transparency and accountability change as new digital tools enter organisations.

Gard Titlestad is a recognised international expert within the field of higher education, research, innovation, and digital transformation. He has comprehensive experience as a senior manager. He has worked for the Nordic countries, for the European Union, and globally. Until 2018 he was Secretary General for the International Council for Open and Distance Education, ICDE. In ICDE, he worked in close partnership with UNESCO on the new Sustainable Development Goals.

Alf Westelius is Professor (Chair) of Digitisation and Management at Linköping University. Applicability and practical relevance guide his interests, and consulting and tutoring have always been important parts of his work. The key to dealing with digitisation affordances lies in how you combine new ways of working, organising, and technology with existing ones. This is what Alf explores in his research.

Gunnar Wettergren is a teacher and researcher at Stockholm University's Department of Computer and Systems Sciences. Gunnar has a long history as a project manager both in the private and academic sectors. Gunnar's primary research interest is project portfolio management. Gunnar has a background in Computer Science.

About the Team

Alessandra Tosi was the managing editor for this book.

Melissa Purkiss performed the copy-editing and indexing.

Jeevanjot Kaur Nagpal designed the cover. The cover was produced in InDesign using the Fontin font.

Melissa Purkiss typeset the book in InDesign and produced the paperback and hardback editions. The text font is Tex Gyre Pagella; the heading font is Californian FB.

Cameron Craig produced the EPUB, PDF, HTML, and XML editions. The conversion is performed with open source software such as pandoc (https://pandoc.org/) created by John MacFarlane and other tools freely available on our GitHub page (https://github.com/OpenBookPublishers).

This book need not end here...

Share

All our books — including the one you have just read — are free to access online so that students, researchers and members of the public who can't afford a printed edition will have access to the same ideas. This title will be accessed online by hundreds of readers each month across the globe: why not share the link so that someone you know is one of them?

This book and additional content is available at:

https://doi.org/10.11647/OBP.0350

Donate

Open Book Publishers is an award-winning, scholar-led, not-for-profit press making knowledge freely available one book at a time. We don't charge authors to publish with us: instead, our work is supported by grants, by our library members and by donations from people who believe that research shouldn't be locked behind paywalls.

Why not join them in freeing knowledge by supporting us:
https://www.openbookpublishers.com/support-us

You may also be interested in:

Inventory Analytics
Roberto Rossi

https://doi.org/10.11647/OBP.0252

B C, Before Computers
On Information Technology from Writing to the Age of Digital Data
Stephen Robertson

https://doi.org/10.11647/OBP.0225

Deliberation, Representation, Equity
Research Approaches, Tools and Algorithms for Participatory Processes
Love Ekenberg, Karin Hansson, Mats Danielson, and Göran Cars

https://doi.org/10.11647/OBP.0108

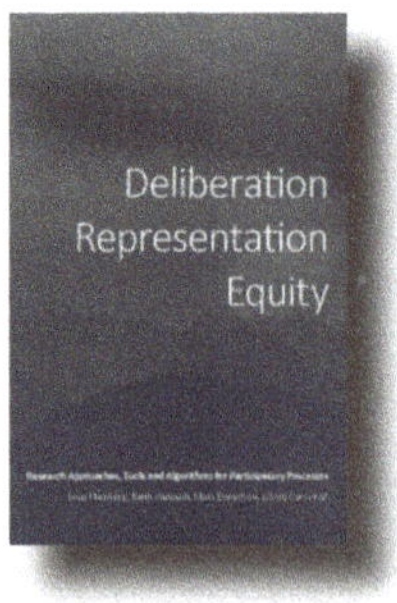

www.ingramcontent.com/pod-product-compliance
Lightning Source LLC
LaVergne TN
LVHW051058210926
848486LV00002B/143